Assessment
Techniques

The Kogan Page Practical Trainer Series
Series Editor: Roger Buckley

'Excellent and challenging' The Learning World, BBC World Service
'Jargon-free and straightforward … sound advice' Personnel Management
'Clear, informative, very practically oriented' The Training Officer

Competence-Based Assessment Techniques

revised second edition

SHIRLEY
FLETCHER

**KOGAN
PAGE**

To Dad, who taught me how to spell

First published in 1992
Reprinted 1992, 1993, 1994
Second edition published 1997
Revised second edition 2000

Kogan Page Limited
120 Pentonville Road
London N1 9JN
UK

Stylus Publishing Inc.
22883 Quicksilver Drive
Sterling VA 20166-2012
USA

© Shirley Fletcher 1992, 1997, 2000

British Library Cataloguing in Publication Data

A CIP record of this book is available from the British Library

ISBN 0 7494 3422 8

Typeset by Koinonia, Manchester
Printed and bound in Great Britain by Bell & Bain Ltd, Glasgow

Contents

Series Editor's Foreword

Organizations get things done when people do their jobs effectively. To make this happen they need to be well trained. A number of people are likely to be involved in this training: identifying the needs of the organization and of the individual, selecting or designing appropriate training to meet those needs, delivering it and assessing how effective it was. It is not only 'professional' or full-time trainers who are involved in this process; personnel managers, line managers, supervisors and job holders are all likely to have a part to play.

This series has been written for all those who get involved with training in some way or another, whether they are senior personnel managers trying to link the goals of the organization with training needs or job holders who have been given responsibility for training newcomers. Therefore, the series is essentially a practical one which focuses on specific aspects of the training function. This is not to say that the theoretical underpinnings of the practical aspects of training are unimportant. Anyone seriously interested in training is strongly encouraged to look beyond 'what to do' and 'how to do it' and to delve into the areas of why things are done in a particular way.

The authors have been selected because they have considerable practical experience. All have shared, at some time, the same difficulties, frustrations and satisfactions of being involved in training and are now in a position to share with others some helpful and practical guidelines.

This revised new edition complements Shirley Fletcher's other book in the Practical Trainer Series – *Designing Competence-Based Training*. The key issue addressed in this volume is how we assess competence. All of us are likely to be familiar with the techniques used to test or assess learning ability or attainment as part of the more traditional training programme. However, assessment of competences is all about actual performance in the work role which involves the trainer in collecting evidence of competent performance from a variety of sources.

The techniques for gathering such evidence are of value to all trainers and in particular to those in organizations that are working towards national standards or which choose to base their training and development on other competence-based systems.

ROGER BUCKLEY

Acknowledgements

The author would like to acknowledge and thank the following for their help in preparing this edition: Employment Occupations Standards Council (EOSC) and Blubeckers Restaurants.

Preface

There has been, and continues to be, much confusion in the last few years regarding the 'competence movement'. The question of what we mean by competence or competency has been compounded by a plethora of technical papers, government edicts and general guidance documents which refer to occupational competence and personal competence. The latest additions, 'general competence' and 'core' competence, do nothing to ease what is increasingly being seen as a bureaucratic maze.

Add to this the further confusion between different competence-based models used worldwide and it is no wonder that employers, trainers, managers and researchers tend to wonder which way to turn next!

This is unfortunate, for competence-based systems have much to recommend them. The flexibility of such systems could provide a much needed boost to the training and education arena, to work performance as a whole and thus to the competitiveness of companies in world markets. This is especially true in the UK.

Competence-based systems operate with two different emphases. In the UK, the national, qualification-driven system focuses on 'standards of occupational performance'. In the USA, the emphasis has been on 'competency development'. Both systems are criticized for not providing an 'overall' package of competency descriptors and each system has its ardent supporters.

However, the national, technical and academic arguments detract from the key benefits that can be drawn from competence-based systems for businesses, whether this be from use of one system or a synthesis of both. Similarly, those who continually attack the new systems are often those who also attack the traditional ones!

Traditional education, training and assessment systems and frameworks have themselves been criticized for many years. Employers complain that 'qualified' people – those who have completed a 'recognized' course of learning – only *know what to do;* they cannot *actually do it.* The costs of such programmes are also a bone of contention (and always will be while employers fail to see education and training of their workforce as an investment).

With competence-based systems, we have the opportunity to introduce training and assessment which focus on *actual performance.* It also provides a framework in which *evaluation of training effectiveness,* as well as *assessment of individual performance* can operate.

Employers have long been asking for a framework in which *measurement* of these important contributors to economic effectiveness can operate. We now have the foundation for this framework.

In this book, which complements several other books on competence-based systems in the Practical Trainer Series, the what, why, when, where, how and who of competence-based assessment are explored in detail. I draw from my own experience at national and organizational level to present a warts-and-all picture of the key principles, methods, components, implications and benefits of competence-based assessment. I also offer practical guidance for those readers who are considering the introduction of this form of assessment – whether that introduction is in connection with defined qualification systems or for other purposes.

Part I provides a foundation for those new to competence-based systems. It deals with three questions: What are the differences between competence-based systems? What is competence-based assessment? How can I use competence-based assessment in my organization? Part II provides practical help in introducing assessment, including training of assessors and the establishment of quality-assurance systems.

Part I FOUNDATIONS OF COMPETENCE-BASED ASSESSMENT

Part I provides a foundation on which to base the plan of your competence-based assessment system. It answers three questions:

- What are the differences between competence-based systems?
- What is competence-based assessment?
- How can I use competence-based assessment in my organization?

Chapter 1 provides examples of competence-based models and outlines the differences between them. It also provides a checklist to help you determine whether the system you are considering is really competence-based.

Chapter 2 outlines the basic principles, concepts and operational implications of competence-based assessment.

Chapter 3 helps you to decide on the uses to which competence-based assessment can be put within your organization.

1

Different Competence-Based Systems

$\triangleright$ SUMMARY $\triangleleft$

This chapter helps you to understand the foundations on which a competence-based assessment system operates. It also highlights the existence of two different competence-based systems and provides you with a general overview of each. Included in this chapter is a checklist to help you decide whether the system you are currently using (or planning to use) is really competence-based.

```
┌─────────────────────────────────────┐
│   Which competence-based system      │
│    am I using/planning to use?       │
└─────────────────────────────────────┘
                  │
┌─────────────────────────────────────┐
│ What are the key differences between the │
│   two main approaches to competence? │
└─────────────────────────────────────┘
                  │
┌─────────────────────────────────────┐
│      How do I know if my system      │
│        is competence-based?          │
└─────────────────────────────────────┘
```

In the UK, national, qualification-driven competence-based systems are based on standards defined by industry. However, this is not the only competence-based approach used around the world.

The confusion that many people experience can involve debates on, for example, competence systems which are:

criterion-referenced	*vs*	criterion-validated
outcome-based	*vs*	behavioural
outcome-related	*vs*	input-related
competences	*vs*	competencies
competence	*vs*	competency

In many cases, the issues of terminology tend to take over and lead to theoretical or academic debates at the expense of real progress.

When considering competence-based assessment systems, the first consideration should always be the needs of the users. Questions such as 'What do we want to assess?' and 'Why do we want to assess?' are far more important at the outset. Without answers to these simple questions, any discussion on technical issues will remain in the circular, theoretical realm.

We will return to this issue at the end of this chapter, where you will be given help in both preparing and answering key questions in your own context. Firstly, there follows a brief review of basics.

Which Competence-Based System?

The competence-based movement has been in existence for some time. From the 1960s onwards, however, there has been an increasing demand in the business world, for greater accountability and more effective means of measuring and managing performance. This has led to research into what makes people effective and what constitutes a competent worker. Consequently, several different models of competence are in use (to meet different needs).

USA – early models in education

It is generally agreed that competence-based *education* has its roots in teacher education – usually referred to as CBET: competency-based education and training – and that its development was fuelled by the US Office of Education's funding for the development of model training programmes for elementary school teachers.

These models included 'the precise specification of competences or behaviours *to be learned*, [note the emphasis on learning] the modularization of instruction, evaluation and feedback, personalization and field experience' (Swanchek and Campbell 1981).

Establishment of these models led to a demand for certification policies which aimed to improve school provision through the reform of teacher education. This became known as performance-based teacher education (PBTE).

As might be expected, the introduction of CBET in the USA caused a strong reaction from the higher education institutions, who perceived this new trend as a threat to their autonomy and academic status. A system of this kind also requires considerable reorganization of resources – an issue which affects the education and training arena at all levels.

CBET was, however, supported by the US Office of Education who promoted the new trend through the National Consortium of Competency-based Education Centers. This consortium established a set of 'criteria for describing and assessing competency-based programs' (see Figure 1.1).

Competency specifications

1. Competences are based on an analysis of the professional role(s) and/or a theoretical formulation of professional responsibilities.
2. Competency statements describe outcomes expected from the performance of professionally related functions, or knowledge, skills and attitudes thought to be essential to the performance of those functions.
3. Competency statements facilitate criterion-referenced assessment.
4. Competences are treated as tentative predictors of professional effectiveness and are subjected to continual validation procedures.
5. Competences are specified and made public prior to instruction.
6. Learners completing the CBET programme demonstrate a wide range of competency profiles.

Assessment

13. Competency measures are validly related to competency statements.
14. Competency measures are specific, realistic and sensitive to nuance.
15. Competency measures discriminate on the basis of standards set for competency demonstration.
16. Data provided by competency measures are manageable and useful in decision-making.
17. Competency measures and standards are specified and made public prior to instruction.

Source: Bourke *et al.* (1975).

Figure 1.1 *CBET criteria for describing and assessing competence-based programmes*

The text also refers to criteria for 'instruction', for 'governance and management' and for the 'total programme'. The emphasis is on *'learning' and 'instruction'* rather than assessment of actual workplace performance. This type of competence specification is most often used as part of a 'competence development programme'. (It is essential to be clear, therefore, whether the key purpose of your proposed competence-based system is the *development of competence* or *assessment of performance*.)

Difficulties arose in the USA because compliance with all the requirements within these stated criteria meant a complete review and reorganization of the education delivery system.

This early model was focused on teacher training and very much centred in the educational forum. Plans to expand this to the vocational sector were hampered by the misunderstanding that the vocational system had always been competence-based! In fact, the US vocational training system, like that in the UK, was one in which curricula were devised centrally for institution-based education and often placed more emphasis on theory and knowledge than on practical application in the workplace. Federal funding was made available to stimulate the use of competence-based systems in the vocational sector but the emphasis remained on PBTE.

Guidance on the development and use of competence-based systems of learning and assessment began to proliferate. A further model was proposed by Elam (1971) and has been used extensively to explain competence-based systems in respect of vocational education and

Essential elements

1. Competences are role derived, specified in behavioural terms and made public.
2. Assessment criteria are competence-based, specify mastery levels and are made public.
3. Assessment requires performance as prime evidence but takes knowledge into account.
4. Individual student progress rate depends on demonstrated competency.
5. The instructional programme facilitates development and evaluation of specific competences.

Implied characteristics

1. Individualization of learning.
2. Feedback to learners.
3. Emphasis on exit rather than admission requirements.
4. Systematic programme.
5. Modularization.
6. Student and programme accountability.

Related desirable characteristics

1. Field setting for learning.
2. Broad base for decision-making.
3. Provision of protocol and training materials.
4. Student participation in decision making.
5. Research oriented and regenerative.
6. Career continuous.
7. Role integration.

Source: Elam (1971)

Figure 1.2 *Characteristics of Elam's early competence-based programmes*

training. It provides a useful starting point – but one word of warning: make no assumptions about the terminology! Recognition of the terms is no guarantee that 'we already do that'. The fact that many aspects of competence-based provision have been tacked on to existing curricula does not make the revised product competence-based! Notice again the use of the terms 'progress', 'learning' and 'programmes' in Figure 1.2.

USA – Hay McBer models

A second widely used model is concerned with the identification of characteristics in superior performers of an occupational role. It is often referred to as the system which relates to 'soft skills', or 'soft competencies'.

The work originates at the McBer Corporation and Harvard Business School. Competencies (note the difference in spelling from the UK 'competences') are derived through use of a form of critical incident analysis, using highly successful or 'excellent' performers as a research group. The resulting underlying characteristics, organized into 'clusters', have been used in management education and training in the USA and UK.

Competence here is defined in terms of the characteristics of individuals. Competence is something which is 'held' or 'owned' by the individual and brought to the occupational role. Examples of the McBer competency clusters are illustrated in Figure 1.3.

The UK competency system

In the early 1970s, the New Training Initiative (MSC 1981) first launched the idea of 'standards of a new kind'. White Papers in 1986 and a review of vocational qualifications in the same year led to the beginning of the Standards Development Programme. The then Manpower Services Commission was charged with managing the development of occupational standards of performance for all sectors of all industries.

The review of vocational qualifications also led to the establishment of the National Council for Vocational Qualifications (NCVQ), now the Qualifications and Curriculum Authority (QCA), which was to take responsibility for the development of criteria for a new framework of qualifications based on these new employment-led standards of competence.

A huge development programme began. 'Industry led bodies' were established and charged with project-management responsibilities for standards development within their own sectors. The Standards Methodology Unit at the MSC (which had become the Training Agency) managed a wide range of projects to establish the methodology for the development of standards and associated assessment and certification systems.

The UK standards of occupational competence (see Figure 1.4) are different in format and in basic concept from those in the McBer system. They are also developed for *all* occupational roles in *all* sectors of industry and commerce. In the UK, competence-based standards reflect the *expectations of workplace performance*. The development of 'personal competences' to supplement these occupationally related standards continues.

Starting on the Right Foot

To say 'we are introducing competence-based assessment' is a very broad statement. If your organization is considering this development, and if

Goal and action cluster deals with the manager's initiative, image, problem-solving skills and goal orientation.

- Efficiency orientation
- Proactivity
- Concern with impact
- Diagnostic use of concepts

Directing subordinates cluster involves a manager's freedom of expression both in terms of giving directives and orders, and giving feedback to help develop subordinates.

- Use of unilateral power
- Developing others
- Spontaneity

Human resource cluster Managers with these competencies have positive expectations about others, have realistic views of themselves, build networks or coalitions with others to accomplish tasks and stimulate cooperation and pride in work in groups.

- Accurate self-assessment
- Self-control
- Stamina and adaptability
- Perceptual objectivity
- Positive regard
- Managing group process
- Use of socialized power

Leadership cluster represents a manager's ability to discern the key issues, patterns or objectives in an organization, and to then conduct himself or herself and communicate in a strong fashion.

- Self-confidence
- Self-conceptualization
- Logical thought
- Use of oral presentations

Figure 1.3 *The competency programme of the American Management Association*

you are charged with the initial research or with the implementation process, then consider the following before making any definitive decisions:

- Which system would best meet our needs?
- What are the implications of each?
- What are the key differences?
- What do we want to assess?
  - occupational competence?
  - personal competence?
  - general competence?
  - all three or any combination?

If this chapter has raised more questions than it has answered then I have achieved my objective. Use of the term 'competence-based' is becoming more common, but unfortunately its correct use is not. For those considering a move in the competence-based direction, I offer the following charts (Figures 1.5, 1.6, 1.7 and 1.8) as a basic reference point and the remaining chapters as a practical guide to that journey. This will be of help in finding your way through the confusion. It will also assist you in making decisions regarding the various assessment systems on offer and their relevance to your organization's needs.

A Comparison of Assessment Principles and Practice

The charts in Figures 1.5, 1.6, 1.7 and 1.8 outline:

- the key differences in principle between competence-based assessment and more traditional forms of occupation-related assessment (in qualification-driven systems);
- the key differences between the different competence-based systems themselves;
- the criteria for ascertaining whether the assessment system you may be offered is really competence-based;
- key questions to ask at the start of your development project.

The remaining chapters then deal with principles, methods and techniques and guidance on implementation in more detail.

Customer Service Level 3 – One Element from Unit 1

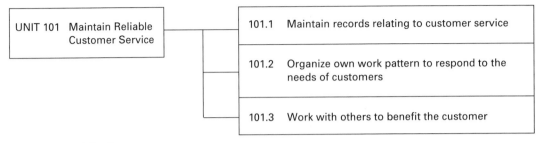

UNIT 101 Maintain Reliable Customer Service	
	101.1 Maintain records relating to customer service
	101.2 Organize own work pattern to respond to the needs of customers
	101.3 Work with others to benefit the customer

Performance Criteria
(a) Opportunities to improve working relationship with colleagues are consistently sought.
(b) Current organizational procedures for monitoring service delivery are regularly evaluated with colleagues.
(c) Communications with relevant outside parties are effectively maintained on behalf of customers.
(d) New contacts likely to benefit customer service are routinely identified through routine scanning of relevant information.
(e) Collaborative work with others is actively used to improve the reliability of service delivery.

Range
Colleagues
1. managers
2. others within the organization

Organizational procedures
3. formal
4. informal

Communication
5. face-to-face
6. written
7. by telephone

Outside parties
8. relevant statutory or regulatory bodies
9. relevant external suppliers

Knowledge
• relevant suppliers, internal and external
• relevant statutory and regulatory bodies and their effect on customer service
• organizational policy relating to service delivery

Understanding
• finding new ways of working with others which benefit the customer
• influencing colleagues to sustain the improved reliability of customer service
• how to use new contacts to improve the reliability of customer service
• working with others in ways that they respect and appreciate how legislation can affect customer service

Figure 1.4 *Example of UK Standards of Competence*
Source: Customer Service Revised Standards (1996) EOSC

	Traditional (course-based)	Competence-based (workplace)
Concept	Assessment of learning ability or achievement	Assessment of actual performance in a work role
Foundation	Curricula, defined centrally by teaching staff/divisional boards	Explicit standards of required performance defined by industry (UK) or by research using 'excellent' performers (USA)
Assessment requirements	Assessment is an integral part of learning programmes	Assessment is independent of any learning programme
Evidence	Assessment evidence drawn from course assignments/exams	Assessment evidence collected from actual workplace performance supplemented by other methods
	Types of evidence predetermined by course syllabus	Types of evidence governed only by rules for quality of evidence
	Assessment is norm-referenced	Assessment is criterion-referenced (UK), criterion-validated (USA), and individualized

Figure 1.5 *Traditional vs competence-based assessment (qualification-driven systems)*

Criterion-referenced competences	Criterion-validated competencies
Standards of performance (competences) developed and agreed by industry (national) or by the organization (company-specific)	Competency clusters developed by research using 'excellent' performers
Assessment of workplace performance	Learning and development of competence/assessment of behaviours
Competence = expectations of employment	Competence = personal characteristics
Standards outcome-based (criterion-referenced)	Standards output-oriented (criterion-validated)
Standards of occupational competence (actual performance at work)	Educational process (competence development)
Agreed benchmark of competent performance	Specifications of 'superior' performance defined by educational research
Product – hard competences	Product – soft competencies

Figure 1.6 *Key differences between main types of competence-based assessment systems*

If you are considering the introduction of a competence-based assessment system and perhaps seeking advice from an external source, the following checklist will allow you to judge whether the proposals presented are truly competence-based.

Is the proposed system:

- based on the use of explicit statements of performance?
- focused on the assessment of *outputs* or *outcomes* of performance?
- independent of any specified learning programme?
- based on a requirement in which evidence of performance is collected from observation and questioning of actual performance as the main assessment method?
- one which provides *individualized* assessment?
- one which contains clear guidance to assessors regarding the quality of evidence to be collected?
- one which contains clear guidelines and procedures for quality assurance?

Figure 1.7 *Checklist for competence-based assessment*

Planning Competence-Based Assessment
Key Questions

1. What do we want to assess?
    (a) Technical competence
    (b) Occupational competence
    (c) Behaviours
    (d) Individual performance
    (e) Group/team performance
    (f) Ability to learn
    (g) Learning achievements

2. Why do we want to assess?
    (a) To measure individual contribution to business objectives
    (b) To measure group/team contribution to business objectives
    (c) To certificate competence to nationally agreed standards
    (d) To confirm competence against company specific standards
    (e) To identify potential for further development
    (f) To confirm outcomes of learning

Figure 1.8 *Key questions for planning the design of competence-based assessment*

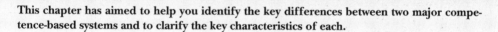

REVIEW

This chapter has aimed to help you identify the key differences between two major competence-based systems and to clarify the key characteristics of each.

The guidance provided in this chapter will help you to decide which competence-based system is best for your particular needs. You need to keep in mind whether your system will:

(a) aim to *develop* competence or to *assess competent performance*, and
(b) be based on behaviours or vocational outcomes, or
(c) be a combination of behavioural and vocational assessment.

2   What is Competence-Based Assessment?

▷   SUMMARY   ◁

This chapter helps you through the initial maze of competence-based assessment systems. It outlines the basic principles on which these systems operate. It also acts as a reference source for your decision-making.

```
┌─────────────────────────────┐
│  What are the common factors of │
│     all assessment systems?      │
└─────────────────────────────┘
         │
┌─────────────────────────────┐
│     What is the purpose of      │
│        (a) traditional and       │
│      (b) competence-based        │
│          assessment?             │
└─────────────────────────────┘
         │
┌──────────────────┐      ┌──────────────────┐
│   How does the   │      │   What makes     │
│ assessment process │──────│ competence-based │
│     operate?     │      │ assessment different? │
└──────────────────┘      └──────────────────┘
         │
┌─────────────────────────────┐
│  What are the implications of   │
│   introducing competence-       │
│      based assessment?          │
└─────────────────────────────┘
```

All Forms of Assessment Have a Common Factor

Assessment is about the *collection of evidence.* All forms of assessment can be included in this description – from everyday activities to the most complex statistical systems.

For example, when shopping for clothes you assess the suitability of various items by matching the qualities of those items to the set of *requirements* you have established for yourself. Your requirements may relate to price, size, colour, style and fit. You will therefore seek *evidence* from price tags and from examination and fitting of the items to help you make a judgement and final choice. Your final choice may allow for some compromise if you cannot find an item which meets *all* your requirements – that is, you will make a decision based on the best match of requirements and evidence.

Similarly, if you were taking a course of learning within a traditional vocational education and training system, you would be assessed by a tutor and/or examiner who would seek *evidence* that you had acquired the required *learning.* This evidence would be in the form of course assignments and probably a final examination, and would be matched against course *learning objectives.* The final decision would be influenced by a 'norm-referenced' process, in other words, your results will be compared with those of other people. You would need to achieve an agreed percentage in order to pass the assessment (or indeed gain a 'credit' or 'distinction').

There are many instances in which we are either assessing or being assessed. In each instance, the assessment concerns the *collection of evidence.* This is, therefore, the common factor within all forms and all types of assessment. So why are there so many types?

Although all forms of assessment concern the use of evidence, each form of assessment may have a different purpose. It is the *purpose* of assessment which will define the nature and process of the assessment system.

The Purpose of Assessment

The purpose of assessment when buying clothes is to collect sufficient evidence to enable you to buy the right clothes at the right price or the closest possible match between your requirements and what is available.

The purpose of assessment within a programme of learning is to collect sufficient evidence to demonstrate that you have *learned* at least the required minimum percentage of the syllabus. If the programme of learning is also linked to an award system, a further purpose may be the achievement of formal recognition that learning has been acquired. This usually takes the form of a certificate or diploma.

In a competence-based assessment system, the purpose of assessment is to collect sufficient evidence that individuals *can perform or behave to the specified standards in a specific role.* If this assessment is also linked to an award system, a further purpose is formal recognition of successful performance.

The Assessment Process

A process is a 'series of actions or events', or a 'sequence of operations'. We could say that *all* forms of assessment involve the following sequence of operations:

- defining requirements or objectives of assessment;
- collecting evidence;
- matching evidence to requirements or objectives;
- making judgements based on this matching activity.

Our 'selecting clothes' assessment would follow the process shown in Figure 2.1, while the programme of learning assessment would follow that of Figure 2.2.

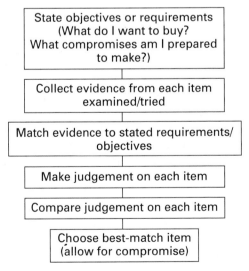

Figure 2.1 *Assessment process – selecting clothes*

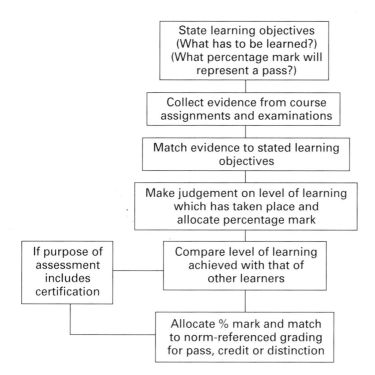

Figure 2.2 *Assessment process – programme of learning*

By comparing the two figures, we can begin to see how the purpose of assessment affects the assessment process and the assessment outcome.

In both examples the basic process of stating objectives, collecting and matching evidence and making a judgement is consistent with all forms of assessment as noted at the beginning of this section. However, at this point, different sequences of action are put into operation because the final *purpose* of assessment differs for each assessment event.

Both assessment events move along a *comparison* route. The first compares items assessed in order to make a *decision about the best item*. The second compares the results of the assessment with the results of other, similar assessments in order to *decide what final grading to apply*.

Both assessment processes follow a comparative approach – they both involve some form of comparison of assessment results. The second example involves 'norm-referencing', where an *average* achievement grade has been calculated and all *individual* achievements are judged against the average. Norm-referencing is the basis of most traditional assessment systems.

Competence-Based Assessment

Figure 2.3 looks at the competence-based assessment process in the same way.

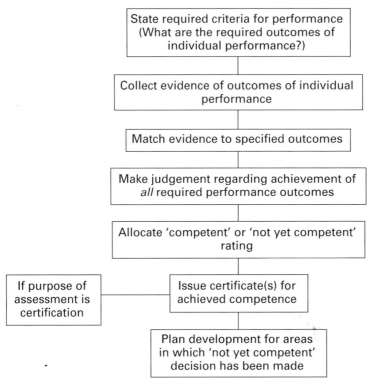

Figure 2.3 *Assessment process – competence-based assessment*

You may notice some key differences in the competence-based assessment approach:

- focus on 'outcomes';
- individualized assessment;
- no percentage rating;
- no comparison with other individuals' results;
- *all* standards (requirements) must be met;
- on-going process (leads to further development and assessment);
- only 'competent' or 'not yet competent' judgements made.

As we have already noted, the *purpose* of competence-based assessment is:

To collect sufficient evidence to demonstrate that individuals can *perform or behave* to the specified standards in a specified role.

We can add to this definition by clarifying that in competence-based assessment we are referring to *work roles* and therefore to *standards of occupational competence*. Occupational competence reflects *performance* at work. Our definition of the purpose of competence-based assessment will therefore look like this:

To collect sufficient evidence of workplace performance to demonstrate that individuals can perform or behave to the specified standards required within a specified occupational role.

This differs drastically from traditional forms of occupational assessment in which evidence collected relates to what has been *learned*. In competence-based assessment, our key concern is *actual performance*. Our focus is therefore, on *what individuals can do* rather than what individuals *know*.

This outlines the *key purpose* of competence-based assessment. The issue of 'perform' vs 'behave' in the definition above will depend on whether we have set vocational outcomes or behavioural outcomes as the basis of our competence system.

Practical Implications of Competence-Based Assessment

The introduction of competence-based assessment at national, organizational or departmental level has wide implications for managers, for trainers, and for those being assessed.

Unlike traditional forms of occupation-related assessment, competence-based assessment can be, and should be, undertaken *in the workplace*, and should be individualized.

Who Assesses?

The first question then is if assessment is to be undertaken in the workplace, who are the assessors?

The most obvious choice is the supervisor or line manager. This arrangement raises a number of questions:

- Do supervisors and managers have time to undertake formal assessment?
- What if the supervisor or assessor doesn't like or has a poor relationship with the person being assessed?
- What skills will assessors need?

What about quality?

The second implication concerns the movement of assessment to a *local* rather than a *central* basis:

- How can quality of assessment be assured if it is undertaken locally by line managers?
- Who trains assessors?
- Who ensures that quality of assessment is maintained?
- Who pays for this?

How valuable is competence-based assessment?

In the UK, competence-based systems have been focused on the introduction of National Vocational Qualifications (NVQs) (and Scottish Vocational Qualifications, SVQs, in Scotland). However, this really concentrates on only one use of competence-based assessment – assessment for certification.

We also need to consider what other purposes competence-based assessment can be put to within our organization, and what resources we will need.

What about training?

Last but not least is the issue of linking competence-based assessment to training. As the assessment system operates on a continuous – rather than one-off – basis, and is operated within the workplace environment, training needs are identified at individual level. Questions here include:

- What systems do we need to ensure that identified training needs are communicated to those who can take relevant action?
- In what way do we need to reorganize our training resources to provide training which meets those needs?

For educational institutions and for business organizations, the issues of resourcing, reorganization and administration are paramount.

All of these questions will be explored, together with possible solutions, in later chapters. For the present, it is important that you begin to think in terms of these issues.

REVIEW ◀

This chapter has outlined the basic principles, purposes and objectives of assessment systems, particularly competence-based assessment. You should make sure you understand these basic principles before beginning work on your own scheme.

3   Purposes and Uses of Competence-Based Assessment

▷   SUMMARY   ◁

This chapter helps you to consider the best ways in which to use a competence-based system within your organization.

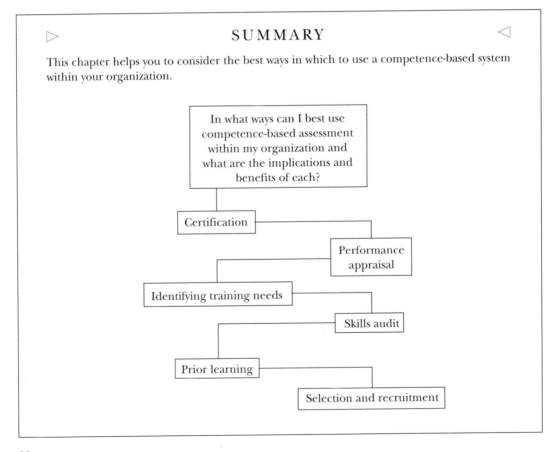

Competences or Competency? Why are We Assessing?

Not all competence-based systems are based on standards defined by industry (as in the UK). They are, however, based on research with *role holders*. In other words, the standards which form the basis of a competence-based system of assessment are developed through research which involves the people who are actually doing the specific work roles.

Obviously, you cannot use a competence-based system for any purpose until you have developed the competence measures. However, once you have the measures developed, they can be used for a whole range of assessment purposes.

One of the first considerations to be given to the introduction of any assessment system is *What is it we want to assess?* This may sound like a silly question, but it is one that is rarely addressed directly because assessment is often based on *assumptions* rather than clear and precise initial planning.

What do *you* want to assess? Are you planning to assess ability to learn (predictive assessment)? Are you planning to assess progress within a development programme (formative assessment)? Are you planning to assess performance (summative assessment)? Are you planning to assess at individual or group level?

Your next question must then be *Why are we assessing?* Is it to find out information about performance which is not currently available? Is it as part of a performance appraisal system? Is it to take a skills audit? Is it for manpower planning or selection and recruitment or the establishment of project teams? Is it for all of these purposes?

Eventually, you will end up with the question *What measures are we using?* This is probably the most important question of all, although it cannot be dealt with in isolation from the others. Assessment concerns measurement – you must therefore know *what* you are measuring, *why* you are measuring it and *what form* of measurement will be used. Only when these questions have been answered can you consider issues of quality of assessment.

To implement competence-based assessment one must assume that the *type* of competency and its measures have generally been agreed. This book does not provide detailed guidance on defining or developing competency statements and measures (for help on this issue, see the reference section).

However, this chapter will help you to clarify some of the issues which affect the development of competency statements by taking you through the possible uses and purposes of such an assessment system.

For the purpose of this and following chapters the terminology used is defined as follows.

Competences	Outcome-based standards of vocational performance (as UK NVQ standards)
Competencies	Behaviourally based statements of competent work-based or personal performance
Competence-based assessment	The collection of sufficient evidence of workplace and/or personal performance to demonstrate that individuals can perform or behave to the specified standards
National assessment system	A nationally defined and agreed assessment system leading to certification of competent performance
Company-specific system	A competence framework designed for a specific business organization, based on business goals and objectives

Purposes of Assessment

1. Assessment for Certification

In a competence-based system, assessment leading to certification refers to 'certification of competent performance', *not* to certification of ability to learn or to completion of a learning programme.

Think this through carefully. There is a huge difference between the various purposes of certification: consider some of the certificates you have seen at various times. What do these certificates actually tell you about the certificate holder? That the certificate holder:

- has *attended* a course of study or learning?
- has *completed* a course of study or learning?
- has demonstrated the *ability to learn to a particular level*?
- has demonstrated that specified theories/facts *have been learned*?
- has achieved a specified percentage grade in a *written* exam?
- has achieved a specified percentage grade in a *practical* test?

In a competence-based assessment and certification system, individuals achieve a certificate when they can *demonstrate performance which meets all the required standards*. Remember, there is no percentage grading, no norm-referencing, no pass or fail – only competent or not yet competent.

Figure 3.1 illustrates these differences between the traditional and competence-based systems.

The traditional view

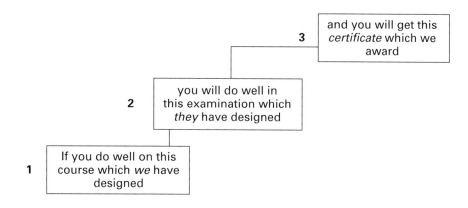

The competence-based view

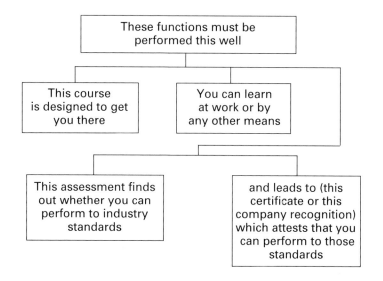

Figure 3.1 *Key differences between traditional and competence-based approaches*

National Vocational Qualifications (NVQs) provide certification by competence-based assessment, as the following case study illustrates.

Case Study: Blubeckers Restaurants Limited
Provided by Ann Lye, Director

1. Brief overview of the organization

Blubeckers Limited is a very successful, privately owned restaurant company. The first restaurant was opened in 1977. Since then, the company has progressively grown to currently six restaurants, with two new branches under construction.

The restaurants are situated in Surrey, Middlesex and Hampshire, providing an informal, friendly and efficient service with an emphasis on consistency and excellence. For customers visiting our ideally located restaurant at Hampton Court, directly opposite the Palace Gates, or our largest restaurant, the Mill House, which benefits from the River Whitewater flowing through its acres of grounds, customer care and satisfaction is successfully achieved.

2. Reasons for introducing NVQs

Blubeckers became an approved assessment centre as a result of demand from industry and professional bodies. Prospective employees were obtaining qualifications at levels required by various employers; however, once the employee started work in their chosen field, little knowledge or understanding of the job undertaken was known.

Through NVQs, employers are able to achieve on-the-job training which will develop employee progression and promotion. This in turn ensures standards are set and maintained, thus creating a stable workforce. Through being able to develop courses for employees, levels of commitment, motivation and staff retention can be maintained in order to run a successful business.

For a candidate for NVQ assessment, the successful achievement and recognition gained from completing a course is obviously very rewarding.

3. Considerations

Prior to becoming an NVQ assessment centre, Blubeckers became involved with Investors in People. The application was made in September 1994 and successful achievement of such an award was granted to Blubeckers in July 1996.

4. NVQs introduced

At present, we offer Catering and Hospitality (Food Preparation and Cooking) at levels 1 and 2 and Catering and Hospitality (Serving Food and Drink) at level 2. In addition, we offer Training and Development at levels 1 and 2, for assessors, verifiers and Company trainers. All staff have the opportunity to carry out such courses. At present though, in the kitchen there are mainly trainee chefs or new employees without any qualifications wishing to learn on the job, and front-of-house, full-time bar and waiting staff in order to progress within the company.

The individuals themselves are the ones who make the decisions whether or not to apply. This includes new employees to the company through to existing employees who want either to extend their current range of skills or to learn a different aspect of the company.

Such developments were a natural progression in the continuing success of the company. By having the opportunity to provide learning and assessment systems within the company, the end result is beneficial for both employee and employer. Better staff means better business.

5. Planning stage

To begin with, in July 1995, we approached Hampshire Training and Enterprise Council for information and advice. This led us to an introduction with Shirley Fletcher, who worked as an external consultant in order to guide Blubeckers into becoming an assessment centre. Ms Fletcher helped us to develop three assessors and one internal verifier. This enabled Blubeckers to apply to City & Guilds to be assessed. On application, an external verifier visited the business and looked at the systems and proposals we had designed. This finally led to Blubeckers becoming an approved NVQ assessment centre in December 1995.

6. Piloting/testing

During the initial stages, Ann Lye and Tanya Evans were working together with Shirley Fletcher. Advice was also sought from City & Guilds. The scheme was tested through meetings and discussions leading to Tanya Evans, Ann Lye and Graham Day becoming assessors.

7. Progress and issues

At the beginning of 1996, quarterly assessors' meetings were scheduled for all assessors and the internal verifier to attend. The meetings are designed as an open forum for discussion, including gathering and collecting evidence, individual candidate needs and progress, review of internal verification system, introduction and use of formalized workplace and assessment reports and discussions involving the introduction of new assessors.

The aims of the NVQ system are to incorporate one Kitchen Assessor and one Front of House in each restaurant within one year. Also, a mapping exercise has been introduced, which involves our current training manual running alongside the requirements of NVQs.

8. Documentation

An Evidence Diary was supplied by City & Guilds, which is still in use today. After testing the suitability of other forms suggested by City & Guilds and Fletcher Consultancy, all other paperwork and documentation has been modified, designed and implemented by Ann Lye. This includes forms and sheets which record the progress and continual assessment of employees throughout the duration of the course. For example:

- NVQ Monthly Candidate Update Form;
- Individual Assessment Plan;
- Workplace Assessment Report;
- NVQ Assessor's File.

9. Quality assurance

There are three levels of assessor, designed to oversee the operation and controls of the NVQ system. An external verifier is employed by City & Guilds to visit the assessment centre to ensure all standards and procedures required by City & Guilds NVQs are adhered to.

An internal verifier is employed by the assessment centre. The responsibilities include scheduling meetings for discussion and assessment, meeting with individuals to maintain records of progress and review their portfolio of evidence, monitoring the assessors, liaising with City & Guilds regarding candidate applications, maintaining up-to-date records of all candidates' progress and advising assessors and candidates of the NVQ process.

Finally, an assessor will be responsible for the individual monitoring of each candidate's progress. In addition, the assessor will be involved in the running and control of the NVQ system and will communicate all findings to the internal verifier.

10. Lessons learned

Planning
Since we have been up and running, a major learning point has been allocating more time and specific dates for meetings and planning. This is to ensure high levels of communication and monitoring. The first Tuesday of every month is now dedicated to such tasks.

Piloting/testing
The role and responsibility of becoming an NVQ assessment centre is much more involved and bigger than we envisaged at the beginning. Six months after becoming an assessment centre, we had 11 candidates throughout the company being assessed.

Documentation
By ensuring regular meetings and discussions with assessors, the style and content of documentation has been reduced but is now more concise.

Quality assurance
Meetings are scheduled quarterly to include candidates, assessors and the internal verifier. Additionally random samples of candidates are taken to assess work so far and record the comments made by the candidate.

General
After six months, the most important key to being a successful centre is simplicity. From experience with candidates so far, the ability to be able to offer qualifications to individuals with learning difficulties is a great achievement for us as a company, and most importantly, for the individual who can progress further.

The problem with assessment and certification

Introducing competence-based assessment can attract criticism from employers. Within a competence-based system or, more specifically, within the NVQ system, assessment leads to certification by a nationally recognized body. This national certification process requires that a quality-control mechanism is put in place – and it is in this respect that complaints about an over-emphasis on 'bureaucracy' are most loudly voiced.

Recent research and development is addressing this issue (see Beaumont Report, 1996).

It is also at this point that issues relating to the unit structure of NVQs are raised. If the main purpose of assessment is certification, and certification takes place on a unit-by-unit and 'whole qualification' (NVQ) basis, then employers are interested to ensure that their employees have access to a full NVQ.

This has presented difficulties. For some companies, the organization or content of work roles means that employees are able to obtain only some of the units required for a full NVQ; they feel that their employees should (or will want to) have access to the full qualification.

Once again, there appears to be a communication block on this point. NVQs are achievable on an individual basis, unlike traditional qualifications which are 'course-led' and achievable on the completion of a set period of study. Individuals can therefore build up their 'record of achievement' one unit at a time. Units may be relevant to more than one sector of industry. It is not, therefore, essential that everyone in every work role should be able to achieve a full NVQ while working in that role. The flexibility of the unit-based system means that individuals can obtain units which are relevant to their current and developmental roles, thus aiding their progression and helping employers to plan training, development and promotional operations.

This issue, and others, were addressed directly within the Blubeckers Restaurant case study.

Key difficulties associated with NVQ assessment include:

- structure of NVQ units (see above);
- bureaucracy and paper-led systems;
- language used in competence-base standards.

These were all highlighted in the Beaumont Report (Beaumont, 1996) which reviewed the top 100 NVQs. Several research projects have been undertaken to improve practice, reduce bureaucracy and encourage greater use of unit certification.

I completed one such project for the National Council for Vocational Qualifications (NCVQ) in 1995/96. The results of this project, which included new guidance for streamlining NVQ assessment, are published by NCVQ in their 'Assessment Guidance for NVQs' (1996). I have also produced a book, *Assessment of NVQs: A handbook for the paperless portfolio* (Fletcher, 1997a), which provides tools and design guidance to help users avoid these pitfalls.

Similar difficulties will arise when implementing other forms of competence-based assessment. Behavioural competencies require assessment practice which is also rigorous and has credibility with users. Quality assurance of competence-based assessment must be a key consideration of design, regardless of the type of competence being measured.

2. Performance Appraisal

Many organizations have performance-appraisal systems. These usually operate on an annual basis and involve an interview with a line manager and use of a pre-interview question sheet.

Most criticisms of this system stem from the use of measures which are very difficult to assess and of rating scales which generally lead to assessors taking the 'middle road' as an easy option.

Competence-based assessment as the basis of performance appraisal provides a more specific measure of performance.

To use the full potential of competence-based assessment within performance appraisal often requires a complete rethinking of the existing process and a broader view of appraisal as one part of a wider performance management system.

Implications and benefits

A competence-based performance appraisal system could provide the following benefits:

- integration of continuous performance management with annual/biannual review and objective setting;
- a common language for appraisal and other HR functions;
- a better tool for managers to monitor and feedback performance, linked to objectives and development needs;
- appraisals measuring actual contribution to business objectives.

Putting this in place has the following implications:

- what measures of competence will be used in both continuous and annual performance assessment (are they consistent?);
- what training will managers need;
- how will achievement of competence link to reward, career development, succession planning.

3. Identification of Training Needs

Competence-based assessment offers an opportunity, through continuous measuring and managing of performance, for managers to identify training needs at individual level.

If such a system is introduced at organization level, the ability to identify these needs, and thus to provide training which is targeted to specific needs, is greatly improved.

Implications and benefits

Operation of a competence-based system for the identification of training needs requires that managers are skilled in identifying real, rather than perceived, needs, in providing feedback, and in identifying those needs which can be dealt with by on-job development. A further added-value aspect of competence-based systems therefore is that managers are encouraged to take more of a development role. However, managers will need appropriate skills to achieve this effectively. Key questions in this context are:

- What training will our managers need in:
  - identifying training needs?
  - coaching?
  - mentoring?
  - opportunity training?
- What communication structure needs to be in place to ensure that training needs are collated?
- What changes do we need to make to our training delivery function to provide modular development programmes?

This last question is often missed. If needs are identified more accurately, there is no longer a need for individuals to attend a 'standard' course – they need only attend courses where on-job development is not available or appropriate, and the course is modular in format and targeted to their specific needs.

At strategic level, identification of training needs as part of a skills audit, using a competence-based system, can assist with the development of corporate training strategies and plans, or indeed with manpower planning activities.

4. Skills Audit

All organizations would probably find it valuable to be able to take stock of their workforce skills. A competence-based system of assessment allows for this to take place either as an initial, introductory process or as the result of collated data from an on-going assessment process.

You may consider introducing a computerized assessment recording system (keeping the Data Protection Act in mind of course). This is particularly useful in organizations which need to put together project teams, each member having specialist skills or expertise.

As an initial assessment, the competency measures can be used to assess current levels of performance (and identify training needs). As continuous assessment, the competence-based system allows for regular monitoring and updating of workforce skill levels.

For example, by providing individuals and their line managers with a copy of the standards which are relevant to their work role, and with guidance on their use, initial assessment will provide an analysis of current skills levels and training needs. As the assessment requires that evidence of competent performance is provided, and this evidence is generated from normal workplace activity, the individual can prove competence through the provision of relevant evidence.

Similarly, in a continuous assessment process, the level of competent performance, and training needs, continue to be identified.

In essence, a competence-based assessment system should make explicit what effective line managers do on a daily basis – *measure and manage performance.* Competence-based assessment should become an integral part of everyday management activity and involve line managers and those being assessed in a continuous process of development and improvement.

Implications and benefits

Again, the measures must be in place before you start, so you may need to invest in this development. The use of accreditation of prior learning (APL) has its own implications and is dealt with in the next section.

The term 'skills audit' has unfortunate connotations. Any introduction in a strong union environment may therefore need careful planning and negotiation. The purpose of the skills audit must be clear if it is to be used as a positive motivator for improvement of performance.

5. Accreditation of Prior Learning (APL)

The APL process provides a useful tool in three areas:

- introducing competence-based assessment;
- taking a skills audit;
- as a staff development process.

APL is an integral part of competency-based assessment, not a separate process. It is one which allows for evidence from past achievements to be included in the total of evidence collected during assessment. There are particular rules of evidence (see Chapter 6) which apply in this context, but there is no reason why APL cannot be as reliable and effective as continuous assessment of performance – as long as quality rules are applied.

Implications and benefits

APL is a useful tool for motivating staff and for introducing competence-based assessment. It requires trained assessors and probably advisers. It can be a very cost-effective process for skills audit. Check carefully about costs-per-head quotations when seeking advice from external sources. In my own in-company work on this issue, I have discovered that employers have been given wildly varying estimates of cost, particularly where APL is used in connection with assessment for certification purposes. In general, check for assessors approved by relevant awarding bodies if certification is one of your objectives. (Chapters 5–8 provide guidance for those of you who are considering the introduction of APL for certification or internal skills audit purposes.)

6. Selection and Recruitment

Again, the issue of having measures developed arises: you cannot assess competence unless you have a clear measure of competence to begin with. However, as noted in the introduction to this chapter, once you have the measures they can be used for a wide range of purposes.

Competence-based measures of performance focus on *outcomes*. If you know what outcomes you require, you can design your recruitment and selection processes around them.

Using the competence measures as a starting point, your recruitment material and interview schedules can be designed to elicit information which directly relates to required performance. (Note the use of the term 'schedules' for interviews – the implication is that questions are pre-determined and follow an agreed format and presentation. This will enable interviews to be conducted in a fair and effective way.)

Implications and benefits

Recruitment and selection processes can be defined with more clarity using a competence-based system. The standards used as a basis for the design of these processes are common across all activities within the organization; there is therefore less chance of a mismatch between staff recruited and staff required. To implement such a system, time must be devoted to the development of interview schedules and training of interviewers. (Again, use of competence-based assessment leads to identification of training needs and requires that training is more systematic and directed to real needs.)

7. Evaluating Training

This is an area which has caused considerable concern but least remedial effort in many organizations. My personal belief is that as long as employers see training as a cost rather than an investment, little action will be taken to evaluate the effectiveness of training programmes. When training becomes an investment issue, the question of gaining the best possible return on that investment becomes important.

With competence-based assessment systems, the measures of competent performance are available for a before-and-after picture to be taken. If measures are used, as they should be, on a continuous basis to measure and manage performance and to identify training needs, then the measurement required to check on the effectiveness of training is already in place.

Training is too often an activity in which individuals are allocated to programmes on a 'grade-related' basis, or are sent to the most appropriate programme on the company's 'menu'. Far too few training consultancies actually make training applicable to the working context. So-called evaluation of programmes is in practice often no more than an enquiry as to the food, accommodation and whether participants liked the trainer.

If your organization needs to evaluate the effectiveness of training – and perhaps the effectiveness of managers' identification of *real* training needs – then a competence-based assessment system provides a framework in which this can be operated.

Implications and benefits

Personally, I believe the 'return on investment' issue is a key one in this context. To establish competence-based assessment as a tool for training evaluation alone would be a costly exercise – but it is unlikely that this would be the case.

The key costs are in development – development of the competence measures and the associated assessment framework. Operational costs are minimal. Once competence measures are established they are available for use in the full range of business activities which have been outlined in this chapter. In effect, their use for training evaluation is a spin-off or added-value aspect of the implementation process.

▶ **REVIEW** ◀

This chapter has briefly outlined the various purposes of competence-based assessment at organizational level. It also makes the key point that once measures are defined (or incorporated as nationally defined standards in the UK), they are available for use in the full range of assessment activities. Further guidance on the many issues, implications and benefits raised in this chapter can be found in the remaining chapters and in the References and Further Reading section.

Part II PRACTICAL APPLICATION

In Part II, you will be taken step by step through the process of competence-based assessment. You may recall from Chapter 2 that our framework of competence-based assessment looked like this:

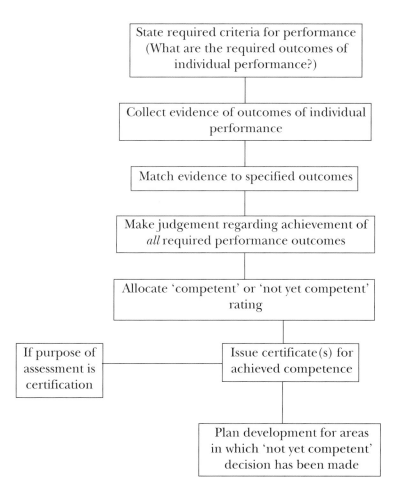

State required criteria for performance
(What are the required outcomes of individual performance?)

Collect evidence of outcomes of individual performance

Match evidence to specified outcomes

Make judgement regarding achievement of *all* required performance outcomes

Allocate 'competent' or 'not yet competent' rating

If purpose of assessment is certification

Issue certificate(s) for achieved competence

Plan development for areas in which 'not yet competent' decision has been made

Chapter 4 begins with this model and outlines issues relating to setting requirements and planning assessment. The remaining chapters deal with the collection and matching of evidence to the specified standards, and with review and follow-up procedures and processes. Chapter 7 also highlights some of the other issues which may need attention due to the knock-on effect of the introduction of competence-based assessment. Chapter 8 deals with quality assurance issues.

Examples of current competence-based assessment systems are included to illustrate key points.

4 Setting Criteria for Required Performance

▷   SUMMARY   ◁

This chapter helps you to familiarize yourself with the structure and content of competence-based standards. It provides guidance on their use and on setting assessment plans for individuals. You will also find help in considering the key factors which can influence effective assessment.

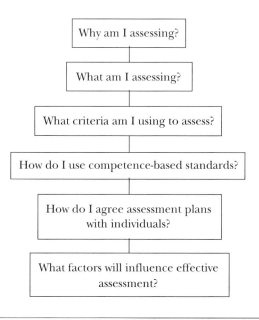

Why am I assessing?

What am I assessing?

What criteria am I using to assess?

How do I use competence-based standards?

How do I agree assessment plans with individuals?

What factors will influence effective assessment?

In Chapter 2, the key features of a competence-based system were outlined. These were

- focus on 'outcomes';
- individualized assessment;
- no percentage rating;
- no comparison with other individuals' results;
- *all* standards (requirements) must be met;
- ongoing process – (leads to further development and assessment);
- only 'competent' or 'not yet competent' judgements made.

These key aspects must be borne in mind when considering the specific requirements of performance to be used within a competence-based assessment system.

Your two key questions at this point are *Why am I assessing?* and *What is to be assessed?*

Why Am I Assessing?

In Chapter 2, competence-based assessment was defined as follows:

To collect sufficient evidence of workplace performance to demonstrate that individuals can perform or behave to specified standards.

Chapter 3 outlined further, more specific, purposes and uses of competence-based assessment, including:

- certification;
- performance appraisal;
- identifying training needs;
- skills audit;
- prior learning;
- selection and recruitment;
- evaluating training.

Your overall reason for introducing a competence-based assessment system may be to raise the level of performance within your organization, or to provide a user-friendly and effective system by which performance can be measured and monitored.

You may choose one or any combination of the specific purposes of competence-based assessment listed above to achieve your overall aim, but you must first be clear about your company's key purpose in introducing an assessment system. You need a clear direction before you begin to answer the next question.

What is to be Assessed?

If we are focusing on performance in the workplace, then what you want to assess is that *performance*. But is it the *process of performing* or the *outcome of performance* that you want to assess? Do you want a one-off demonstration of that performance, or do you want to know that people can perform to a specified standard over a period of time? Are you going to assess on an individual or a group basis? Will you need to assess simply *what people do* or also *how well it is done?*

In a competence-based system, as our key features list shows, the focus is on *outcomes* of performance and assessment of *individuals* over a *continuous period.*

A further key point is whether you are assessing competence or excellence. Do you want to set common standards of performance which you can use as a benchmark for competent performers? Do you wish to add a further benchmark of 'excellence'? What are the implications of doing this? If everyone has to meet 'excellent' standards will you be raising the level of performance or risking losing good workers? Will you have a reward system attached to these standards and will excellence gain a higher reward than competence? Is this system to be linked to certification? Is this certification to include national recognition by an external body, or is it to be company certification only?

In a competence-based assessment system, there is no grading of results, only a simple judgement of 'yes you have met the standards' or 'no, you have not met the standards yet'.

In deciding *what* you are going to assess, therefore, you need to begin with the *key aim* of assessment within your company.

Establishing Criteria for Performance

In the UK, national standards of occupational competence for all sectors of industry are being published at all levels. These standards, defined by industry, provide an agreed benchmark of competent performance for occupational roles within each sector.

In the UK, they are also incorporated into National Vocational Qualifications (NVQS). In the USA, similar standards are available as the basis of competency-development programmes. Both forms of standards are illustrated later in this chapter.

These standards will provide you with a sound starting point on which to make your decisions about the standards or criteria for performance which you need to set. They are outcome-based, reflecting expectations of workplace performance, and have been agreed through consultation with role holders.

They do, however, reflect an agreed benchmark of competence (UK) or 'excellent performers' (USA). If you are seeking to establish company-specific standards of excellence and/or to incorporate your company's mission statement and objective into the final standards, then further work will be needed. Should you wish not to make use of national or other available standards, but to develop your own, then you may use a range of methods. Current standards development methodology uses functional analysis. General guidance on this development issue was given in Chapter 3.

Of key importance is the list of features of a competence-based system provided at the beginning of this chapter. When you set your 'requirements' or 'standards' of performance for use in a competence-based system, these key features must form a central part of your development process. You may need consultancy support to achieve this.

Three examples of outcome-based standards of performance follow, taken from both the UK and US systems. Competence-based standards can be defined for all occupations, as these examples illustrate.

You will notice that in Figure 4.2, the example has 'range indicators' rather than 'range statements'. This is because the management field is 'generic' – that is, managers work in all occupational areas. Range indicators therefore serve as a guide for users in all occupations and can be made into more specific range statements by detailing the range to match the occupational context.

The third example (Figure 4.3) is from the US competency model and illustrates the 'clusters' which can be used as a basis for the design of programmes to develop competence.

You will notice a difference in structure between the UK and US standards. In the UK, the use of functional analysis has led to standards which are very explicit in terms of the required outcomes of actual workplace performance while the US system focuses on 'personal attributes'.

There have been criticisms of both systems. Some believe that the UK system focuses too much on the performance of work activities and not enough on the personal effectiveness of individuals. Others believe that the US system focuses too much on personal effectiveness and not enough on the work activities. The UK system does have a set of 'personal competences' – illustrated at Figure 4.5 in the following section. As you will see, this structure is similar to that used in the USA.

Your choice for use of standards must depend upon the objectives of your assessment system. Guidance on the purpose and objectives of assessment systems was given in Chapter 2. You might like to review that

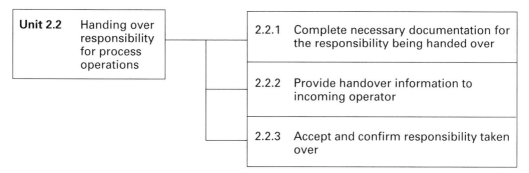

Element 2.2.1: Complete necessary documentation for the responsibility being handed over

Performance criteria

(a) All documentation required by procedures and/or necessary for the incoming operator is completed accurately and legibly.

(b) Documentation is assembled and passed to the incoming operator as specified in procedures.

(c) Any missing or incomplete documentation which would prevent the handover being carried out fully is brought to the attention of the appropriate authority.

Range

Handover situations: During a shift at the appropriate point in an operating cycle, at the end of a shift.
Oral and written information

Operations: Moderately complex process operations and related tasks, involving several different unit operations and some problem solving

Plant/equipment: Moderately complex plant and equipment, with some control instrumentation, several interactions between items of equipment and people, and with a number of parameters within the operator's control

Evidence requirements

The candidate should:

- demonstrate completing documentation for at least one handover

For all activities specified in the range the candidate should:

- explain the consequences of not keeping accurate and up-to-date records for this activity
- describe the correct procedure to follow in the event of documentation being missing or incomplete

Figure 4.1 *Example of competence-based standards (UK) – Process Operations (CIA)*

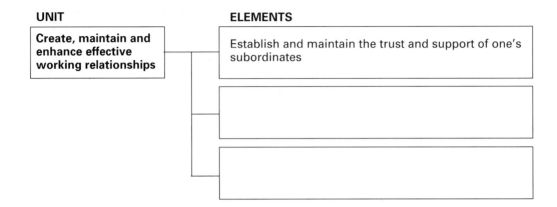

Element 7.1: Establish and maintain the trust and support of one's subordinates

Performance criteria

- Time is taken with subordinates to establish and maintain honest and constructive relationships
- Subordinates are encouraged to offer ideas and views and due recognition of these is given
- Where ideas are not taken up, the reasons are clearly given
- Subordinates are consulted about proposed activities within an appropriate timescale and encouraged to seek clarification of areas of which they are unsure
- Subordinates are sufficiently informed about organizational policy and strategy, progress, emerging threats and opportunities
- Promises and undertakings to subordinates are realistic and are honoured
- Subordinates are given appropriate support in any situations which involve people outside the manager's team
- Where there is concern over the quality of a subordinate's work, the matter is directly raised and discussed with him or her

Range indicators

Subordinates are all those within the manager's direct line responsibility
Subordinates include – staff (permanent, temporary, full/part-time); subcontractors; trainees/students placed with the manager's team
Communication may be instigated by – the manager; the subordinate
Information giving and consultation takes place both – formally; informally
Information giving and consultation is through the means of – team meetings; one-to-one discussions; telephone conversations; written communication

Figure 4.2 *Example of competence-based standards (UK) – management (Management Charter Initiative, 1991)*

Human resource management cluster

Managers with these competencies have positive expectations about others; have realistic views of themselves; build networks or coalitions with others to accomplish tasks, and stimulate cooperation and pride in work groups.

Accurate self-assessment
　　The ability to appraise one's strengths and weaknesses realistically.

Self-control
　　The ability to subordinate one's personal needs or desires to those of the organization.

Stamina and adaptability
　　The ability to sustain long hours of work and be flexible in adapting to change.

Perceptual objectivity
　　The ability to be relatively objective about others' views and not limited by subjectivity.

Positive regard
　　The ability to express a belief in others' ability to perform and to improve.

Managing the group process
　　The ability to stimulate others to work effectively together in a group setting.

Use of socialized power
　　The ability to influence others through group effort.

Figure 4.3 *Example of competency-based standards (USA) – human resource management cluster*

chapter before continuing with any plans for introducing a competence-based assessment system.

As a general guide, if you are aiming to assess the actual outcomes of workplace activity, the UK structure illustrated provides a basis on which this can be implemented. If you are seeking to assess personal effectiveness, then the US themes and clusters, or the UK personal competence model would be more appropriate.

Using Standards of Competence

Standards of occupational competence, whether in UK or US format, provide guidance to the assessor on three key aspects of competent performance:

	UK	*USA*
What has to be achieved	Element	Cluster
How well it must be achieved	Performance criteria	Competency
In what contexts/conditions	Range Statement	Descriptor

Within this system, assessors will assess the elements or clusters of competence, performance criteria and range statements. A number of elements or clusters grouped together form the first level of certification within a vocational award.

Individuals must demonstrate evidence which can be matched to *all* specified standards, across the full specified *range* of activities. This is because a 'competent individual' is someone who can perform:

- to the specified standards;
- consistently;
- over a range of contexts or conditions.

Examples of the structure of standards of competence are given in the following figures.

Figure 4.4 illustrates the framework for the US competency system. This uses 'themes' and 'clusters' to illustrate the areas of competence required. This framework is similar to the UK personal competences model shown in Figure 4.5 and focuses on 'competence' as a personal attribute, rather than an expectation of workplace performance.

Figure 4.5 illustrates the UK personal competence model. As noted above, it is much easier to see similarity between this and the US themes and clusters illustrated in Figure 4.4.

It is easy to see why the two systems become confused. There are similarities between the US and UK systems in the personal competence structure. However, the structure of UK standards for occupational roles is quite different.

It is important to remember that the key difference between the two systems is the concept on which development of the standards is based. In the UK, standards reflect the expectations or outcomes of workplace performance; in the US system, standards reflect the personal attributes of individuals who have already been recognized as excellent performers.

When using these standards, keep these key concepts in mind. This will help you to focus on the objectives of your assessment.

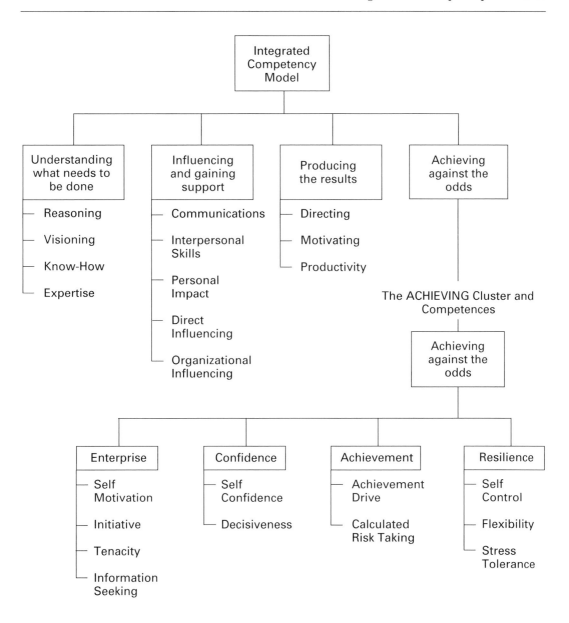

Figure 4.4 *Structure of competency descriptors (USA)*

PERSONAL COMPETENCE MODEL

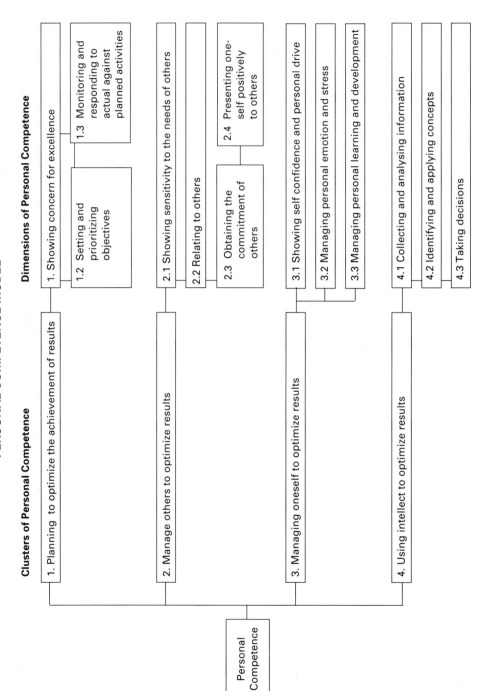

Figure 4.5 *Structure of personal competences (UK) (Management Charter Initiative 1991)*

Agreeing Assessment Plans

As competence-based assessment systems operate on an individual basis, the assessor must agree an individual assessment plan with each person to be assessed. This will involve establishing which units or clusters of competence the individual and the assessor feel can be realistically assessed within the individual's current job role. Some account of development activities may also be taken.

It is essential that an assessment plan is agreed so that the individual knows he or she is being assessed on a continuous basis, and is aware of the form which that assessment will take.

Competence-based assessment is an iterative process – that is, the assessment plan will constantly be reviewed and updated as individuals develop and achieve competence. If the assessment system is linked to certification processes, particularly to national certification, this review and update will also involve recommendation for award of unit or full certificates.

To be truly effective in planning an individual assessment, the assessor must understand the principles of competence-based assessment and be skilled in the use of various assessment methods. 'Planning assessment' in the competence-based context does not mean 'setting up a skills test' or arranging an examination.

Establishing an Assessment Plan

Figure 4.6 illustrates the stages involved in agreeing an assessment plan. *This must be undertaken with each individual for whom you have line management/assessment responsibility.*

The following text uses the term 'unit' to refer to the first level of assessment which leads to achievement of formal recognition. Readers using a US system should therefore substitute 'cluster' for 'unit'.

Why does the individual want to be assessed?

You must first agree on the reasons for assessment. Is the individual keen to achieve national certification? Are they seeking promotion? Are they seeking training and development? Is this an integral part of the company performance management system/appraisal?

Does the individual understand the system?

Make sure the individual understands the structure of the units and the standards on which they are built. Also check that the individual

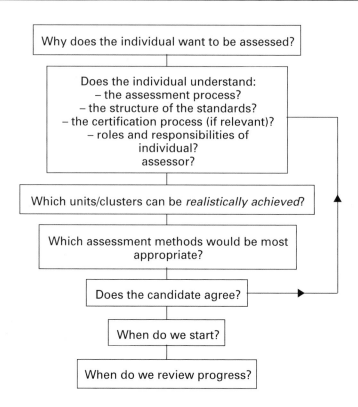

Figure 4.6 *Establishing an assessment plan*

understands what is involved in the assessment process – that he/she will be assessed on a continuous, not a one-off, basis. The roles and responsibilities of the individual and the assessor must be made clear. (The assessor's role will be outlined in Chapter 5.) The individual's role and responsibilities include:

- bringing to the attention of their designated assessor, evidence which they feel is relevant to on-going assessment (including evidence from past experience);
- agreeing an assessment plan with the line manager.

Which units can the individual realistically achieve?

You must negotiate with the candidate the number of units which realistically reflects their *current* work role. You may also work with them to identify units which relate to their training or future development needs, but you must keep in mind that the individual must be in a position, or have the opportunity, to provide actual *evidence* of performance.

What methods of assessment would be most appropriate?

As we have noted already, *observation of natural workplace performance* must be the primary form of assessment. However, you should consider operational constraints and identify those areas which may require supplementary assessment methods.

When do we start?

Set a clear start date for assessment. Make sure the assessment records are ready for use (including the awarding body log book if appropriate). It is essential that clear and accurate records of assessment are kept, although the system does not have to be elaborate and should be user-friendly. If you are working within an assessment system linked to formal recognition by an awarding body then you may find that pro forma for assessment records are provided by that awarding body. You may wish to modify these or develop your own. Of course, if you are using your own company system, your documentation will have been devised and developed in-house.

Influences on Assessment

When planning assessment, the assessor must be aware of various influences on the assessment process. The following should be used as a general guidance note in this respect.

Assessment should be *unobtrusive* and should not interfere with normal workplace activity. All assessors can be influenced by a number of factors and it is helpful to be aware of the most common influences so that you can try to avoid them.

A sense of direction

Unplanned assessment will result in inaccurate judgements. Always be clear about what evidence you are looking for in any assessment situation. This means being familiar with and understanding the specified standards.

An illusion of validity

It is very easy to observe someone or to review written evidence and conclude that 'this is good'. The issue at hand is not whether or not an individual does 'good work'; the issue is whether the evidence you are *currently assessing* provides *valid proof* that the required standards are being met. Evidence can be of high quality but have nothing whatsoever to do with the particular area of competence which you are assessing!

Stereotyping

Stereotyping is never useful in an assessment situation. Your concern as an assessor is to collect and evaluate relevant evidence of actual performance. This has nothing to do with categorizing people.

Halo and horns effects

A very common source of inaccurate judgement is due to preconceived ideas about a person's performance. These ideas may be based on the fact that you actually like the person concerned (they have a halo), or that you don't like them (they have horns) – or that they usually do good or excellent work. The reverse works as well: maybe they do or don't like you! None of these considerations should affect your judgement. Your concern is the actual evidence presented.

Hawthorn effect

People act differently when they know they are being assessed. Competence-based assessment is *continuous* and should therefore be carried out under normal working conditions on an everyday basis. We have already noted that assessment should also be unobtrusive.

Contrast effects

Competence-based assessment is *individualized* assessment. It is concerned with individual performance, not a comparison or contrast with how other people perform. You should be careful to avoid comparing and contrasting the group of candidates for whom you are responsible.

REVIEW ◀

This chapter has taken you through the initial steps of competence-based assessment – setting criteria and establishing an action plan. The following chapter moves on to consider the actual collection of evidence.

5 Collecting Evidence of Competence

▷ SUMMARY ◁

This chapter helps you to choose the most relevant and effective assessment methods and outlines the roles and responsibilities of those involved in the assessment process.

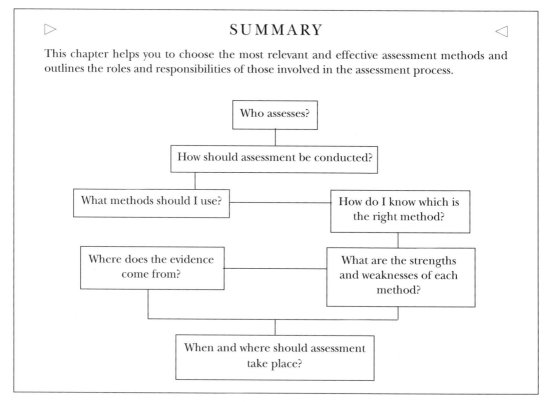

Assessment is about making judgements. A skilled assessor, in any context, is one who is able to review evidence which has been presented and make a confident decision of 'competent' or 'not yet competent' based on that review.

Assessors must be able to establish and agree a clear *assessment plan* with individuals. They must also be aware of *influences on assessment*. These issues were dealt with in Chapter 4.

All of this also requires, however, that assessors are skilled in the choice of *methods* of assessment and that they understand the strengths and weaknesses of each method. They must also be aware of the *sources* of evidence.

In this chapter, we look at the who, when, where and how of competence-based assessment. We explore the roles of assessors and methods of assessment together with the strengths and weaknesses of each.

Who Assesses?

An assessor's role is to review individual candidates' evidence of performance and to make a decision, based on that evidence, regarding the competence of each individual in his or her work role. This is an important and responsible position in which to operate. To be effective, assessors need answers to questions such as:

- How do I know what competent means?
- Where does the evidence come from?
- How do I choose the right assessment methods?

There are no magic answers. The quality of assessment, however, lies in the skills of the assessors and in their understanding of the concepts and principles of competence-based assessment. A skilled assessor is able to adopt new and creative approaches to assessment based on this clear understanding. Competence-based assessment is *individualized* assessment – each individual may produce different or unique collections of evidence of performance, thus providing a different or unique challenge to the assessor. The assessor must therefore adopt a flexible and creative approach to this challenge.

If competence-based assessment is *individualized* and *focused on performance* then the best person to assess is a first-line manager or supervisor.

An assessor within a competence-based system should be someone who is in regular contact with the individual and therefore has the opportunity to observe and monitor actual performance in a realistic *working environment.*

The role of a workplace assessor can be summarized as follows:

- A workplace assessor is usually a line manager – because a line manager is the best person to observe natural workplace performance.

- The workplace assessor is responsible for judging *evidence of performance* and ensuring that this evidence is of the correct *type* and *quality* to ensure that a confident decision about the sufficiency of evidence to meet required standards is achieved.
- The workplace assessor may use a range of assessment methods but the primary form of assessment must always be *observation of performance. Feedback* should be given to individuals on a regular basis and *training needs* will be identified during the course of assessment.
- The workplace assessor is also responsible for *recording assessment.* Details of evidence and of judgements made must be entered on an assessment record.

This creates a new perspective in many organizations. In a competence-based system, the workplace assessor will be a line manager; all line managers must therefore be trained in the skills and application of competence-based assessment. This has considerable long-term benefits: managers become more effective at measuring and managing performance and operate on a more people-oriented basis. A learning culture also develops. However, achievement of these outcomes requires an initial investment in the training of line managers. This issue is also a key point for British Telecom, as outlined below. (The knock-on effects of introducing competence-based assessment are also outlined in more detail in Chapter 7.)

The British Telecom Experience

The trainer-training groups in British Telecom decided to go for a competence-based assessment approach as it offered a complete assessment approach and therefore helped to avoid duplication of assessment in a variety of roles. British Telecom used to operate a category system for trainers where the same skills may be used within a particular category, but with a different emphasis.

British Telecom found that 20 activities (competences) previously identified by in-house research would fit into the national system of assessment.

The key difficulty of introducing competence-based assessment, from the viewpoint of British Telecom, is that of training the workplace managers in the principles of the new system.

Managers will need to be very clear about what it is they are looking for; they will need to apply common standards and to give feedback in a developmental way.

British Telecom provides training for managers in training manager support workshops but believes it is also helpful if the workplace managers undertake some of the 20 identified activities themselves on the trainer development programme.

A clear decision has been made that assessment will be undertaken by line managers. Issues of quality and relevance will be uppermost within British Telecom and it is expected that central monitoring of standards will remain an in-house priority.

Accreditation of prior learning will, it is believed, be a part of the assessment system. Plans to operate this in the most cost-effective and efficient way will be considered.

Multiple assessors

When we talk of a workplace assessor, we usually refer to a 'designated' assessor. Within a competence-based assessment system, each individual should have a designated assessor responsible for recording evidence and 'signing off' satisfactory achievement of competence within a particular area (usually a unit) of competence.

However, as we shall see when we look at sources of evidence (p. 72) a number of assessors can (and often should) be involved in the assessment process. Many people may observe an individual's performance – senior managers, peers, trainers and tutors; all have relevant evidence. An assessor may use these other people as sources of evidence, or they may take a more formal role in supplying evidence on a regular basis. As a rule of thumb, one should remember that the use of multiple assessors can increase the reliability of assessment. However, to keep communication lines clear, only one assessor should have the responsibility for formally recording achievement. (Note also the use of the term 'achievement' rather than 'completion' – this helps to keep your mind focused on *outcomes* rather than training or learning *inputs*.)

How does the assessor know what 'competent' means?

The assessor in a competence-based system is guided in the assessment process by the specified standards of performance. These were outlined in Chapter 4.

Key issues for assessors

Assessment is about *generating* and *judging* evidence. Different methods of assessment can be used, at different times, to produce evidence of different types.

There are many assessment methods. For example:

- observation of performance;
- skills test;
- simulation exercise;
- project or assignment;
- oral questioning;
- written examination;
- multiple-choice question paper.

Some of these methods provide evidence of *performance*, some provide evidence of *knowledge* and/or *application of knowledge and understanding*.

Assessors may use all or only a few of these. Decisions on which methods to use and on how and when to use them will be influenced by four key components:

- what is to be assessed (the standards);
- the assessment framework (the units or clusters);
- the context of assessment (operational constraints);
- skills of the assessor.

The first component – what is to be assessed – was explored in Chapter 4. Competence-based assessment must always start with matching what people actually do to the specified standards of performance. If you are not using nationally agreed standards, then your own must be in a format which clearly indicates the *outcomes* which individuals must achieve.

The second component – the assessment framework – again depends upon the system you are using. In the UK certification system of National Vocational Qualifications, your framework will consist of *units of competence*. If you are using a different model, your framework may be *clusters of behaviour* or competencies as behavioural measures. Whatever your system, it should be in usable chunks – each chunk representing an area of activity which has real meaning in the workplace. This is essential if you are linking your assessment to certification and reward systems.

The third component – the context of assessment – is crucial to the successful operation of your assessment scheme. In an ideal situation, each individual to be assessed will have a line manager as a designated assessor. Each designated assessor will be monitored by a verifier or quality assurance assessor (see Chapter 8), and each verifier will in turn be monitored by an external verifier if your system is part of a National

Vocational Qualification. However, ideal situations do not often exist!

Your particular operational constraints must be taken into account and issues such as lines of communication and accountability must be paramount in these considerations. But these are not the only issues: operational constraints affect the choice of assessment methods, and assessors will need to tailor the choice of assessment method to the operational context.

The skills of the assessor – the fourth component – are therefore of utmost importance, which is why assessors will need training and development (see Chapter 8). Assessors need skills in the selection and use of assessment methods, and they need an understanding of the strengths and weaknesses of each method. They also need to make the best use of various sources of evidence in addition to being fully aware of the many influences on assessment. The remainder of this chapter deals with these issues.

Sources of Evidence

In order to select the most appropriate and effective assessment methods, an assessor must have a clear understanding of the various sources of evidence. This section reviews the following key sources of evidence of performance:

- multiple assessors;
- performance at work;
- specially set tasks/projects/assignments;
- questioning;
- historical evidence.

Multiple assessors

Earlier in this chapter, we briefly reviewed the idea of multiple assessors – a variety of people who have contact with the individual being assessed and who therefore can provide evidence of that individual's performance. One *source* of evidence, therefore, is other people who have this contact.

If we are to make best use of this source, however, we need to have clear lines of communication. People need to know that they have a role in providing evidence.

In your own context, consider who these people might be. For example:

- senior managers;
- tutors and trainers;

- peers and co-workers;
- customers;
- contacts in other divisions/departments.

Basically, anyone with whom an individual has contact within their normal working activity can be a source of evidence. But take care – your approach to each source will need to be planned. You will also need to make sure that the evidence you receive reflects the performance of the particular individual, and is not clouded by that person's involvement in team activities. All sources must be carefully considered in terms of the quality of evidence provided. (The issue of quality is dealt with in the next chapter.)

Performance at work

The best evidence comes from actual workplace performance. Remember, competence-based standards reflect *outcomes* of performance; where better to collect evidence of achievement of these outcomes than in the realistic, everyday working environment?

Observation of actual workplace performance should always be an assessor's primary *form of evidence collection.*

Performance on specially set tasks

Where observation of normal workplace activity is not possible, special tasks or assignments can be set to *generate* the required evidence. Because it is produced in a 'false' or 'simulated' setting, evidence provided by this route will not be of the same high quality as that generated by normal workplace activity. However, evidence produced by simulated methods will *contribute* to continuous assessment and help the assessor make decisions about the individual's competence across the specified range of activities.

There are times when a simulation or skills test or project will be an essential means of generating evidence. For example, an assessor cannot set fire to a building, or shut down equipment and machinery to assess whether an individual knows how to deal with such an emergency. Similarly, where licensing is required, such as with fork lift truck drivers, health and safety requirements would prohibit assessment in real working situations until the licence had been obtained.

Other issues also come into play. Competence-based assessment requires that individuals are assessed across the full range of activities specified within the standards. Individuals do not always have the opportunity to demonstrate their competence on all types of equipment or machinery. For example, a welder may need to demonstrate competence in the use of MIG, TIG and arc welding, but may not have an opportunity to do so for some time if the particular work in hand requires only two out of the three methods. In this type of circumstance, use of specially set tasks, projects, assignments and tests can generate the evidence required.

Questioning

It is often the case that observation of normal activity and specially set tasks do not provide sufficient evidence. For example, if an individual needs to be assessed across a wide range of contexts or conditions, or in the use of a wide range of equipment or machinery, the assessor may have to spend years waiting for, or trying to create, the right opportunity!

In assessing competence, the assessor is attempting to collect evidence that demonstrates an individual's performance to required standards. This includes *application* of knowledge and understanding – it is not 'knowing' itself that is important in competent performance, but what individuals *do* with that knowledge.

If you want to know that an individual is able to drive a car on a clear day, with little traffic about, you might observe their performance by sitting in the car with them. However, if you also want to know that they can drive the same car, or different cars, in rain, snow, sleet, hail, high winds, thunderstorms, in light and heavy traffic, and on motorways, A and B roads and dirt tracks, you might take years to assess them this way!

Your basic aim as an assessor in this context, and in all other competence-based assessments, is to collect sufficient evidence to make a confident judgement that the individual can perform to the required standards across the full range of specified activities.

One very simple way of finding out what you need to know is to ask. In the assessment context, your questions need to be carefully framed to elicit the *evidence* you are seeking. You might ask 'What if…' to elicit evidence of performance across the range of activity. You might set a series of open, written questions to assess that an individual is able to apply relevant knowledge and understanding to activities which require decision-making, or problem-solving. For example, assessing a doctor's performance across the full range of diagnoses, medicines and medical tests applied to patients could take forever unless a written form of evidence collection was used!

Historical evidence

The term 'historical evidence' has been used to refer to evidence of past achievements and often occurs in literature and guidance on the accreditation of prior learning (APL).

Evidence from past achievements can be valuable in competence-based assessment and often forms part of the on-going assessment process.

Again, the *quality* of evidence is of paramount importance and the 'rules of evidence' must apply (see Chapter 6).

In a sense, we might say that all evidence is historical, since once it has been produced it is immediately in the past! However, this source of evidence can, when used effectively, help to fill the gaps when an assessor is attempting to collect evidence across the full range of an activity.

Choosing the Right Assessment Methods

Assessment methods include:

- observation of performance;
- skills tests;
- simulation exercises;
- project or assignment;
- oral questioning;
- written examination;
- multiple-choice question paper.

We noted earlier that some of these methods provide evidence of *performance* and some provide evidence of *knowledge and understanding*. You will also recall that it is *application* of knowledge and understanding that is of key interest in a competence-based assessment system.

When considering the use of various assessment methods, an assessor must keep these questions in mind:

- What evidence do I need?
- How much evidence do I need?
- Which methods will provide quality evidence?

The following pages provide guidance on the use of each of the assessment methods listed above, with these key questions in mind. This guidance refers to the selection of assessment methods; guidance on quality of evidence follows in Chapter 6.

Observation of performance

Strengths
- Provides high-quality evidence of competence.
- Is undertaken (or should be) as usual part of line manager's responsibility.

- Individuals become accustomed to ongoing assessment.
- Provides continuous assessment basis.
- Evidence is produced regardless of whether it is used for assessment.

Weaknesses
- Opportunities to demonstrate competence across full range of activities may be limited.
- Interference of 'local' standards/procedures may affect time allocated to workplace assessment.
- Assessor/assessee relationship.

Key Issues
- Need for trained assessors.
- Use of multiple assessors.
- Need for clear lines of communication and quality-assurance measures.

Specially set tasks: skills tests, simulations, projects, assignments

Strengths
- A useful tool for generating evidence where opportunities for assessment across the full range are limited or prohibited by health and safety regulations.
- Can be off-site and therefore avoid noisy or disruptive environments.
- Test conditions can be standardized for skills tests.
- Time for testing can be effectively allocated.

Weaknesses
- Removed from realistic working conditions.
- Individuals react differently in a test situation.
- Structure of assignments and projects often very loose.
- Difficulties in predicting exactly what type of evidence will be generated.

Key Issues
- Need for planning and structure.

Oral questioning

Strengths
- Valuable tool for collecting evidence across full range of activities (ie, providing supplementary evidence).

- Valuable tool for collecting evidence of underpinning knowledge and understanding and its application in the workplace.
- Can be rigorous, and standardized with planning and structure.

Weaknesses
- Assessors can often answer their own questions!
- Evidence collected by this method alone would not be sufficient to assign competence.
- Least likely to reflect or represent real working conditions.

Key Issues
- Need for trained assessors with effective questioning techniques.
- Requires largest inferential jump to assigning competence.

Written examination

Strengths
- Valuable tool for assessment in areas where knowledge forms a key component of competent performance (eg, information providers).
- Can be well structured to elicit key areas of knowledge and understanding.

Weaknesses
- Also assesses ability to write and construct written material.
- Needs skilled assessors to judge responses.
- Time away from workplace required to complete the examination.
- Time for assessors to review and mark responses.

Key Issues
- Danger of assumption that 'knowing' means 'able to do'.
- Often unstructured or unplanned.
- Supplies supplementary evidence of actual performance.

Multiple-choice question papers

Multiple-choice question papers provide a useful tool for assessing knowledge of a particular topic. They need careful construction and are usually put together by subject experts who are also skilled in the use of this form of assessment. The basic model of a multiple-choice question paper is, as its name implies, a question followed by several possible answers for the candidates to choose between.

Strengths
- Well-designed questions can be standardized.
- Elicits key knowledge/understanding in short timescale.

Weaknesses
- Always a 25 per cent possibility of correct answer being chosen at random (where four possible answers are given).
- Needs skilled designer to prepare item bank and question paper.
- Time away from work to complete test needed.

Key Issues
- Time and skills needed for design, delivery and marking.
- Supplementary evidence only – not direct evidence of actual performance.

When and Where Should Assessment Take Place?

In planning competence-based assessment, one of the key aims should be to make it flexible so that candidates can be assessed in a variety of ways. An assessor should also take into account any operational constraints.

Wherever possible, assessment should take place *in the workplace* with *observation of normal workplace activity*. This may not always be possible, either because the opportunity to assess across the full range of activity is limited, or because the noise within the working environment makes questioning or discussion difficult.

Where assessors are attempting to assess field staff, further difficulties arise. How can a manager assess his staff when they are out at customers' premises all day?

Competence-based assessment may, therefore, take place in the workplace or off the job. It should be continuous, making the best use of naturally occurring evidence (from normal work activity). Assessors will need to be able to set up and manage other forms of assessment, however, in order to ensure that high-quality and sufficient evidence is generated, collected and recorded before competence can be assigned to an individual.

Assessors must first understand the basis on which a competence-based assessment system operates. They must be clear about the principles of assessment and the requirements for high-quality evidence of performance. They must be aware of and develop skill in the use of various assessment methods and be able to use any combination of methods to meet the operational constraints in which they operate. Only when assessors have been trained in these skills can the assessment system operate effectively.

Effective operation begins with the establishment of assessment plans. This planning process was outlined in Chapter 4. The selection and use of assessment methods, and planning of the location and timing, all contribute to the overall quality of the assessment system.

 REVIEW

In this chapter, the process of collecting evidence has been explored. Well-planned collection of evidence is critical to ensure that the right quantity and quality of evidence is available for matching to the specified standards.

Chapter 6 explores the next steps – matching of evidence to standards and making judgements about individual achievement of competence.

6 Matching Evidence to Standards

> SUMMARY <

This chapter helps you to understand and apply the rules of evidence and the rules of assessment. These rules are critical aspects of competence-based assessment. It also explains the range of terminology used within this phase of competence-based assessment.

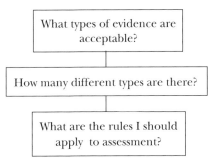

Introduction

The quality of a competence-based assessment system depends, as we have noted earlier, on the skills of the assessor. A key assessor skill concerns making judgements about the quality of evidence collected. Chapter 5 explored various assessment methods, together with the strengths and weaknesses of each. In this chapter, we look at the quality of evidence which is generated from these various assessment methods.

As a general rule, evidence generated from normal workplace activity will be of the highest quality. We can then move down a scale of quality as illustrated in Figure 6.1.

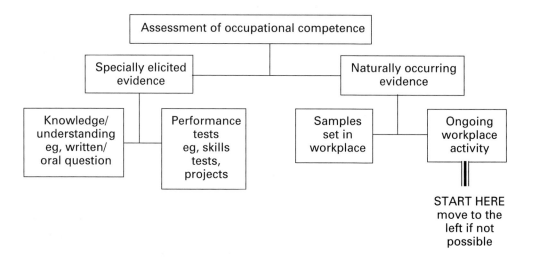

Figure 6.1 *Quality of Evidence of Occupational Competence*

Types of Evidence

Another area of general confusion for those new to competence-based systems occurs when discussions about *types* of evidence takes place. Once again, a variety of terms tends to be used interchangeably, often including:

- performance evidence;
- knowledge evidence;
- direct evidence;
- primary evidence;
- indirect evidence;
- supporting evidence;
- supplementary evidence;
- historical evidence.

In this initial section, these terms will be defined so that further exploration of rules of evidence can be undertaken without the added clutter of confusing terminology.

Performance evidence

This term has been used in earlier chapters and refers specifically to evidence of an individual *actually doing something*. For example, performance evidence of an individual undertaking a selection interview would be actual observation, or a video recording of that interview. Similarly, performance evidence of an individual completing a regular or requested maintenance check would be observation of that check being undertaken. Performance evidence is one form of *direct* evidence. It is also one of the required *primary* forms of evidence within a competence-based assessment system (see below).

Knowledge evidence

This term refers to evidence which indicates an individual's ability to recall, apply and transfer knowledge within a working environment. It is usually collected by questioning techniques and often by the use of 'What if…' questions.

The application of relevant knowledge and understanding is essential to competent performance and therefore must be assessed. Evidence of the application of knowledge and understanding within a working context is also a *primary* form of evidence of competence within a competence-based assessment system.

Primary evidence

The two definitions above referred to this term. Within a competence-based assessment system, the *primary* types of evidence are those which provide information about *actual* performance or the *application* of knowledge and understanding within *realistic* (normal) workplace activity.

Direct evidence

This is evidence which gives clear information about the candidate's performance. It will take the following forms:

- actual products of performance;
- results of observation of performance;
- results of questioning by the assessor.

These three forms of evidence also represent *primary* evidence (see above).

Direct evidence about some aspects of performance can also be obtained from skills tests, projects and assignments. However, such evidence is usually referred to as *supporting* or *supplementary* evidence (see below).

This is the simplest form of evidence for an assessor to use in matching to standards, but is often the most difficult to collect because of the time required to observe or question the individual or to examine finished products.

Indirect evidence

Indirect evidence provides the assessor with information *about* the individual and may take the form of:

- references or letters of validation;*
- photographs of completed work;
- audio tapes;
- trophies or awards;
- letters from customers/colleagues;
- production records;
- training records.

Many other forms of evidence may come into this category. It is important to remember that in a competence-based system, an assessor is dealing with *individualized* assessment. This means that the types of evidence presented, particularly where historical evidence is included (see below), will be unpredictable. Assessors must become used to dealing with unfamiliar and new forms of evidence. In this context, confidence in the use of rules of evidence, discussed later in this chapter, is critical to success.

Supporting or supplementary evidence

As the terms imply, supporting or supplementary evidence is that which adds to the main (or direct) forms. There is, therefore, some comparison between indirect and supporting and supplementary evidence. These terms are often used interchangeably.

Evidence from skills tests, projects and assignments is often termed supporting or supplementary; this leads to considerable confusion since this type of evidence can also be referred to as 'direct' (see above).

Use of these terms, as in many contexts, depends upon the perspective being adopted. If the discussion concerns the direct/indirect dimensions, then evidence from skills tests, projects and assignments will be direct because the evidence collected in this way *directly* reflects *part of* the required performance. However, if the discussion concerns primary

*A letter of validation is a form of reference, but one which provides specific information relating to the standards of performance. This form of reference is often provided by individuals as part of an accreditation of prior learning process (see 'Historical evidence').

versus supporting/supplementary evidence (see above), then skills tests, projects and assignments will be viewed as supporting/supplementary evidence. This is because these test situations are simulated and do not fully reflect realistic workplace activity as it would be undertaken on a normal day-to-day basis.

Historical evidence

Historical evidence is that which provides the assessor with information about an individual's past achievements. It may take any form and include those listed under the primary, supporting, direct and indirect headings above. Historical evidence therefore can be the most difficult to assess, but it can also provide one of the most valuable sources of evidence. Assessors will need skill and confidence if the credibility and quality of the assessment system is to be maintained.

Methods and Quality

Two sets of rules are applied within a competence-based system. The first refers to the *methods* of assessment and the second to the *quality* of evidence collected.

You might consider these two sets of rules as similar to rules applying to the legal profession.

In a court case, it is possible that *sufficient* evidence has been collected in order for a jury to make a confident judgement about guilt or innocence. However, technicalities relating to *how* the evidence was collected can make the sufficiency issue irrelevant.

The same rules apply in your workplace assessment. You may have sufficient evidence, but if the methods of collecting that evidence were invalid, the quality of evidence is affected.

So how can you ensure quality and sufficiency and thus make confident judgements in your assessment role?

Six key concepts must be kept in mind. These concepts relate both to quality of assessment method used and quality of evidence assessed. They are illustrated in Figure 6.2 and outlined in more detail in the following text.

```
┌─────────────────────────────────────┐
│                                     │
│       Rules of assessment           │
│                                     │
│          Transparency               │
│            Validity                 │
│           Reliability               │
│                                     │
└─────────────────────────────────────┘


┌─────────────────────────────────────┐
│                                     │
│        Rules of evidence            │
│                                     │
│            Validity                 │
│          Authenticity               │
│            Currency                 │
│           Sufficiency               │
│                                     │
└─────────────────────────────────────┘
```

Figure 6.2 *Key concepts of methods and quality*

Rules for Assessment Methods

Transparency

If something is transparent, it is open and clear to anyone who takes time to look at, or through it. A competence-based assessment system should be clear to all involved. If standards are accessible, easily understood and have real meaning to the users, and if the assessment plans and methods are well thought out then roles and responsibilities are more easily conducted.

Validity

A well-planned assessment is one in which the assessor and the individual being assessed are clear on *what* is to be assessed and *what* evidence will be generated. In addition, the types and forms of evidence will provide realistic proof of the specified standards. A common example of invalid assessment (and invalid evidence) would be a written test of practical skill. A *valid* assessment would be observation of reactions to a fire alarm (particularly when the time for testing of the alarm was not known in advance by the individuals).

As an assessor, think firstly of your objectives in assessment. Ask yourself what you need to find out (what evidence you need) about this person's performance. Then ask whether this assessment method will provide that evidence.

Reliability

An assessment system is only of real value if assessors in different locations would make the same judgement about the same candidate based on the same evidence. A well-designed assessment system builds in tests of reliability through quality control and monitoring of assessment. Your in-company assessment scheme will only be reliable if two different assessors provided with the same collection of evidence reach the same conclusion about the competence of the individual to whom the evidence refers. This type of testing activity should form part of assessor training (see Chapter 8).

Rules of Evidence

Validity

The same issue – assessing what is supposed to be assessed – arises when considering evidence. The key question for assessors to ask about each piece of evidence is 'What does this evidence tell me?' It may tell you something about the specified standards or it may tell you about some other related activity.

For example, if you were assessing maintenance engineers, you might receive documentation referring to completed work. What does this documentation tell you? Does it tell you that the work was completed to the correct safety standards? Does it tell you that the work completed was as requested by the customer? Does it tell you that the work was completed using the correct parts and that they were all fitted correctly? Does it tell you if the customer was satisfied?

In fact, the documentation may only tell you that the engineer is able (or not, as the case may be) to complete paperwork correctly, neatly and in accordance with company procedures!

Remember, the issue of validity is critical. Ask 'What does this piece of evidence actually tell me about this individual's performance?'

Authenticity

How do you know that the evidence presented to you was actually produced by the named individual? Was it produced by the individual alone, or as part of a team? These questions are particularly relevant when assessors are dealing with 'historical' evidence, but still have to be kept in mind when current evidence is being considered.

If an assessor is to attribute competence to an individual based on the evidence presented, then the issue of authenticity must be addressed.

Currency

Once again, this is of particular relevance to evidence from prior achievement (historical evidence) but should not be ignored in on-going workplace assessment. The key here is to focus on the standards as your starting point.

It is very easy for assessors to fall into the trap of making assumptions about evidence. This can be due to the many influences on assessment (see page 51), or due to lack of planning of assessment (page 49) or due to lack of application of rules of assessment (page 72). Most often, however, falling into the 'assumption trap' is caused by assessors failing to refer (and to re-refer) to the specified standards as their starting point.

Evidence is only current if the information it provides the assessor matches that specified within the standards.

Sufficiency

Once assessors have managed the collection of evidence and the application of rules of validity, authenticity and currency, one question remains: Do you have *enough* evidence of the right *quality* to make a *confident* judgement about competence?

This question of sufficiency has caused considerable difficulties for new assessors who frequently ask how to decide what is enough.

Here we come back to the key principles of competence-based assessment and to the format which standards of occupational competence take. A basic rule for competence-based assessment is that *all of the standards must be assessed*. This means that evidence must be collected to demonstrate that an individual has performed the element and its associated performance criteria across the full specified range of activity before that *element* can be 'signed off'. In addition, this signing-off activity for each element must be completed before the unit of competence can similarly be signed off and a certificate issued for that unit.

The issue of providing evidence for all performance criteria and across the full range sounds like a horrendous task for assessors. If this task is approached on the basis that one piece of evidence is required for each criterion and for each aspect of the range then this would be true. However, contrary to general belief, this is not the case (see NCVQ,

1996). The issue of matching evidence and making judgements about competence is explained in the next section on matching evidence and judging competence.

I end this section with a checklist which I have found very useful for new assessors. It also leads us nicely into the next section.

Applying rules of evidence: checklist for assessment

- All of the standards must be assessed.
- Evidence should relate clearly and directly to specified standards.
- There should be sufficient evidence to cover the full range of contexts or contingencies specified within the standards.
- There should be no comparison or contrast between candidates – evidence relates directly to individual assessment.
- Evidence should be traceable to its source (effective record keeping is important).
- Evidence should be generated in realistic conditions using valid assessment methods.
- The assessment process should put no additional pressure on candidates or assessor.

Matching Evidence and Judging Competence

The checklist in the previous section forms a useful guide for assessors in the matching and judging stages of competence-based assessment. The following text provides more detail to help assessors use the checklist and thus to develop and maintain confidence in their assessment role.

All of the standards must be assessed

Only two judgements are possible in competence-based assessment – 'competent' or 'not yet competent'. Because the performance criteria relate to *critical* aspects of performance, this means that all criteria must be met. Because true competence entails transferability of skills and knowledge, evidence of performance across the specified range must also be collected.

The evidence should relate clearly to the standards

There are a number of issues relating to rules of evidence. These include validity, currency, authenticity and sufficiency and are discussed earlier in this chapter.

Sufficient evidence must be generated in realistic conditions

Competence-based assessment assesses *workplace* activity. Assessment should therefore take place in a realistic working environment and relate to normal working practice.

The assessment process should be individualized, but should not put additional pressures on the candidate

As an assessor, you need to assess each individual in their normal working practice. Assessment should be unobtrusive and should relate only to the specified standards.

The assessment process should not put additional pressures on the assessor

Assessors in competence-based systems are usually line managers. Competence-based standards are designed to make explicit what people do in their normal working roles. They should therefore provide assistance to managers in their supervisory role and not increase their workload to an unmanageable degree.

How much evidence?

We come back to the question of sufficiency of evidence and to a concept which assessors invariably find difficult at first. As noted in the first part of this chapter, one misconception which causes problems on the 'sufficiency' front is that one piece of evidence must be found for each performance criterion (Figure 6.3).

In fact, one 'package' of evidence will provide valid information for all performance criteria. It may even provide valid information about performance criteria in different elements, or different units. Figure 6.4 illustrates this.

Assessors have expressed initial concerns that competence-based assessment will generate mountains of paperwork, that each individual will need to collect piles of evidence which has to be stored somewhere and judged on a one-to-one basis with each performance criterion. As Figure 6.4 illustrates, this is not the case. Assessors will only develop the confidence to make such judgements, however, through practice. It becomes clear, therefore, that building such practice into assessor training can help develop this confidence.

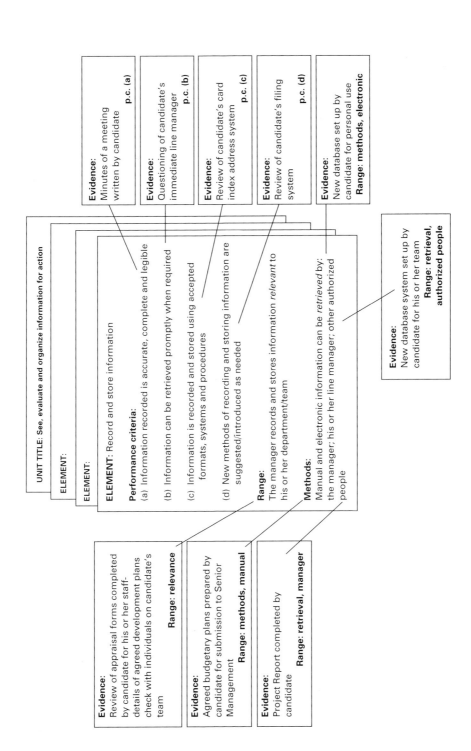

Figure 6.3 *Incorrect approach – one piece of evidence for each performance criterion*

UNIT TITLE: See, evaluate and organize information for action

ELEMENT:

ELEMENT:

ELEMENT: Record and store information

Performance criteria:

(a) Information recorded is accurate, complete and legible

(b) Information can be retrieved promptly when required

(c) Information is recorded and stored using accepted formats, systems and procedures

(d) New methods of recording and storing information are suggested/introduced as needed

Range:
The manager records and stores information *relevant* to his or her department/team

Methods:
Manual and electronic information can be *retrieved* by: the manager; his or her line manager; other authorized people

---

1.
'Packages' of Evidence to meet all relevant p.c. and range

2.
Questioning to cover contingencies

For example:

Package 1
New database set up by candidate for customer records – review of this and testing of its use with the candidate provides evidence for *all* performance criteria and 'electronic' aspect of range and for 'access/retrieval' requirements.

Package 2
Report on review of appraisal forms:
– review of this report provides evidence for p.c. (a), (b), (c)
– questioning provides evidence for p.c. (d)
'Package' provides evidence for range as 'manual' and 'retrieved by'

Figure 6.4 *Correct approach – matching evidence of performance to standards*

► REVIEW ◄

This chapter has outlined the key issues relating to the matching of evidence to performance standards and explained the many different terms used. All assessment activities should be accompanied by feedback and follow-up action; the next chapter looks at these peripheral activities.

7 Review and Follow-up

⊳ S U M M A R Y ⊲

This chapter briefly outlines the peripheral activities and knock-on effects involved in the introduction and operation of competence-based assessment. It provides guidance on planning and implementing these activities.

```
┌──────────────────────────────────┐
│   What if evidence shows that an  │
│   individual is not yet competent?│
└──────────────────────────────────┘
               │
┌──────────────────────────────────┐
│   How is evidence of performance  │
│            recorded?              │
└──────────────────────────────────┘
               │
┌──────────────────────────────────┐
│    What needs to be in place to   │
│    provide follow-up training?    │
└──────────────────────────────────┘
```

Identifying Training Needs

In conducting on-going assessment of performance, an assessor will automatically identify training and development needs. When collecting evidence of performance, 'gaps' in this evidence will emerge. These may be due to lack of opportunity to demonstrate competence. They may also be due, however, to lack of experience, skills or knowledge.

The competence-based assessment system therefore provides a working model for the identification of training needs – as long as the assessor is skilled in recognizing which gaps are due to training needs and which to lack of opportunity!

Such is the 'knock-on effect' of introducing competence-based assessment within an organization. Once supervisors and line managers start to use the assessment system, their skills (or the need to develop them) also receive highlighted attention. Line managers need to develop skills in providing feedback and in recognition of training needs, to name but two.

In addition, the organization's procedures get some attention. It is only when assessors attempt to find quality evidence, and when they begin to ask key questions such as 'What does this evidence actually tell me about Joe Bloggs's performance?' that possible improvements in the procedural and administrative systems start to emerge.

For example, in the last chapter, we considered documentation which might be completed by an engineer and asked what it actually told us about the work completed by the individual engineer. Questions like this can lead us to the conclusion that our recording system is perhaps not all it should be – or that our engineers have not been trained in its use!

When we think about *identifying training needs* therefore, we are considering both assessor and assessee. Through the collection of evidence, the assessor will identify the needs of the assessee. However, the process of collecting and judging evidence will in itself highlight the assessor's own training needs!

Recording Assessment

If your organization is going to go to all the trouble of perhaps developing its own competence-based standards and assessment system, or introducing a nationally devised one, then it would be a shame if the whole system was found not to work because the records were inadequate.

The system for recording assessment needs to be both simple and efficient. Assessors need space to record *what* evidence they have judged, *when* they judged it, and the *method of assessment* used. There also needs to be space for the assessor to record that the element has been achieved (when sufficient, high-quality evidence has been collected and matched to the specified standards).

These records may be used, within a national, organizational or professional vocational qualification system, as the basis for recommendation for award. It is essential, therefore, that the records used provide a solid

Evidence Assessment Record

Name: _____

Description of Evidence	Performance Criteria											Range/Contexts	Location of Evidence	Assessor		Verifier	
	a	b	c	d	e	f	g	h	i	j	k			Sign	Date	Sign	Date

I have reviewed this evidence and I am satisfied that sufficient evidence has been collected to demonstrate competence in this element

Assessor: _____ Date: _____ Internal/External Verifier: _____ Date: _____

I have received feedback on my assessor's judgement
during the collection of this evidence: _____ Date: _____

Unit No: [   ] Unit Title: [   ] Element No: [   ] Element Title: [   ]

Figure 7.1 *Example assessment record*

basis on which a quality-assurance system can operate. An example of an assessment record is given in Figure 7.1.

Recording Achievement

The assessor only needs to record positive evidence (achievement) on a record such as that in Figure 7.1. Evidence which indicates a training need can be passed on to the relevant personnel, or may lead to the assessor providing on-job development.

Here again, the question of procedures arises. Does your organization have procedures which allow supervisors and line managers to pass on identified training needs? Do these procedures actually lead to action being taken to meet those needs?

It may be that the introduction of competence-based assessment leads to a review of your procedures in connection with the identification of training needs and the provision of required training.

Providing/Arranging Follow-up Training

As noted above, assessors will need to be skilled in the identification of training needs. However, they will also probably require skills in coaching and on-job development. One might argue that these are skills that supervisors and line managers should have anyway – but in reality, few do. Managers, particularly in the UK, do not have key 'people skills' which help them to make the most of their human resource.

A second issue relates to the procedural question already raised. What procedures does your organization have for:

- passing up information on identified training need?
- providing training and development on a modular basis?
- developing training programmes on a modular basis?
- designing and developing programmes based on explicit standards of performance?

Again, the knock-on effect of introducing competence-based assessment begins to become clear.

If the assessment system is to be used to the full, then supporting systems of training and development for all staff, including those who take on an assessor role, must be put in place. A competence-based assessment system provides a valuable foundation on which to measure, manage and maintain high-quality performance within an organization.

However, this can only happen if the implications of introducing the system are carefully considered and plans for peripheral activities are put into action at an early stage.

The next issue to be addressed is that of quality assurance. Chapter 8 explains the key issues and provides general guidance on this matter.

REVIEW

This chapter has outlined the peripheral issues of recording assessment and quality assurance. Although 'peripheral', these issues should not be dismissed! Any assessment system is only as good as its supporting infrastructure. You should, therefore, give careful thought to the design of your supporting framework and its operation.

8 Quality Assurance Issues

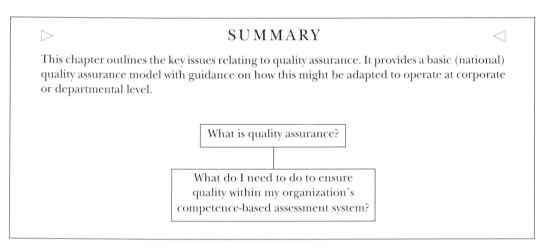

▷   S U M M A R Y   ◁

This chapter outlines the key issues relating to quality assurance. It provides a basic (national) quality assurance model with guidance on how this might be adapted to operate at corporate or departmental level.

What is quality assurance?

What do I need to do to ensure quality within my organization's competence-based assessment system?

Introduction

There is little point in developing and introducing a competence-based assessment system unless an effective quality assurance model is put in place to ensure that standards, and the credibility of the system are maintained.

There are several aspects to quality assurance within competence-based assessment systems. These vary depending upon whether your organization introduces a nationally approved system, such as that relating to National Vocational Qualifications (NVQs) in the UK, or whether you operate your own in-house system.

However, whether your system operates in-house, and with or without certification, key issues to be addressed in the design and/or establishment of a quality-assurance system will be:

- selection of assessors;
- training of assessors;
- monitoring of assessors.

If your system is also linked to certification, either in-house or national, other issues will need to be addressed, such as approval of assessment sites, and procedures for certification.

All these issues are dealt with in the following sections.

Selection of Assessors

Assessors are key personnel within a competence-based assessment system. You will wish to consider the main characteristics/technical requirements for assessors within your organization. If you operate within a national certification system, you may well find that the selection criteria are already established; nevertheless, these criteria will include the following:

- experience in the occupational role;
- experience in supervision/line management;
- willingness to undertake assessment.

The last may seem strange, but it is essential. If line managers are not willing to undertake assessment, then they will not undertake the assessment thoroughly, and you will have created a situation in which the credibility of the system is threatened. You will need to know why line managers are unwilling: do they feel threatened themselves by the new system? (Remember, it highlights their skills, or lack of them.) Do they see it as extra workload? (They will need initial briefing to overcome this, as well as detailed training and development.)

You will need to explore and overcome these initial barriers to effective operation of your assessment system.

You may try a pilot programme to begin with. In this way you can choose your pilot group and make use of those people with the commitment and drive to help you make the system work. People usually feel less threatened, and put up fewer barriers, when they see a system actually operating, and operating well. Plan your pilot carefully and make sure everyone knows what is going on.

Training of Assessors

This is vital. Assessors are no different from anyone else. Would you take on new operatives, or new managers without providing training? (Some organizations may answer yes to this!)

Everyone needs to learn what the expectations of a role are. They need to understand the importance of the role activity and the procedures which need to be followed. Assessors need to understand several aspects of the competence-based system:

- principles of competence-based assessment;
- what makes it different from other forms of assessment;
- using standards of competence;
- rules of assessment;
- rules of evidence;
- methods of assessment;
- room for flexibility and creativity;
- roles of assessors and individuals;
- the quality-assurance structure in which the assessment system operates;
- benefits of the assessment system.

You should ensure that a training programme is provided for assessors immediately before the system is put into operation. Selected assessors should be briefed prior to the formal training, so that they can prepare their staff and deal with any concerns which may arise.

Assessors will also need follow-up support. You should consider establishing 'assessor networks' – opportunities for assessors to meet and discuss concerns, difficulties and successes. All of this activity contributes to the quality of the assessment system and encourages commitment and involvement. The network activity also provides an opportunity for assessors to discuss and identify any common training needs which may arise, such as feedback skills, coaching, further training in assessment methods, interpersonal skills and so on.

Monitoring of Assessors

The process of monitoring assessment is usually called *verification*. Your competence-based assessment system should operate within a verification framework. The extent of this framework will depend upon the extent of your system. For example, an in-house system leading to company certification of individual performance might have a three-tier

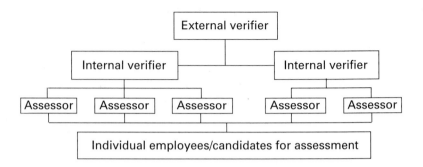

Figure 8.1 *Basic verification framework – national certification*

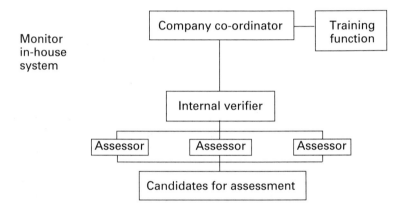

Figure 8.2 *Verification framework for in-company model of competence-based assessment*

system, whereas one linked to national certification would have as many as seven tiers. Figure 8.1 illustrates a basic verification framework for a nationally certificated competence scheme. A model for an in-company system is illustrated in Figure 8.2.

Each assessor needs to be monitored to ensure reliability of assessment – that is, that the same judgement would be reached by more than one assessor when the same collection of evidence of competence is assessed.

To achieve this, you will need someone who monitors the assessors (an internal verifier) and a central coordinator.

The remainder of this chapter outlines the responsibilities of these key roles and other quality-assurance procedures which can be applied at national and at corporate or departmental level.

Verification Frameworks: Roles and Responsibilities

Workplace assessor

A workplace assessor is usually a line manager, since a line manager is the best person to observe natural workplace performance.

The workplace assessor is responsible for judging *evidence of performance* and ensuring that this evidence is of the correct *type* and *quality* to ensure that a confident decision on sufficient evidence to meet required standards is achieved.

The workplace assessor may use a range of assessment methods but the primary form of assessment must always be *observation of performance*. *Feedback* should be given to individuals on a regular basis and *training needs* will be identified during the course of assessment.

The workplace assessor is also responsible for *recording assessment*. Details of evidence must be entered on an *assessment record*.

The workplace assessor will be monitored by an *internal verifier*.

Internal verifier

An internal verifier is usually someone who operates in-company at the next line-management responsibility level. The verifier's role is to oversee assessment and make sure that quality-control procedures are maintained.

An internal verifier will sample assessments and countersign assessment records. He or she is monitored by an *external verifier* (or company coordinator).

External verifier

An external verifier is usually an employee of an awarding body or institution and visits approved assessment sites on a regular basis. You will have an external verifier if you operate a UK National Vocational Qualification (NVQ).

The external verifier will wish to see individuals' records of assessment and may also sample evidence collected. He or she will check that quality-control systems are fully operational and will report back to the awarding body or institution on any difficulties encountered.

The external verifier, appointed by the national awarding body (or the company coordinator in an in-company system), has responsibility for monitoring the overall assessment process and for passing on recommendations for certification to the awarding-body management structure. This is where a possible seven-tier system comes into play (see Figure 8.3).

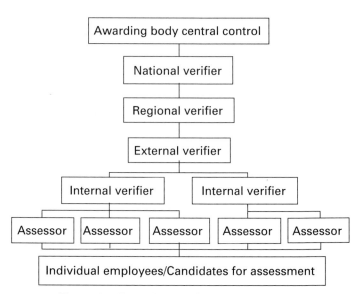

Figure 8.3 *Extended verification framework*

Approval of Assessment Sites

If your organization operates within a national assessment system, it is likely that you will be required to go through an approval process for each site at which you wish to operate assessment.

If you operate your own in-company system, you will still want to ensure that a common system operates at all locations or in all subsidiaries. The following guidelines on the approval and monitoring processes which operate within the UK system at national level can therefore be applied at corporate level by substituting 'corporate body' for 'awarding body' and 'subsidiary' for 'assessment centre'.

The approval process usually requires the payment of a registration fee after certain aspects relating to operation of the assessment have been checked against criteria set by the awarding body. These include:

- trained assessors;
- use of approved recording systems;
- internal monitoring (verification).

As the awarding bodies have to recoup their own quality-monitoring costs, they make a charge for registration of assessment centres and for materials, the latter being centrally devised. (You do not have to use national awarding body materials.)

This is helpful in establishing a common system across all occupational roles within an industry sector. However, it does cause some difficulties for organizations which operate within several sectors, each of which may have their own assessment documentation and their own requirements for training of assessors. For example, in your organization you may have managers, administration and clerical staff and those who operate in various technical roles – at least three or four 'industry sectors'. If you have to operate a different assessment and recording system for each, the training and resourcing costs start to look ominous!

Some awarding bodies require that your appointed assessors are trained using a specific programme. This actually goes against the grain: a key principle of competence-based assessment and qualifications is that training to a level of competence should be available by a wide range of routes and methods. To say that assessors can only be deemed acceptable (and by implication, competent) if they are trained by one route is therefore stepping outside the principles in which the system itself should be operating.

Procedures for Certification

Once again, if you are introducing a nationally recognized system, the procedures for certification will be included (or should be) in the initial briefing materials provided by the awarding body(ies).

This usually includes procedures by which the record of assessment – which may be a logbook provided by the awarding body – is signed by the assessor and countersigned by the internal verifier once sufficient evidence of competence has been collected. The record will then continue through the quality-assurance framework to the external verifier and thence to the central office of the awarding body where computer records will be updated and certificates issued.

Certificates can be issued on a unit-by-unit basis as well as a full qualification (ie, a required number of units). In a company certification scheme, where the corporate body would be the awarding body, a similar set of procedures would need to be established. A computerized database to store records of achievement and issue of certificates would be essential where large numbers of unit-based certificates were awarded.

▶ **REVIEW** ◀

This chapter has briefly outlined the key quality-assurance issues within a competence-based assessment system. Further guidance can be found in the References and Further Reading.

9 Assessment Strategies

In 1999, the Qualification and Curriculum Authority (QCA), formerly the NCVQ, issued guidance jointly with the Scottish Qualification Authority (SQA) to all Standard Setting Bodies (SSBs) – many of which are National Training Organizations (NTOs) for the development of assessment strategies for NVQs and SVQs.

This guidance asked all NTOs to prepare a detailed strategy for assessing NVQs and SVQs. This built on the previously published *Common Accord* (NCVQ, 1996) – a document to which all national awarding bodies had agreed in order to standardize quality procedures and improve customer focus in NVQ delivery.

Each NTO's assessment strategy must address some key issues. Many of these are relevant to business organizations and are therefore useful to consider in relation to in-house assessment systems:

- the proposed methods of achieving external quality control of assessment;
- the extent to which simulated working conditions may be used to assess competence and the required characteristics of simulation;
- the aspects of standards that should always be assessed through performance in the workplace;
- the requirements for the occupational expertise of assessors and verifiers.

These are all issues that businesses should consider, whether introducing NVQs/SVQs or their own competence framework.

External Quality Control

Is your competence-based assessment system to be linked to external standards and qualifications? If so how will your external quality control system operate?

Simulation vs Workplace Performance Evidence

Coming back to 'what do you want to assess' – to what extent will you allow simulation to be used within your assessment system? What constitutes acceptable simulation? What are the risks?

Occupational Expertise of Assessors and Verifiers

When you have reviewed the section on 'who will assess' and planned the development of your assessors, bear in mind that line managers are not always the best assessors in terms of specific competences being assessed. Check that you set clear criteria for your selection and development of assessors and verifiers.

The move towards industry-defined strategies for assessment within the NVQ/SVQ structure means that there will be more flexibility within the system, with NTOs having more involvement in defining, through industry consultation, the requirements for implementation and quality assurance.

References and Further Reading

Beaumont, G (1996) *Review of 100 NVQs and SVQs: A report submitted to the Department for Education and Employment*, NCVQ, London.

Bill, L (1990) 'The Comparability of Examination Systems and Certificates used in the Various Countries of Europe', paper to the 16th International Conference, Maastricht, International Association for Educational Assessment, June 1990.

Bourke, J B, Hansen, J H, Houston, W R and Johnson, C (1975) *Criteria for Describing and Assessing Competency Programmes*, Syracuse University, NY, National Consortium of Competency Based Education Centers.

Boyatzis, R E (1982) *The Competent Manager*, Wiley, New York.

Burke, J W (ed.) (1989) *Competency Based Education and Training*, Falmer Press, London.

CBI (1994) *Quality Assessed: The CBI review of NVQs and SVQs*, Confederation of British Industry.

DfEE (1998) *Mapping Guidance: Key/Core skills in NVQs and SVQs*, Department for Education and Employment.

Elam, S (1971) *Performance Based Teacher Education: What is the state of the art?* American Association of Colleges of Teacher Education, Washington DC.

Fletcher, S (1997) *Designing Competence-Based Training*, 2nd edn, Practical Trainer Series, Kogan Page, London.

Fletcher, S (1994) *NVQs, Standards and Competence: A practical guide for employers, managers and trainers*, 2nd edn, Kogan Page, London.

Fletcher, S (1993) *Quality and Competence*, Kogan Page, London.

Fletcher, S (1997a) *NVQ Assessment: A handbook for the paperless portfolio*, Kogan Page, London.

Fletcher, S (1997b) *Analysing Competence: Tools and techniques*, Kogan Page, London.

Fletcher, S (1997c) *Competence and Organizational Change: A handbook*, Kogan Page, London

Management Charter Initiative (MCI) (1991) *Implementation Pack*, MCI, London.

Mansfield, B and Matthews, D (1985) *Job Competence: A description for use in vocational education and training*, FESC/ESF Core Skills Project, Bristol.

Mitchell, L (1989) 'The Definition of Standards and their Assessment', in Burke, *op cit.*

MSC (1981) *A New Training Initiative: Agenda for action*, Manpower Services Commission, Sheffield.

MSC (1986) *A Review of Vocational Qualifications in England and Wales: Final report*, The Stationery Office, Norwich.

NCVQ (1988) *Information Note 4 (November)*, NCVQ, London.

NCVQ (1995) *Criteria and Related Guidance*, NCVQ, London.

NCVQ (1996) *Assessment of NVQs*, NCVQ, London.

NCVQ (1996) *Implementing Standards for Assessment and Verification*, 2nd edn, NCVQ, London.

NCVQ (1997) *Assessment of NVQs and SVQs*, NCVQ, London.

NCVQ (1997) *The Awarding Bodies Common Accord*, NCVQ, London.

Qualifications and Curriculum Authority (1998) *Standards and Vocational Qualifications in Continuing Professional Development (CPD): QCA discussion paper no. 1*, July, QCA, London.

Qualifications and Curriculum Authority (1999) *Developing an Assessment Strategy for NVQs and SVQs*, QCA, London.

Swanchek and Campbell (1981) 'Competence/performance-based Teacher Education: the Unfulfilled Promise', *Educational Technology* June, pp 5–10.

Training Agency (1988–90) *The Development of Assessable Standards of Occupational Competence*, Standards Methodology Unit, Moorfoot, Sheffield.

Training Agency (1989) *Development of Assessable Standards for National Certification: Guidance notes*, Training Agency, Sheffield.

Training Agency (1990) *Competence and Assessment*, issues 6–12 and special editions, Training Agency, Sheffield.

Index

The Open University

T357
Structural integrity:
designing against failure

BLOCK 2
FRACTURE MECHANICS

PARTS 1 AND 2

This publication forms part of an Open University course T357 *Structural integrity: designing against failure*. Details of this and other Open University courses can be obtained from the Student Registration and Enquiry Service, The Open University, PO Box 197, Milton Keynes MK7 6BJ, United Kingdom: tel. +44 (0)845 300 60 90, email general-enquiries@open.ac.uk

Alternatively, you may visit the Open University website at http://www.open.ac.uk where you can learn more about the wide range of courses and packs offered at all levels by The Open University.

To purchase a selection of Open University course materials visit http://www.ouw.co.uk, or contact Open University Worldwide, Michael Young Building, Walton Hall, Milton Keynes MK7 6AA, United Kingdom for a brochure. tel. +44 (0)1908 858793; fax +44 (0)1908 858787; email ouw-customer-services@open.ac.uk

The Open University
Walton Hall, Milton Keynes
MK7 6AA

First published 2007.

Edited and designed by The Open University.

Typeset by SR Nova Pvt. Ltd, Bangalore, India.

Printed in the United Kingdom by The University Press, Cambridge.

ISBN 978 0 7492 1853 9

1.1

INTRODUCTION TO BLOCK 2

INTRODUCTION TO BLOCK 2

Block 1 introduced you to stress analysis: determining and quantifying the stress in components and structures. Block 2 is about how we design parts knowing that they may contain flaws, or may develop flaws in service from wear, fatigue or degradation.

Ideally, once a component or structure has been fabricated, we would like it to have an infinite life and never need to be maintained. In reality, this is unattainable: cost constraints in manufacture, limits to materials properties, fundamental physical limits and the need for pragmatic engineering mean that manufactured objects do not last for ever. Components wear and corrode, and structures such as aircraft suffer from fatigue cracking. Some products will contain flaws or cracks from the moment of their construction; and, although this may be an unwanted state of affairs, it's something that needs to be understood and accounted for in design. Cracks in materials can, as you might expect, cause failures to occur at significantly lower applied loads than would otherwise be the case.

Part 1 of this block introduces you to the application of the theory of fracture mechanics to engineering parts, primarily made from metals, that contain cracks or flaws. I shall cover different industrial sectors, from nuclear reactors to aeroplanes, where the theories are applied in different ways according to the types of structure and the way that they are used. I will address the practical aspects of applying theories concerned with the behaviour of cracked bodies, and provide an appreciation of the underlying fundamentals that inform those theories: hence the title of 'Practical fracture mechanics'.

Part 2 looks in detail at the phenomenon of fatigue, where cracks can initiate and then grow in a material even in the absence of an obvious initial flaw. The consideration of fatigue loading is a critical part of the design process, as the progression from a pristine component to a broken one can be surprisingly rapid under certain loading conditions.

Part 3 looks at *how* materials fail on the microscale, and how a structure can resist the development of cracks and damage.

Part 4 covers the very important topic of degradation in service. Key to the success of any product is that it is able to survive the conditions in which it operates, and very few materials are entirely resistant to attack from the elements – not everything can be made from gold …

Part 5 looks at an extension of fracture mechanics to cases where significant plasticity may be associated with the growth of a crack in a material, and how assessments of possible failures are performed in such cases.

Finally, in Part 6, the block ends with some case studies exemplifying the concepts that you have met throughout this course.

Associated with this block are three calculators, written in Microsoft® Excel, which are provided on the course DVD to save you the labour of repetitive calculations: the '*K* calculator', the 'Fatigue calculator' and the 'R6 calculator'. In the first part of this block you will learn to perform the calculations longhand and then gain some acquaintance with the K calculator. Later on in your studies, the use of the calculators takes over. The calculators are to aid teaching of the engineering, so that the important teaching points are not overwhelmed by repetitive sums. You will be able to use the calculators to answer continuous-assessment questions, but you will not have the calculators in the exam room, so try not to anticipate the use of the calculators to do the exercises that are set longhand.

CONTENTS

1   INTRODUCTION

1.1   Introduction to fracture mechanics

Fracture mechanics is the study of cracked structures under load. Engineers now routinely buy and run plant and machinery that is cracked, whereas once the idea that a bought and paid-for piece of equipment might contain cracks was unacceptable. George Irwin, the founder of modern fracture mechanics, said that in the 1940s 'it was not considered mannerly to talk about cracks in newly fabricated structures'.

The presence of cracks in safety-critical structures is inevitable, particularly when they are fabricated by welding. This means that high-pressure gas pipelines in suburban areas, nuclear pressure vessels (usually a little further away from major population centres), and chemical plant containing dangerous substances are commissioned and used cracked. Despite this, failures under static load are rare nowadays. There are two major reasons for this: metals are now much 'cleaner' (containing fewer flaws), have very good properties and are well characterized, and the safety of critical structures is assured by ▽ **proof testing** ▽.

▽ Proof testing

Proof testing is a technique whereby components that are not up to specification can be identified before entering service. The usual principle employed is to expose the components briefly to conditions more severe than they would be expected to endure in service. A badly flawed component is likely to be destroyed by a proof test, so it is not undertaken lightly. Clearly a failure during proof testing is less harmful than an unexpected failure in service. One important assumption of this approach is that exposure to the more severe conditions during proof testing does not in itself damage the component.

Proof testing is often used on safety-critical components that may contain flaws or defects and are relatively highly stressed in service. For example, ceramic grinding wheels are exposed to large stresses as they are spun at high speed in operation. Furthermore, they necessarily contain porosity that is used both to remove swarf and to supply coolant to the workpiece. If large enough, a pore can act as a defect that grows catastrophically in service, leading to fracture of the wheel. As wheel fracture is clearly undesirable, wheels are spun to 1.5 times their operating speed in a steel tank before they leave the factory. As the maximum stress in a grinding wheel is proportional to the square of its speed ($\sigma \propto v^2$), this proof test thus requires each wheel to survive 2.25 (i.e. 1.5^2) times its service stress before being allowed into service.

Proof testing has always been a godsend to engineers, as a proof-tested metal pressure vessel, for example, is in a better condition for service after testing – assuming that it survives! When a vessel is loaded well above its design load during proof stressing, stresses around notches and cracks exceed yield and so the material plastically deforms, usually without further cracking. This plastic deformation causes defects to be blunted, stress distributions to be evened out and, when the load is removed, residual compressive stresses to be left in what would otherwise be potentially dangerous areas.   △

In this part, I am going to consider primarily engineering metals, of which by far the most common are steels. The principles can be applied to other classes of material, but they find most application when designing with metals.

Ferrous metals of all kinds are very much cleaner than they were half a century ago; fewer impurities mean that they are much tougher and so less prone to dangerous, brittle fractures. The presence of notches, other stress raisers that are necessary in a particular design, and cracks introduced during fabrication is less of a problem than it was. However, there is plenty of safety-critical plant in operation that is half a century old, and failure assessments of such plant are routine to ensure that they continue to operate safely.

Historically, plant became heavier (because of the need for thicker sections to support operation at higher temperatures and pressures) at the same time as stronger, less-tough materials were being used. Concern over the behaviour of such structures in the presence of cracks – for example, vessels in the nuclear industry – stimulated research into fracture mechanics in order to consider, and so prevent, potential failure events. As ever, industrial development and regulatory procedures are triggered by accidents and the fear of accidents.

For example, in an aircraft structure made from forged and rolled metal that is riveted together, cracks are unlikely to be present when the plane is brand new; but they do grow by fatigue in service under repeated loading and unloading during flight and on the major loading excursions during landing and take off. If, as is likely, you have travelled in an aeroplane, you have certainly trusted your life to a cracked aluminium structure. Many cracks in an airframe are minor, but the economic life objective is for 19 out of 20 aeroplanes to exceed 20 years of operation without major fatigue cracking in the primary structure. This means that, in a structure that just meets this design objective, 1 out of 20 aeroplanes may crack prior to 20 years of service. These statistics predict that in a large fleet of aeroplanes the earliest fatigue cracking could occur as early as midway through the aeroplane's design life.

The prediction of fatigue crack growth based on fracture mechanics concepts is a very powerful tool for assessing crack growth in the airline industry. For example, the limit to stable growth of a fatigue crack occurs when the (long) crack grows in a fast, unstable fashion by tearing through the thin panels (Figure 1.1) and possibly by brittle failure through thicker spars. So, if you can calculate the growth rate of a crack you will be able to determine whether failure is imminent or not.

At the other end of the design spectrum are structures that are designed for infinite life, and so don't have such problems. For example, the designer of a monocoque car structure is far more concerned with crumple zones that dictate the plastic collapse of a car body in a crash. However, the designer of a car is not as concerned with the need to minimize weight as the aircraft designer: aeroplanes designed like cars would remain firmly land-bound.

Different industries use different metals in different sizes under different design constraints, and so they use our understanding of how cracks grow and how cracked structures might fail in different ways. The designer of the light, thin-walled, aluminium pressure vessel that is a civil aeroplane (military aircraft are not pressurized) has a completely different set of problems from the designer of the four-inch-thick, hot, steel pressure vessel that is a nuclear reactor. Although the understanding of cracked metal under load is built on the same theoretical and

Figure 1.1 Part of the body of the Aloha Airlines Boeing 737, which lost a section of the fuselage owing to fatigue cracking

practical foundations in both cases, the resulting engineering practice is completely different. As a result, experience shows there is little or no movement of specialized engineers between, say, Rolls Royce Marine and British Aerospace.

The theories that we have to describe the dynamic behaviour of a crack growing under an increasing load are, quite frankly, not very good. However, the notion that engineering is built on the ability to predict a type of behaviour as exactly as possible is naive. Engineering practice is a combination of theories, analysis, experiment and codes that produces conservative, and therefore reliable, results. Safety factors collect together the variabilities in materials and the uncertainties in the design and assessment processes (again, these are industry specific) to produce reserve factors on load that are acceptable.

A key factor in all the industries that have to live with cracks is the inspection processes. Cracks that break the surface can be found by observant aircraft cleaners or by painting with special paints, and cracks buried in the body of a part might be found using non-destructive techniques (NDT) based on X-rays or ultrasonics. Again, the inspection methods vary with different industries and the characteristics of their products, but inspection procedures are integral to the design and operation of safety-critical structures and plant in all industries.

1.2 Materials properties and testing

You know from Block 1 that engineering materials under load are routinely characterized using a tensile test to measure yield stress (or 0.2% proof stress) and tensile strength: a structure designed to carry two-thirds of its yield stress is regarded as highly stressed.

Stress is the engineering measure that takes the geometry out of a problem; doubling the cross section of a bar at the same time as doubling the axial load leaves the stress on the section the same. Stress has the property of *similitude*: if I know the stress in a small laboratory specimen will be the same as that in a large component or structure, I can perform an assessment of the one based on the results from the other. So stress is the *lingua franca* that allows us to relate the result of my laboratory test to your huge, expensive structure on which many lives and jobs depend.

At the beginning of the twentieth century it was found that tensile test results were not sufficient to characterize the failure of notched parts, particularly when the notch is sharp – as it is with screw threads, for example. Similitude did not work, which was a huge shock, as it was expected that increasing the cross section would reduce the stress and so improve the design of the part. In fact, in the presence of a sharp notch this simply isn't the case.

A new type of test was needed. The test that was developed to characterize the toughness of a material, as opposed to its tensile strength, was the Charpy test – a test that is still used today. In a Charpy test, a high load is applied to a sample using a swinging hammer that strikes a notched bar (this is not a shock load, as the hammer swings relatively slowly). The toughness of the bar is measured by the energy lost from the hammer in fracturing the bar. Brittle fractures absorb less energy than ductile fractures.

 DVD

The Charpy test can be seen as part of the 'Liberty ships' programme on the DVD; tensile testing is shown in the 'Testing of materials and structures' programme.

The pendulum machines used in a Charpy test are cheap, simple and quick to use for making measurements at a range of temperatures. Such tests are carried out according to the procedures of international standards that capture both custom and practice in order to ensure that their results are compatible across test-houses in different countries. The resulting Charpy V-notch energy (CVN or C_v) is a measure of toughness. However, it cannot be used to predict the failure of a large structure from the performance of small specimens; the CVN value measured in the Charpy test does not have the property of similitude, and cannot be used to predict failure in a larger structure. But it does provide a good, qualitative idea of whether a failure might be brittle or ductile, and it is hugely practical:

> It can readily be seen that in the use of these very small test pieces lies one of the chief merits of the whole system, it being possible to cut specimens from crop ends of shafts, odd scraps from machinery and very often from the finished product without injuring its strength or appearance, further the cost of preparation of the specimen is very small, and storing and recording of the fractured sample for future reference is greatly simplified.

E. G. Izod talking about his own version of the Charpy test.

Engineers in the early 1900s were attempting to identify 'brittle steel'. Nowadays, the idea that a *material* is brittle can be grossly misleading. Rather, we would have you classify *fractures* as brittle. An example of our favoured, pedantic statement is 'glass is a material that normally fractures in a brittle fashion', rather than the more conversationally normal 'glass is a brittle material'.

Some steels will fail in a dangerous manner by brittle fracture at a particular size (say that of a pressure vessel), but fail in a safer fashion by energy-absorbing ductile mechanisms at a smaller size (say that of a test specimen). Together with the need for materials characterizing numbers, this led to the development of the modern fracture toughness test that is currently embodied in BS EN ISO 12737:2005. The fracture toughness test involves growing a fatigue crack in a specimen, then carefully loading it to failure while monitoring the applied load and the opening of the crack.

Therefore, the fracture toughness test is expensive, and so it has not superseded the Charpy test; buying a value of fracture toughness to British Standards costs about £300 per number at the time of writing, whereas a Charpy test is about a tenth of the price, with a 10% discount for the usual set of three. But the more costly test does give similitude: the fracture toughness value at which the small sample fails will be the same as that at which the large pressure vessel fails, if it fails by brittle fracture.

I turn now to the use of engineering theory. Numerical analysis has transformed engineering. Almost all modern engineering practice in structural and failure analysis is built on the use of computers to perform numerical analyses using finite element (FE) software – this is the only way that our theories can be applied to complex geometries. An FE analysis that is specific to your problem is expensive, and so the results numerical analyses of important (common) problems are captured on data sheets or encapsulated in other software. Here I shall combine numerical analysis with theoretical models and the results of testing in exactly the same way that they are combined in current industrial practice.

The practical fracture mechanics techniques that you will learn in this block are those that are in current use: people earn their living in this way.

1.3 The story so far

There are several key messages that I want you to take away from reading this introduction:

- Proof testing to loads above the design load benefits metal structures.

- Cracks in operating structures are common.

- Structures containing cracks are routinely inspected and assessed.

- Tensile tests scale (i.e. show similitude), but some toughness tests do not.

- There are traditional and modern standards for measuring toughness.

2 LINEAR-ELASTIC FRACTURE MECHANICS

2.1 Brittle and ductile fracture

A perfectly brittle failure leaves no visual trace of plasticity on the broken surfaces of the specimen. So, the two broken halves of a part that has failed in such a manner can be fitted back together perfectly, showing only a line of separation on the surface – remember the broken mug you saw in Block 1 Part 3. Brittle fractures propagate extremely quickly, moving at between about 40% and 100% of the speed of sound in the material. Figure 1.2 shows a brittle, flat fracture in a small, steel specimen that initiated from a fatigue crack grown from a machined notch.

The fragment in Figure 1.2 is half of a specimen that fractured when loaded in bending. The load–deflection trace (Figure 1.3) was linear until the bang of a fast fracture was heard. If the specimen had been unloaded before fast, brittle fracture broke it into two pieces, then the trace would have gone straight back to the origin. A fracture of this type is known as *linear-elastic*: linear because the path is a straight line and elastic because the load trace goes up and down the same path.

By way of a complete contrast, look at the fracture surface in Figure 1.4. A specimen made from a different steel, of a similar size to that shown in Figure 1.2, has failed from a fatigue crack in a way that shows evidence of considerable plastic deformation during failure: the heavily distorted fracture surface means that the two halves of the test-piece cannot be fitted back together. The massive plasticity associated with such a failure generates a non-linear load–deflection curve, as shown in Figure 1.5.

Figure 1.2 and Figure 1.4 show different steels that fail in different ways when tested under the same conditions with samples of about the same size. However (and this is one of the major issues in fracture mechanics), a specimen that fails in a ductile manner in a small section can fail in a fast, brittle fashion in larger sections. The implication of this is profound: in the presence of a crack, increasing

DVD

Toughness testing using samples such as those shown in Figures 1.2 and 1.4 is covered in the 'Toughness testing: Corus case study' programme on the DVD. You have not yet been introduced to all the concepts in that programme, but you may want to watch it now and revisit it later.

Figure 1.2   A flat, brittle fracture

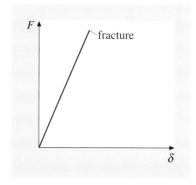

Figure 1.3   Linear load–deflection trace from a toughness test

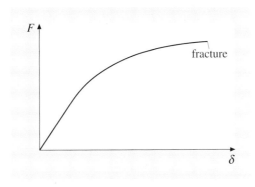

Figure 1.5   Non-linear load–deflection trace

Figure 1.4   A distorted, ductile fracture

the size of the part does not necessarily improve its performance because the same metal can fail in different ways depending on the size of the section containing an initiating flaw.

2.2 The linear-elastic fracture mechanics equation

The most dangerous form of failure in a cracked structure is brittle fracture. As we have seen, where a crack interacts with the right conditions of specimen geometry and loading, metals that show significant ductility in a simple tensile test will fail in a brittle manner, with no apparent plastic behaviour at all.

Fortunately, although our theories for cracks growing dynamically under a gradually increasing load are not all that good, the theory that predicts the onset of fast, brittle fracture is quite remarkable in its accuracy. The linear-elastic fracture mechanics (LEFM) theory is a unique mechanics solution for an infinitely sharp crack in a body under load where the material's response to applied loading is linear.

There is no assumption or incorporation of plasticity in LEFM theory. However, in a cracked metal body under load there is always some plasticity at a crack tip. If a crack tip were infinitely sharp, then the stress ahead of the crack would shoot off to infinity; in practice, plasticity intervenes to blunt the crack (Figure 1.6). There is a very small amount of yielding at the crack tip (called *small-scale yielding*), but it doesn't matter what happens in this region because it is the surrounding elastic field that controls the fracture event; hence the stress in the fracture mechanics equation is the far-field stress. This is the argument that allows us to use LEFM theory for metals, and effectively to ignore the small plastic region around the tip of the crack.

One reason that LEFM theory is remarkably useful is that there is a *pattern* of stresses ahead of a crack tip (Figure 1.7) that is always of the same form for the same mode of loading; only the magnitude of this pattern depends on the loading and the geometry of the component.

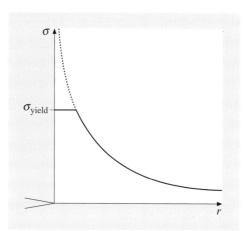

Figure 1.6 The magnitude of the stress field at a distance r from the crack tip would tend towards infinity as r goes to zero, but there is always some plasticity that limits its maximum value

Note that the stress intensity factor has no relation to the stress concentration factors you encountered in Block 1, which are a result of changes in geometry.

The magnitude of the stress field is embodied by a single parameter, the *stress intensity factor* K_I. It's a good name because K_I sums up the stress state at the crack tip in just one number, its intensity. If two cracks have the same intensity number, then the material ahead of the crack tip is in exactly the same loaded state. How useful is that?!

So, how do we determine K_I? The simplest of all geometries for studying crack problems is a conceptual one. Figure 1.8 shows a centre crack in an infinite plate in tension, for which case there are only two parameters that K_I can depend on: the far-field stress σ, which characterizes the load, and the length of crack, defined as $2a$ by convention for an embedded crack; this crack length is the only measure of geometry for an infinite plate.

We find that the stress intensity factor K_I is related to stress and the square root of the crack length and we write $K_I \propto \sigma\sqrt{\pi a}$, and deduce that its units are the unusual MN m$^{-3/2}$, or MPa $\sqrt{\text{m}}$. The π, though inconvenient, is there for historical reasons.

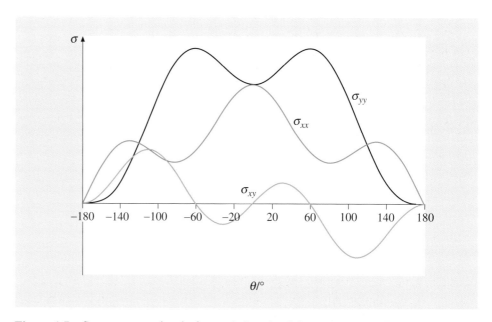

Figure 1.7 Stress pattern ahead of a crack for a load that acts to open the crack faces

To take account of different geometries, say an edge crack rather than a centre crack (Figure 1.9), we put in a dimensionless number to produce the LEFM equation:

$$K_I = Y\sigma\sqrt{\pi a} \tag{1.1}$$

where $Y = 1$ for an embedded crack in the notionally infinite plate shown in Figure 1.8. For an edge crack in an infinite plate (Figure 1.9), where by convention the length of crack is defined as a, $Y = 1.12$. Values of Y are found in handbooks – more on this later.

You may have come across the LEFM equation previously. If you haven't, fear not, as with only four variables it is easy to understand. However, you will need to know the definitions of the variables in this equation to be able to apply it in practice.

To summarize:

- The LEFM equation is the key equation for studying fracture. It describes fast, brittle fracture where there is no gross evidence of plastic deformation on the fracture surface.

- K_I is the crack-tip characterizing parameter, called the stress intensity factor. It is a measure of the magnitude of the stress field near a crack tip. The stress intensity factor applies to sharp cracks. Like stress, the stress intensity factor can be used to compare different problems: any crack in a body that has the same K_I as another crack in another body is effectively in the same condition.

- Y is a dimensionless parameter that accounts for the geometry in which the crack is contained.

- σ is the stress in the body of the material away from the crack (the so-called far-field stress).

- a is the length of an edge crack or one-half the length of an embedded crack.

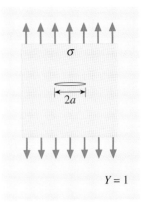

Figure 1.8   Centre crack in an infinite plate

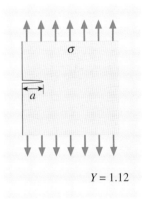

Figure 1.9   Edge crack in an infinite plate

EXAMPLE

A bar contains a 4 mm edge crack, and is loaded with a far-field tensile stress of 100 MPa. If the value of Y is 1.2 for the geometry concerned, what is the value of the stress intensity at the crack tip?

SOLUTION

Using Equation (1.1) the stress intensity is:

$$K_I = Y\sigma\sqrt{\pi a}$$
$$= 1.2 \times 100 \text{ MPa} \times \sqrt{\pi \times 4 \times 10^{-3} \text{ m}}$$
$$= 13.5 \text{ MPa } \sqrt{\text{m}}$$

Note that the far-field stresses in Figure 1.8 and Figure 1.9 act in such a way as to open the crack. The subscript 'I' in K_I indicates that the crack is being loaded by such stresses normal to the direction of the crack opening.

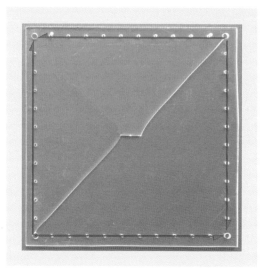

Figure 1.10   Cracking in shear from a central saw cut in a Perspex plate

Clearly, it is possible to have remote stresses that act in a different direction, relative to the crack, from those shown in Figures 1.8 and 1.9.

Figure 1.10 shows a Perspex® panel loaded in pure shear, as indicated by the arrows around the edges. So, in the plane of the crack the crack-tip stress pattern will be caused by shear stresses, but note that the crack did not grow in the direction of its original plane. Instead, the two cracks grew from the central saw cut in the direction dictated by the maximum opening load stresses, not in the directions dictated by the remote (shear) stresses.

EXERCISE 1.1

Draw the directions of the principal tensile stresses that open the crack on Figure 1.10.

However, in fibrous materials with weak interfaces in the direction of the central saw cut, a crack might grow in the direction of the shear loading and in this case the subscript II is used, i.e. K_{II}, to distinguish that the crack is progressing under the influence of a different mode of loading; but in common, homogeneous materials cracks grow in the direction dictated by the maximum opening stresses. In this part, I am going to deal only with cracks being opened by stresses normal to the direction of the crack. If the subscript is not present in a paper or book, then you can assume that K refers to the opening K_I; you can also make the same assumption in this course. The different possible modes of loading a crack are shown in Figure 1.11; by far the most prevalent in practice is mode I.

With the single parameter K_I you can characterize the crack driving force in any loaded component. So, if K_I in my specimen is the same as K_I in your complex and expensive plant, then, as long as there is not much plasticity present (i.e. LEFM is a valid theory to use), my crack-tip conditions are the same as yours; and when my (cheap) specimen goes bang I can use the result to predict when your expensive plant will fail and charge you a fee for the service. So, unlike the Charpy measure of toughness, an LEFM measure of toughness can be used to predict failure.

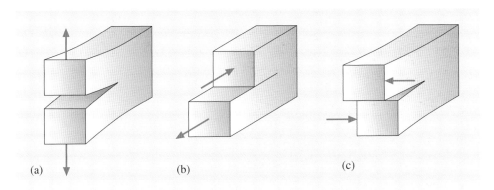

Figure 1.11   The three modes of loading a crack: (a) tensile opening (mode I); (b) in-plane sliding or shear (mode II); (c) anti-plane shear (mode III)

Another way of considering K is as a crack-driving parameter: for a given geometry, you can keep increasing the load and so increase K_I at the crack tip. This is analogous to increasing the load and so increasing the stress in a section. However, just as is the case with stress, there comes a point at which the material can no longer resist the stress intensity. In the case of stress, the stress that causes plastic deformation to occur is known as a yield stress (or in practice define a 0.2% proof stress). The yield stress is a material property. In fracture mechanics, the material property is known as the *fracture toughness* of the material – K_{IC} for the case of K_I. This material property is a limiting value on the mechanics driving force of stress intensity.

So, the essence of LEFM is contained in the equation:

$$K_I = Y\sigma\sqrt{\pi a} = K_{IC} \text{ at failure} \tag{1.2}$$

The values of the variables in the fracture mechanics equation are often uncertain. For example, materials properties and/or crack lengths might be unknown ('no records, Guv, it was built in 1950, you know') and so values will need to be assumed. How such problems are dealt with depends on industrial practice, experience, and agreed standards.

LEFM is a theory of brittle fracture: the lowest energy fracture that can occur in a metal. With common, modern steels in ordinary-sized sections, such fractures occur rarely, and yet LEFM is a useful theory simply because it can produce conservative results. If a simple stress analysis produces a result that is either correct or lower than that which would be achieved by a more complex (and, therefore, more expensive) analysis, then the simple analysis will be used if its results are acceptable: there is no point being more accurate than is required to solve a problem. Such analyses are called lower-bound solutions; any decision based on such an analysis will be a conservative decision.

This goes against the simple view that the aim of engineering analysis is to predict what *will* happen, if you are designing, or what *did* happen, if you are troubleshooting or doing lucrative forensic engineering.

The difficulties in applying the LEFM equation lie in deciding whether it is appropriate to a problem and what are sensible values to use in a specific, practical context.

2.3 The parameters of linear-elastic fracture mechanics

In this section I shall consider each of the variables in the fracture mechanics equation in turn, with a view to assigning some values to them and practising calculation with the fracture mechanics equation.

2.3.1 Fracture toughness K_{IC}

K_{IC} is the material property that predicts fast, brittle fracture when $K_I = K_{IC}$. K_{IC} is measured from a test conducted to a standard such as BS EN ISO 12737, or ASTM E399. Table 1.1 gives some indicative values of K_{IC}.

Table 1.1 K_{IC} values for a range of materials

Material	K_{IC}/MPa $\sqrt{m}$
Modern, high-strength steels	50–200
Older, lower-quality steels	down to 40
Titanium alloys	50–100
Aluminium alloys	20–40
Cast irons	6–20
Glass	0.5

Clearly, the range of K_{IC} values for different metal alloys is wide, which is because toughness depends critically on the type of alloy and the state of its heat treatment. Notice that an aluminium alloy can have a toughness value the same as that of a cast iron, which, perhaps, illustrates the danger of referring to materials as being brittle. Aluminium alloys are not very tough, in absolute terms, but they are usually used in thin sections, so brittle failure tends to be unusual. However, Figure 1.12 shows an aircraft spar that has failed in service with very little plastic deformation visible on the fracture surface.

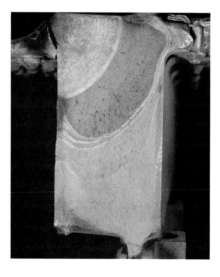

Figure 1.12   Failed aircraft spar

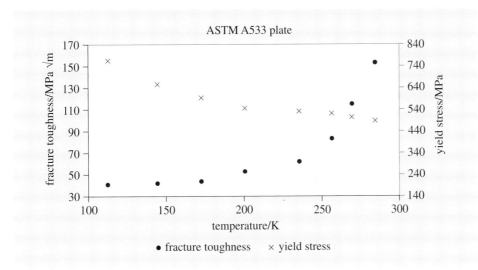

Figure 1.13 Relationship between yield stress and toughness

For a particular alloy that can be heat treated to produce different strengths, we usually find that high strength is 'bought' at the expense of toughness and that for a particular alloy at different temperatures the strength and toughness are inversely related. Figure 1.13 shows the relationship between yield stress (strength) and toughness for a high-quality steel plate. This remarkable dataset shows that the yield stress of this steel increases by 58% while the fracture toughness falls by 73% as the temperature falls: an example of the ▽ **ductile-to-brittle transition temperature** ▽. High strength and high toughness are difficult to achieve at the same time.

▽ Ductile-to-brittle transition temperature

In general, the toughness of materials tends to fall as the temperature is reduced. The energy-absorbing mechanisms in materials that lead to good toughness tend to work better when there is some thermal energy to help activate them.

Many steels exhibit an extreme example of this, with a sharp transition from ductile failures to brittle failures over a relatively narrow range of temperature.

This is most pronounced in ferritic steels, where the crystal structure is body-centred cubic. If that means nothing to you, don't worry. Austenitic steels, which have a face-centred cubic structure, do not show a pronounced transition. This is an example of how the structure of a material on the atomic scale can have an influence on its macroscopic mechanical behaviour.

For an example of how the ductile-to-brittle transition can have a significant influence on the performance of steels in practice, watch the 'Liberty ships' programme on the course DVD. △

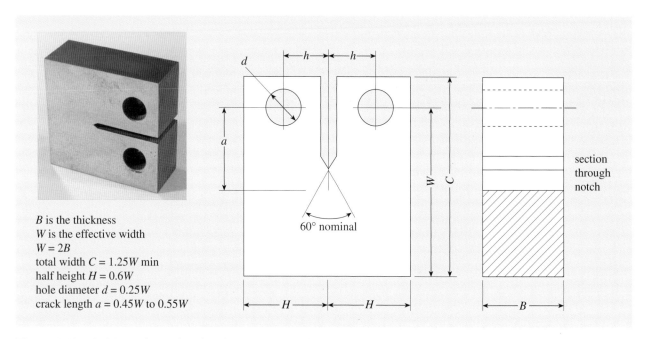

B is the thickness
W is the effective width
$W = 2B$
total width $C = 1.25W$ min
half height $H = 0.6W$
hole diameter $d = 0.25W$
crack length $a = 0.45W$ to $0.55W$

60° nominal

section through notch

Figure 1.14 A CT specimen showing the recommended ratios from BS EN ISO 12737

Material properties such as K_{IC} need to be measured, and engineers depend on standards to specify how they are measured, so that data from different sources can be compared and used reliably. Standards reflect the traditions in different industrial sectors. To measure K_{IC}, the geometry of the test-piece being loaded is important: the aircraft industry likes the compact tension (CT) specimen shown in Figure 1.14, whereas bend specimens (Figure 1.15) are favoured by the pipeline and pressure-vessel industries. There are various historical factors lying behind such traditions; the standards are written to allow for both approaches, and for the results obtained from the different approaches to be comparable. The geometry and loading of a bend specimen serve to magnify the load on the cracked ligament, which is a benefit to industries that use tough materials; in contrast, the CT geometry is useful because it is economical with material.

Both test specimens have a notch from which a fatigue crack is grown into the body of the material; the intention is to grow the crack to a sufficient length that it is away from any effects of the tip of the notch and the loading pins.

A valid fracture toughness test needs to produce a flat, low-energy, brittle fracture. If a range of specimens with varying thickness B is tested, it is found that the load needed to cause fracture gets progressively lower as the test-piece gets bigger. The failure load is asymptotic to a minimum value, as shown in Figure 1.16; it is this minimum value that is the materials property K_{IC}. The purpose of a standard document is to recommend a set of procedures that will produce a 'true', valid value of K_{IC} economically, i.e. without using overlarge test-pieces. Figure 1.16 also shows what are called 'shear lips' on the edges, i.e. free surfaces, of the advancing crack front. These shear lips are produced by the unconstrained plasticity at the free surface.

Look back to the small specimen shown in Figure 1.2, where there are no shear lips. If the metal being tested is not very ductile, then the plasticity ahead of the fatigue

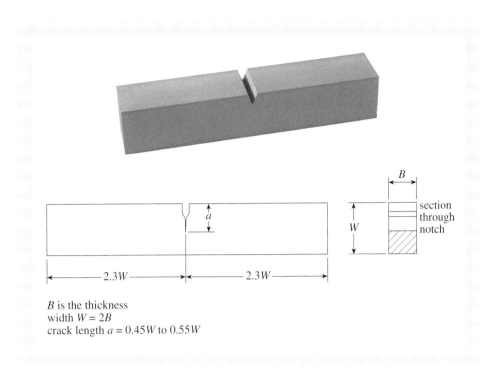

B is the thickness
width *W* = 2*B*
crack length *a* = 0.45*W* to 0.55*W*

Figure 1.15   A bend specimen

crack tip is small and relatively easily contained by a small body of elastic material; hence, a small test specimen is fine. If the metal is ductile, then the larger plastic zone needs more elastic material to contain it; hence, a large test specimen is needed.

The stress state along a crack front is complex. In the centre of the crack the material ahead of the tip is in plane strain; at the free surface the material is in plane stress. It is this change in stress state that creates a larger plastic zone along the crack front, which is shown in Figure 1.17.

DVD

For an illustration of the variation of the stress state along the crack front, watch the 'Plane strain animation' programme on the DVD.

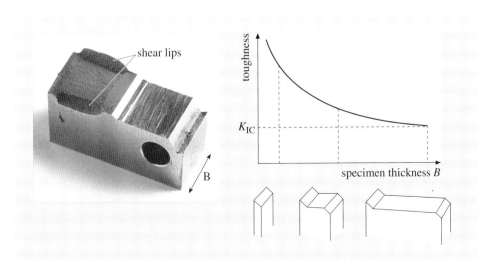

Figure 1.16   The effect of specimen thickness on the toughness

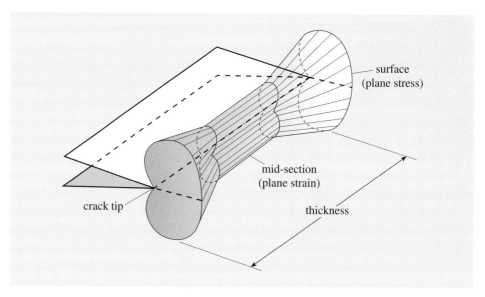

Figure 1.17   The shape of the plastically deformed material and how it varies at the crack tip (usually referred to as the crack-tip plastic zone)

When the shear lips are small compared with the total surface of flat fracture, this is a sign that most of the material is in plane strain, and the test is likely to produce a valid LEFM fracture toughness.

The rule of thumb adopted by standards is that the key dimensions of cracked specimens need to be about 50 times greater than the size of the crack-tip plastic zone in order to produce valid LEFM conditions. British Standard BS EN ISO 12737 gives these size criteria for LEFM specimens as:

$$B, a \geq 2.5 \left(\frac{K_Q}{\sigma_{\text{yield}}} \right)^2 \tag{1.3}$$

i.e. both the specimen's final crack length before it is fractured and its thickness B need to exceed this value, calculated from K_Q (the provisional value of K_{IC} when the test is complete). In practice, an estimate of K_{IC} will be made beforehand in selecting an appropriate specimen size.

SAQ 1.1 (Learning outcome 1.1)

(a) An aluminium alloy has an estimated toughness K_{IC} of 32 MPa √m and a yield stress of 380 MPa. What value of B will be needed to obtain a valid measure of K_{IC}, according to British Standard BS EN ISO 12737?

(b) Use Equation (1.3) to calculate what the Standards recommend for the thickness B at the extremes of temperature for the steel shown in Figure 1.13.

The answer to SAQ 1.1 shows that a remarkably wide range of sizes can be necessary for fracture toughness tests, which are genuinely seen in practice. The photograph

Figure 1.18   Little and large; the small specimen is about 20 mm in width

in Figure 1.18 was taken in the laboratories at Corus. The bottom specimen is half of a broken CT sample of a nuclear pressure-vessel steel; on top is a whole CT sample made from a high-strength, low-ductility steel.

If you have, or can buy, a valid fracture toughness for your material, in the relevant condition and at the temperature of interest (this might not be the design temperature, but, say, some thermal shock temperature that is lower than the operating temperature), then you are well on the way to applying LEFM.

Often valid LEFM-based toughness data are not available. Safety cases are needed for plant routinely designed and built from materials without K_{IC} data; indeed, much existing plant has little or no original documentation. By far the most common toughness data available, achievable or affordable is a measure of C_v.

The Charpy test is a cheap and cheerful swinging-hammer test, compared with the more complex and instrumented K_{IC} test. There is, of course, some commonality in the values obtained from the two tests for the same material, as both measure fracture resistance, albeit in different ways: see ☑ **Charpy test correlations** ☑.

DVD

The practice of a Charpy test is shown in the 'Liberty ships' programme on the DVD.

☑ Charpy test correlations

Charpy energy measurements of toughness cannot be used predictively, unlike K_{IC} values. Because the Charpy test values are specific to the size of sample measured, they cannot necessarily be extrapolated: there is no similitude. However, they are ubiquitous and cheap, so there is a continuing, strong interest in relating the results of a Charpy test to a K_{IC} value. So, what are the problems?

Figure 1.19 shows the results of Charpy tests on a ferritic steel at a range of different temperatures.

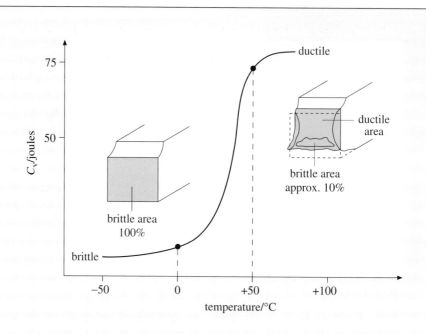

Figure 1.19   Charpy test results

For this material, at this size and at low temperatures, the fracture process does not consume much energy, the fracture surface sparkles and the two halves fit back together: the fracture is by brittle cleavage on this 'lower shelf' of the diagram.

On the 'upper shelf' there is a small sparkling area surrounded by dull, deformed fracture surface (dimpled rupture) that has consumed much more energy during its creation: the fracture is ductile, the two halves do not fit back together and gross plastic deformation is seen close to the free surfaces.

The temperature halfway between the upper and lower shelves is called the transition temperature or the ductile-to-brittle transition temperature.

Not all engineering metals show such a sharply defined change in fracture with temperature. There is a striking difference between the fracture behaviour of austenitic and ferritic steels, for instance.

Typically, a Charpy specimen is about 10 mm wide, and, as K_{IC} is sensitive to size, relating Charpy results to fracture toughness values is very difficult. However, it is also critical whether, at the operating temperature, an engineering part will cleave or tear. If an engineering structure is bigger than 10 mm, then Charpy test results will not necessarily translate from specimen to structure. Charpy energy values cannot be used to predict the performance of an engineering part; they are a property of the test.

All these arguments militate against the likelihood of a useful general relationship between Charpy toughnesses and K_{IC}; but the need cannot be ignored! So, there are many published correlations in the literature that are specific to particular materials and that try to distinguish between fractures on the upper and lower shelves, and through the transition regime when these materials are ferritic. British Standards give advice on using a master curve based on Charpy results; however, guidance in standards is conservative, hedged around with conditions and not applicable to older steels.

Modern pressure-vessel steels with C_v values no greater than 70 J and no less than 7 J were studied in 1973 to produce the expression $K_{IC} = 14.7C_v^{0.5}$, with a scatter band of $\pm15\%$. A recent Structural Integrity Assessment Procedure for European Industry (SINTAP) document suggests a lower bound relationship for steel of $K_{IC} = 12C_v^{0.5}$, which is a little lower than the bottom of the scatter band of the 1973 study. The SINTAP recommendation is the only relationship that we shall use here.

EXERCISE 1.2

(a) What range of fracture toughnesses is obtained between C_v values of 7 to 70 J:

   (i) using the 1973 expression $K_{IC} = 14.7C_v^{0.5}$

   (ii) using the SINTAP expression?

(b) What proportion of the range of fracture toughnesses for steels does this cover?

(c) What would be the expected Charpy toughness, using the SINTAP relationship, for an aluminium alloy with a toughness of 30 MPa √m?

Key concepts

The key concepts to take away from this section are:

- Values of K_{IC} for engineering metals cover a wide range. A 'tough' material might have a K_{IC} of 30 MPa √m, though many steels have values in excess of 100 MPa √m.

- Alloying metals and heat treating them can produce high strength, but at the expense of toughness.

- Fracture toughness tends to fall with reducing temperature.

- The stress state along a crack front in a fracture toughness specimen changes from plane strain in the centre to plane stress at the edges.

- Plane stress failure produces shear lips at the edges of the specimen.

- CT and bending specimens are specified in international standards for the measurement of K_{IC}, and a valid fracture toughness measurement requires most of the fracture surface to be under plane strain conditions.

2.3.2 Geometrical factor Y

The dimensionless factor Y in the fracture mechanics equation accounts for the geometry in which the crack is present and the size of the unique stress pattern within that geometry.

EXERCISE 1.3

(a) What is the value of Y for a centre crack in an infinite plate under tension, and how is the length of the centre crack expressed?

(b) What is the value of Y for an edge crack in an infinite plate under tension, and how is the length of the edge crack expressed?

If a plate is of finite size (as, of course, is always the case in reality), then the crack tip is affected by the free boundary and K_I is larger than is the case when the boundary is far distant. This is because the stress field in the presence of the crack depends on the geometry in which it exists. Y accounts for this geometry effect: the closer the tip is to the boundary, the higher the value of Y and so the higher the value of K_I.

Equations that describe the change in Y are obtained from curve fitting of FE solutions; they are available in handbooks, just like the stress concentration factors you saw in Block 1. The convention in these handbooks is usually that an embedded crack is $2a$ long and an edge crack is a long (Figures 1.8 and 1.20 are examples of embedded cracks, whereas Figures 1.9 and 1.21 show edge cracks). Embedded cracks have two tips, so 'two tips $2a$' is a useful aide-memoire. The same convention has come to be used on the width of the plate: $2W$ where the crack is embedded, W when it is an edge crack.

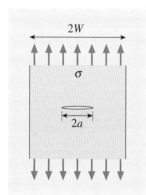

Figure 1.20 Embedded crack in a plate of finite width

All the Y relationships that you will need in this block are in the calculators on your DVD, which you will use in a while. You will never have to remember a specific value for Y for a particular geometry, though it's helpful if you remember that $Y = 1$ occurs only in the case of an embedded crack in an infinite plate. In this part, I shall just consider these two geometries of an embedded crack and an edge crack where the boundaries affect the value of Y.

For illustration, the equation for a through-thickness centre crack in a plate of finite width in tension, Figure 1.20, is:

$$K_I = Y\sigma\sqrt{\pi a} = \left[\frac{1 - 0.025\left(\dfrac{a}{W}\right)^2 + 0.06\left(\dfrac{a}{W}\right)^4}{\sqrt{\cos\left(\dfrac{\pi a}{2W}\right)}}\right]\sigma\sqrt{\pi a}$$

Note that, in this equation, as the plate widens and so a/W becomes smaller, then Y approaches unity, i.e. the value for an infinite plate.

An edge crack in a finite-width plate (Figure 1.21) is not, as one might think by considering symmetry, the equivalent of half an embedded crack, because the slope at the centre of the gaping crack in an infinite plate is constrained, whereas it is free at the mouth of an edge crack. (Imagine an embedded crack: at its centre the slope of the two surfaces is constrained to be horizontal before curving down to the opposite tip. If you imagine an edge crack as half of an embedded crack, then there is nothing on the other side to constrain the slope of the two surfaces.) This freedom to gape can be thought of as effectively 'moving' the load to the crack tip, and thus increasing K.

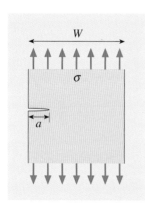

Figure 1.21 Edge crack in a plate of finite width

For an edge crack in an infinite plate (Figure 1.9) under tension $Y = 1.12$, so:

$$K_1 = Y\sigma\sqrt{\pi a} = 1.12\,\sigma\sqrt{\pi a}$$

The equation that takes into account the width of a finite edge-cracked plate is:

$$K_1 = \left[1.12 - 0.23\frac{a}{W} + 10.55\left(\frac{a}{W}\right)^2 - 21.72\left(\frac{a}{W}\right)^3 + 30.39\left(\frac{a}{W}\right)^4\right]\sigma\sqrt{\pi a}$$

Comfortingly, in this equation Y approaches 1.12 as the plate becomes wider and a/W becomes smaller.

Note that in both of these geometries the crack is infinitely long out of the plane of the paper.

EXERCISE 1.4

Figure 1.22 shows the Y calibration curve for a plate in tension with a through-thickness edge crack.

(a) By reading directly from the curve, estimate Y when the crack is one-quarter of the way through the thickness W of the plate.

(b) Estimate the percentage change in Y as the crack grows to (i) one-half and (ii) three-quarters through the thickness.

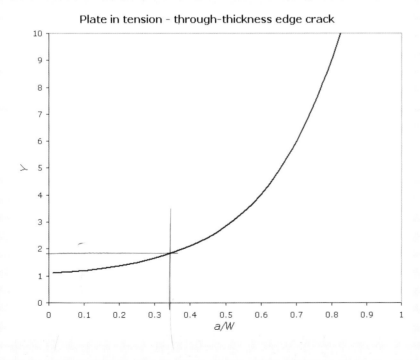

Figure 1.22   Y calibration for an edge-cracked plate loaded in tension

The answer to Exercise 1.4 shows that, as a crack grows, the value of Y can increase dramatically. So, either knowing or making an assumption about the nearness of a crack front to a boundary is critical to the practice of fracture mechanics.

The 'K calculator' is in the computer-based activities section of the DVD.

Figure 1.22 comes from the 'K calculator'. Open the spreadsheet now. The first sheet is called 'Brittle fracture'. You can choose different calibration factors from the drop-down menu. Select the option for a plate in tension with a through-thickness edge crack and then look at the second sheet titled 'Y calibration'. The graph of Y against a/W should look like the one in Figure 1.22.

SAQ 1.2 (Learning outcomes 1.2–1.4)

Have a look at how Y changes with a/W for an edge-cracked beam or plate in pure bending, rather than in tension, using the K calculator and repeat Exercise 1.4.

Notice from the answer to SAQ 1.2 that K_I does not increase with crack length anywhere near as rapidly under bending as under tension. This is because the stress distribution in bending varies from tension to compression across the section, so there are compressive stresses ahead of the crack.

I now want to consider a plate or beam with an edge crack that finds itself in a combination of a tensile stress field and a bending stress field.

EXERCISE 1.5 (BLOCK 1 REVISION)

Sketch the distributions of stresses in a beam or plate under a combination of a tensile and a bending load.

I am most interested in a crack that finds itself subjected to the maximum tensile stresses; Exercise 1.5 showed that this occurs where the stresses of σ_{tension} and σ_{bending} combine to open the crack.

I have two very different Y calibration curves for tension and bending, and clearly I cannot simply choose one of them, arbitrarily, and use it for $\sigma_{\text{tension}} + \sigma_{\text{bending}}$. No, in stress fields of different forms the general rule is that the K values are added, not the stresses that cause them. So, I need to use the two Y calibration curves for the different stress distributions and add the resulting K values to produce a crack-driving parameter for the case of combined tension and bending.

(Note that Y calibration curves can be found using either the applied stress or the applied load. In the K calculator for an edge-cracked plate under tension and in bending I have used stress.)

EXERCISE 1.6

Calculate, longhand, the combined K for a through-thickness crack that has grown one-quarter of the distance from the tensile surface (i.e. $a/W = 0.25$) in a piece of 10 mm × 30 mm bar (Figure 1.23) under a tensile stress of 100 MPa and a bending stress that varies from +100 MPa to −100 MPa.

Figure 1.23   Bar with a through-thickness edge crack subject to tensile and bending stresses

Let's now consider further the far-field stress by which a crack is opened.

2.3.3 Far-field stress σ

The stress in the fracture mechanics equation:

$$K_I = Y\sigma\sqrt{\pi a}$$

is the far-field stress distribution in which the crack finds itself (computed from simple mechanics equations, handbooks or specific, expensive numerical calculations). K_I deals with the complex stress field at the crack tip – there is no application of a stress concentration factor. It is a common mistake to throw in a few stress concentrations for luck.

In this block I shall be quite cavalier about using the nearest available stress distribution to that of a particular problem with which I am concerned – so long as it is of a similar form.

For example, let's consider an edge crack in the wall of a pipe that is under pressure (Figure 1.24). Modelling the stress distribution in the pipe wall as a membrane stress, the crack can be considered as acting in a tensile stress field calculated using:

$$\sigma = p\frac{r}{t} \tag{1.4}$$

where p is the internal pressure, r the mean radius of the pipe and t is the wall thickness (as long as the mean pipe radius is much larger than the wall thickness).

The calculated value of stress can then be entered directly into the fracture mechanics equation using the Y calibration for an edge-cracked, finite-width plate. Note that

In the terminology of pipes, a 'membrane' stress is one that is uniform through the pipe wall: for example, a stress caused by the internal pressure in a thin-walled pipe. This distinguishes such a stress from a bending stress in the pipe wall that varies through the wall thickness.

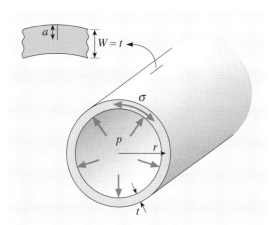

Figure 1.24   Stress in a pipe wall

this calibration does not take into account the curvature of the pipe wall; there are such calibrations but I don't have one to hand, so we will use what we have and assume that, as long as the radius is large compared with the wall thickness, the error involved will be small. So, let's do it, longhand again.

SAQ 1.3 (Learning outcomes 1.4–1.6)

(a) A thin-walled pipe carries a pressure of 15 MPa. It has a mean radius of 120 mm and a wall thickness of 10 mm. Ignoring curvature effects on the stress distribution and the value of Y, calculate K_I for an internal edge crack that is a quarter of the way through the pipe wall.

(b) If the pipe was made from steel, would you expect this crack to cause a brittle failure at this pressure?

Remember: Y calibration curves for different geometries are different for different stress distributions and so stresses that require different calibration curves cannot be added – only the resulting K_I values can be added. The crack in a combination of a tensile stress field and a bending stress distribution that we considered earlier produced two values of K that were added to produce the combined K, which could have been compared with a value of K_{IC} for a specific material.

These stress distributions, which result from different external loadings, are relatively easy to deal with because their values are usually known. Analysis becomes much more difficult when self-equilibrating, internal residual stresses, commonly introduced during welding, are encountered. In general, design stresses are easily evaluated, but residual stresses created during fabrication are much more difficult to assess because their values are not known, are not easily measured, and can be very high.

Their unknown values make the specific orientation of a crack relative to the direction of the residual stresses of secondary interest. So, being good, conservative engineers, we usually assume the worst: that the residual stresses are opening the crack, i.e. they are tensile. If residual stress distributions are of the same form, or can be assumed to be of the same form, as the external stresses, then the stresses can be added and one Y calibration curve used. Otherwise, different calibration curves are needed and the K values are added.

SAQ 1.4 (Learning outcomes 1.5 and 1.7)

The cracked pipe in SAQ 1.3 was made from steel with a yield stress of 400 MPa. It was pre- and post-weld heat treated, so tensile residual welding stresses of about 20% of yield might also be present and opening the crack. Calculate the crack-driving force K_I in the presence of both design and residual stresses; again, do this longhand.

SAQ 1.4 shows how residual stresses can affect fracture processes, if they add to an existing tensile stress to increase K_I.

The industrial terminology for the design stresses is *primary* stresses, and for the welding residual stresses that act over a short distance it is *secondary* stresses.

In addition to the significant uncertainties introduced by residual stresses, there is great potential for introducing further uncertainty when crack lengths are considered – after all, we didn't deliberately introduce the confounded things!

2.3.4 Crack length

The length of the crack is denoted by a in the fracture mechanics equation. Given that parts aren't deliberately manufactured with cracks in them, their size, therefore, is measured by some non-invasive process such as radiography or ultrasonics, is assumed as part of a design process, or is seen after a part has failed. In some cases the presence of a crack is assumed even if none is detected by inspection. For a safety-critical part, if a detection system that can measure cracks down to 2 mm is used and no crack is found, then assuming there are cracks of 2 mm present, which have only just been missed, is only prudent.

Crack lengths in the handbooks of Y calibrations are always regular geometries, such as semi-circles, ellipses, lines or circles. In practice, cracks are irregular and so one makes conservative assumptions about their shape. For example, if an embedded crack is triangular you might model it as a circle that envelops the triangle – particularly if you happened to have a Y calibration curve for an embedded, circular crack.

Cracks that are introduced during the fabrication of welded structures can also grow by fatigue in structures that are cyclically loaded.

Fracture mechanics comes into its own when a crack is found. Does one:

- stop the plant immediately

- order the crack ground out and rewelded (then worry about whether this has made the problem better or worse because of what it might have done to the residual stresses and the material properties)

- run the plant at a lower loading until the part can be replaced

- tell the plant manager that it is OK to keep running the plant without any remedial action and risk having to explain to the judge why it was a good decision, despite the explosion having killed the maintenance engineer?

LEFM calculations that show a good safety factor are fine for these types of problem because they are the lowest energy failure. If a failure under load were to occur not by brittle fracture but by ductile tearing mechanisms, then the calculation will simply give an extra margin for safety.

Keeping heavily loaded, cracked plant and aeroplanes in operation requires the active management of cracks using non-destructive inspection techniques. However, inspection cannot be performed in a simple 'Is there a crack there and, if there is, how big is it and what do we do about it?' sort of way. For example, a typical story (taken from the power-generation industry) runs like this:

- We haven't found any cracks on inspection, so let's assume that we could have found any and all cracks longer than 6 mm (this was the standard figure in the industry at the time, although improved NDT techniques now reduce this figure).

- So, we will assume there is a crack that is 6 mm long, which we haven't found, and that it is in the worst place, i.e. loaded by the maximum opening stress amplitude.

- We know our loading cycles exactly, and so can estimate that a 6 mm crack, if one exists, will grow by fatigue to 8 mm in a year.

- We also calculate that the crack has to grow to 16 mm before the (conservative) LEFM theory says that catastrophic failure will occur and the whole shooting match blows up and kills everyone in the building.

- So, we will inspect every year and have a safety factor of two on the critical crack length, or whatever seems comfortable.

Now comes the brilliant bit.

- After a year, we reinspect and can't find a crack, so there never was a 6 mm crack and it hasn't grown to 8 mm as estimated.

- So, the clock starts again, assuming that a 6 mm crack has just been missed; and if this cycle carries on the plant can run for ever.

- Five years down the line the NDE industry guarantees (in writing, and on the back of their insurance certificate) that with their new kit they can find all cracks over 3 mm.

- They find one 3 mm long and call it 'Sally'.

- Running the (conservative) calculations again we work out that it will take 5 years for the 3 mm crack to grow to 8 mm, based on a safety factor of 2.

- After another couple of years Sally is still 3 mm long so they time the NDE to coincide with the repainting schedule, which costs £20k, and they have to remove some paint to do the NDE anyway.

- Fifteen years down the line Sally is still 3 mm long and so the failure-assessment process clock is still reset to zero at regular intervals.

This is the key to what fracture mechanics provides: a means of assessing whether or not a crack is *safe*.

If a crack is found in a structure, then the possible courses of action (which include the sort of fracture mechanics assessment just outlined) can be constrained by the context of the problem: see the input ☑ **Cracking in nuclear plant** ☑.

2.3.5 Review of the parameters

- K_{IC} is measured in your own laboratory, bought from a test-house, guessed from experience or converted from Charpy values.

- Y is looked up in a handbook of common geometries or calculated using an FE program. I have given you a calculator on the DVD that contains the Y values that you will need during this course (more on this later).

- σ is the far-field stress calculated from a mechanics equation, looked up in a handbook or calculated numerically (in fracture mechanics there are *no* stress concentration factors calculated from the presence of the crack!).

- a is measured or estimated; pay for non-destructive evaluation/testing (NDE/NDT), and assume they have only found all cracks of the length they have written into the contract and that there is one that is just a tiny bit smaller that they haven't found.

☑ Cracking in nuclear plant

At the time of writing there are significant cracking problems at British Energy's Hunterstone B and Hinkley Point B advanced gas-cooled nuclear reactors that have been operating for over 200 000 h. The component most affected is called a bifurcation, a junction between two curved pipes within the heat-exchanger circuit, of which there are 528 per reactor.

Crack measurement by eddy-current testing (not an easy business, see Figure 1.25) reports a typical crack growth rate of 0.1 to 0.2 mm per year – although some have grown 1 mm per year.

Figure 1.25   Inspection of the heat exchanger of a nuclear reactor

This particular context, of the nuclear industry, is illustrated by this extract from an article quoting Andy Spurr (British Energy's chief technical officer):

> Spurr said that the vast majority of cracks are too insignificant to warrant repair and the rest are treated using one of four options:

- Remelt affected area.

- Replace the bifurcation.

- Internal plugging.

- External plugging.

> The chosen option depends on the particular crack and bifurcation. Spurr said that plugging is not an attractive option because it can lead to the degradation of the boiler's surface area. However, each boiler can accommodate 'quite a lot of plugging' before there is any reduction in output. Asked whether replacement of the boilers was an option, Spurr said it was highly unlikely as it would be 'practically, very, very difficult to execute.'

> 'British Energy's bifurcation blues' (2006) *Nuclear Engineering International*, 22 November.
> http://www.neimagazine.com/storyprint.asp?sc=2040465

3 LINEAR-ELASTIC FRACTURE MECHANICS IN PRACTICE

LEFM theory is useful notwithstanding that most overload fractures in engineering metal parts will not be brittle. If you can show that a crack in a part will not grow by fast, brittle fracture, then any plasticity involved in the fracture process will make it more difficult for the crack to grow, effectively providing an added safety factor. So, a satisfactory safety case based on an LEFM analysis means that the practitioner may not need to go any further, even though the eventual failure will not be brittle.

In this section you will practise using the fracture mechanics equation in ways that are used in industry and with issues that are important to industry.

DVD

The 'K calculator' is in the computer-based activities section of the DVD.

ACTIVITY 1: USING THE *K* CALCULATOR WORKBOOK

Open the *K* calculator; you will see a spreadsheet for entering variables into the fracture mechanics equation. You have already seen that the 'Brittle fracture' sheet has an interface for inputting variables and a drop-down menu for choosing the *Y* calibration curve appropriate to a particular geometry and loading. Now choose the 'Plate in tension – through-thickness edge crack' geometry from the drop-down menu. What you should see is shown in Figure 1.26.

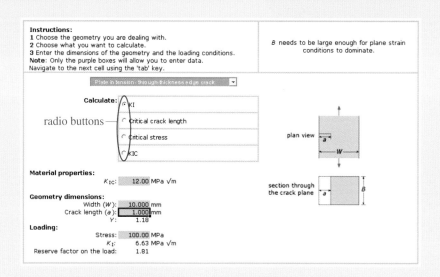

Figure 1.26   The 'Brittle fracture' interface for an edge-cracked plate in tension

You can choose from four different types of calculation by using the 'radio buttons' highlighted in Figure 1.26. Try the different radio buttons and you will see different data boxes highlighted in purple. These purple boxes are where you put data in and the values in the white boxes are calculated by the spreadsheet.

These calculations happen automatically for three of the radio buttons, but the critical crack length button has an additional purple 'Calculate' button, which you must click on in order to trigger a solution.

The first radio button calculates K_I and shows the value of Y for variations in a, W and stress. If K_{IC} is given a value, then it also calculates a reserve factor on load (which is the ratio of K_{IC} to K_I).

EXAMPLE

Try putting in the values from SAQ 1.3 of stress = 180 MPa, $W = 10$ mm and $a = 2.5$ mm. Leave the fracture toughness of the material box empty. Does the answer match your answer to SAQ 1.3?

SOLUTION

The calculator is a little better at reading graphs than I am. It gives a K of 23.94 MPa $\sqrt{m}$ and returns a value for Y of 1.5 (Figure 1.27). Good enough, I reckon.

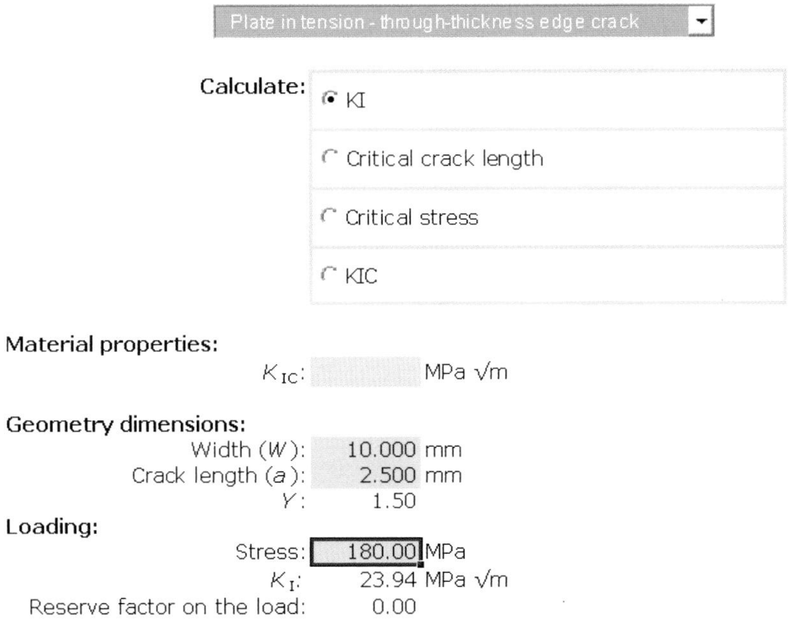

Plate in tension - through-thickness edge crack ▼

Calculate: ⦿ KI

    ◯ Critical crack length

    ◯ Critical stress

    ◯ KIC

Material properties:
K_{IC}:   MPa $\sqrt{m}$

Geometry dimensions:
Width (W):   10.000 mm
Crack length (a):   2.500 mm
Y: 1.50

Loading:
Stress: 180.00 MPa
K_I: 23.94 MPa $\sqrt{m}$
Reserve factor on the load: 0.00

Figure 1.27   Plate in tension with a through-thickness edge crack – $K_I \approx 24$ MPa $\sqrt{m}$ and $Y = 1.5$

EXAMPLE

Now input a value of K_{IC}, to find one that will return a reserve factor on the load of 2.

SOLUTION

As you might expect, a K_{IC} of double the value of K_I does the trick (Figure 1.28).

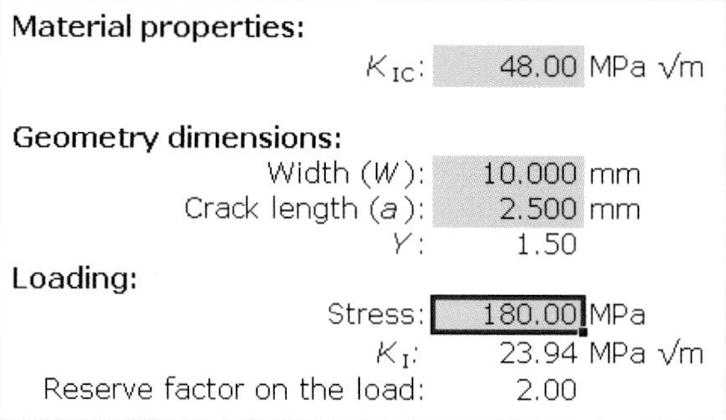

Material properties:
K_{IC}:   48.00 MPa √m

Geometry dimensions:
Width (W):   10.000 mm
Crack length (a): 2.500 mm
Y: 1.50

Loading:
Stress: 180.00 MPa
K_I: 23.94 MPa √m
Reserve factor on the load: 2.00

Figure 1.28   Plate in tension with a through-thickness edge crack – the reserve factor is 2 when $K_{IC} \approx 48$ MPa √m

Now click the 'Critical crack length' radio button, which brings up the additional 'Calculate' button. Given a value for W, a K_{IC} for the material and an applied stress, this calculates the critical crack length at which brittle fracture will occur.

EXAMPLE

For the bar in Exercise 1.6, where $W = 10$ mm, and a stress of 180 MPa, determine the critical crack length if the toughness of the material is 100 MPa √m.

Hint: remember to hit 'Enter' after adding each value and then to click on 'Calculate'.

SOLUTION

The calculator gives a critical crack length of 6.0 mm.

EXERCISE 1.7

Assume now that there may be some lower-toughness weld metal in the pipe, so the crack could find itself in material with a toughness of 40 MPa √m.

Do you expect the critical crack length to cause failure to be longer or shorter? Use the calculator to produce a value.

Let's turn now to the 'Critical stress' radio button. If I know the crack length, the geometry and the material toughness, then I can calculate the stress that would cause brittle failure.

EXAMPLE

Still working on the edge-crack geometry, put a tiny crack into the 10 mm section and a reasonable toughness value for a steel. What is the stress that would cause brittle failure?

SOLUTION

I put in 100 MPa √m for the toughness and 0.1 mm for the crack length, which produces a stress of 5043 MPa (Figure 1.29)!

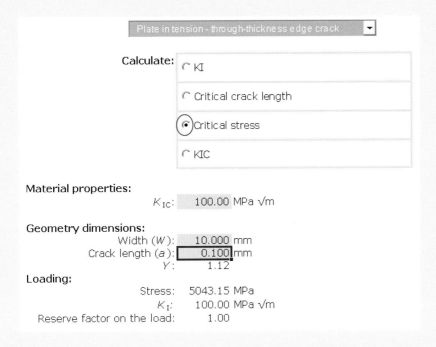

Figure 1.29   Plate in tension with a through-thickness edge crack – the critical stress is 5043 MPa

Well, if you can produce a steel with a toughness of 100 MPa √m and a yield stress of about 5000 MPa, it's about time to consider retiring rich. Any real steel would have yielded way before brittle failure could take place. The calculation is correct in so far as it goes, but *it doesn't address failure by any mechanisms other than brittle fracture* – I shall return to this issue later in the block.

Finally, the radio button labelled K_{IC} allows you to calculate the fracture toughness of a material from the conditions that were in place when brittle fracture took place. This is particularly useful for forensic engineering. If you have an obviously brittle fracture surface and know the loadings on the part that broke, then you have, in effect, a toughness test.

EXAMPLE

Keep using the through-thickness edge crack calibration.

If you have a broken aluminium part that has failed in a brittle fashion at a crack length of 1 mm in a 10 mm section at a nominal stress of 90 MPa, what is the fracture toughness of the material?

SOLUTION

I get a fracture toughness of about 6.0 MPa $\sqrt{m}$ (Figure 1.30). This is a very low value of toughness that should appeal to the Sherlock Holmes in you: perhaps there are some other loadings or the part has been improperly used?

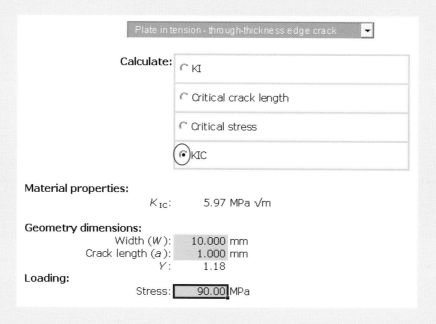

Figure 1.30   Plate in tension with a through-thickness edge crack – the fracture toughness of the material is approximately 6.0 MPa $\sqrt{m}$

3.1 Applying fracture mechanics

What now follows is a series of exercises and SAQs that form a design narrative. Work through these using the K calculator. I will draw out the key concepts as the narrative progresses.

At the heart of the design of a chemical plant is a steel, thin-walled pressure vessel that is fabricated by welding. It is a safety-critical design that has the facility for an emergency shut-down by being flooded with cold water. The emergency shut-down procedure generates long-range thermal stresses that act in the same way as the stresses generated by the pressure in the vessel, i.e. over the whole of the structure. In addition, there are welding residual stresses that act over a short range, a few millimetres around the weld, and that are self-equilibrating. The issues I am introducing here are significant to such a design, they are not simply examples to provide practice – although they do this as well.

Imagine that you are the plant designer concerned with the structural integrity of a thin-walled pressure vessel where chemical reactions take place under pressure. The high-quality steel plate from which the vessel will be made is well characterized and it is 16 mm thick. You know that its toughness on the ductile upper shelf is 140 MPa √m and on the brittle lower shelf it is 80 MPa √m, and that the transition temperature is somewhere between 0 and 10 °C. The tensile membrane stress in the vessel during normal, high-temperature operation is 300 MPa and the NDE procedures will guarantee finding all surface-breaking cracks above 4 mm in length.

EXERCISE 1.8

What will be the reserve factor on load during normal high-temperature operation of your design? Use the higher toughness value.

EXERCISE 1.9

The vessel is flooded with cold water on emergency shut-down, which induces a thermal shock loading that effectively increases the operating stress by 50%. Is the vessel still safe? (You can assume that the thermal stresses just add to the tensile membrane stress, so the same calibration factor can be used; and again, use the higher toughness value.)

So far the analysis has used the upper-shelf toughness value. If you don't know whether the steel is on the lower shelf when flooded with cold water on emergency shut-down, then unless the toughness at this temperature can be ascertained, or measured, you must use the conservative value of 80 MPa √m, i.e. the lower-shelf toughness. This reduces the reserve factor on load to an unacceptable level of just above unity (Figure 1.31), which doesn't allow much room for errors and unknowns. So this calculation is somewhat worrying.

SAQ 1.5 (Learning outcomes 1.6, 1.8 and 1.9)

You have paid for an FE analysis of the thermal loading transient that shows that it is more appropriate to treat the thermal stresses as bending stresses. How does this affect the result of your analysis?

(Hint: you will have to use more than one of the calculator load models, and add the K values by hand – the calculator won't do this for you.)

Now, a very important factor in the development of a safety case for a pressure vessel is the possible residual stresses within it. Every pressure vessel will have a weld of some sort associated with it, whether as part of the fabrication of the vessel itself, or the connection of pipework associated with the addition and removal of the vessel's contents.

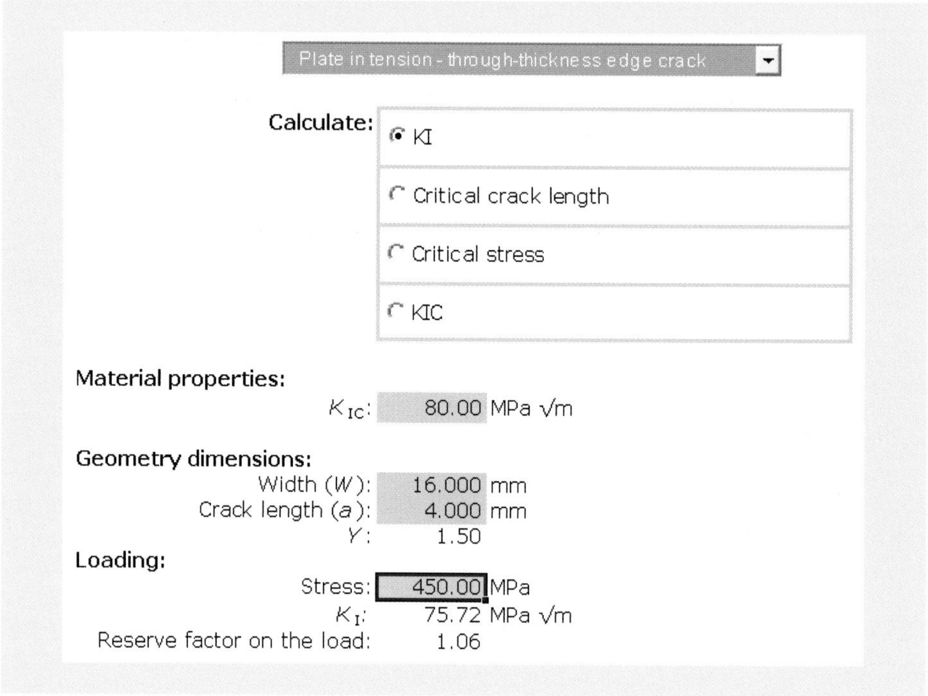

Figure 1.31   The effect on the reserve factor of using the lower toughness value

You need to redo the safety case, taking into consideration the probable tensile residual stresses due to welding; the assumption is that the residual stresses act in concert with the loading stresses and with the thermal stress to open a possible crack. The yield stress of the material is 500 MPa. As a rule of thumb you can assume that if the weld is pre- and post-weld heat-treated to high standards there might still be residual stresses that are 20% of yield present. If the weld has not been heat-treated, the regulators require you to assume a worst case, i.e. that the residual stresses are equal to the yield stress of the material.

You will need to analyse the design under both assumptions. So far we have calculated that the K due to the design load is 50 MPa $\sqrt{m}$ and due to thermal shock is 18 MPa $\sqrt{m}$. The residual stress will add further to these values.

SAQ 1.6 (Learning outcomes 1.6–1.9)

Include the effects of residual stress in the calculation of the total K:

(a) during normal operation

(b) during thermal shock when an emergency shut-down occurs.

What do the results tell you about the operation of the design, given the toughness data for the material?

The fracture mechanics analysis suggests that your design is not robust enough to stand up to emergency shut-down. There clearly needs to be some amendment to the design of the vessel.

SAQ 1.7 (Learning outcomes 1.9 and 1.10)

Suggest at least two possible changes to the design of the vessel that will mean it can be constructed and operated safely.

If your NDE contractor buys a new piece of kit that can guarantee to find flaws over 3 mm long, is this the salvation of your design?

SAQ 1.8 (Learning outcomes 1.6–1.10)

Redo the calculations using a flaw size of 3 mm. Can the vessel now be operated safely:

(a) without weld heat treatment

(b) with weld heat treatment?

Neither of the reserve factors calculated in SAQ 1.8 inspires confidence, so I'm afraid you will have to increase the wall thickness to avoid potential brittle failure. Life would also be much easier if the material were on the upper shelf at 0 °C, so perhaps you should contact the steel supplier?

What you should know and be able to do so far

You have used the K calculator workbook extensively for analysing various inputs to a typical design problem. The workbook compares calculated values of K_I with the fracture toughness K_{IC}, and the difference gives a safety factor in terms of a reserve factor on load. You should now be confident in calculating safety factors in structures loaded by primary and secondary stresses using the K calculator, or longhand using Y calibrations and the fracture mechanics equation.

One of the key skills in analysing engineering problems is the ability to make appropriate simplifications. One of the aims of the design narrative you have just followed has been to introduce you to a sequence of steps where simplifications are necessary to obtain a solution simply. You must be prepared to make simplifications in order to solve a problem.

3.2 Plastic collapse

I shall now introduce one of the most important lessons in the understanding and use of LEFM: that it is possible to use the theory outside its applicability, and so make mistakes.

Consider the design of the plant that we followed through the previous section. The nominal design stress is 300 MPa and the thermal stresses are 150 MPa, giving a total of 450 MPa, which is a gnat's whisker away from the material's yield stress of

500 MPa. A structure experiencing two-thirds of the yield stress is considered to be a highly loaded structure, and this is 90% of yield.

So, could your design fail by yielding? Certainly it could.

EXERCISE 1.10

Use the K calculator to calculate the critical stress for your 3 mm edge crack.

If the stress in the whole of the wall thickness exceeds the yield stress of the material, then your design will fail by plastic collapse. So, for a 3 mm crack the whole of the wall thickness will exceed the yield stress of the material and fail by plastic collapse, long before brittle failure. Of course it won't literally collapse: it will blow up (think of bubble gum), but 'plastic collapse' is the proper term for this type of failure.

Plastic collapse is the other end of the failure spectrum to LEFM. Bend a piece of wire, such as a paper clip, a small amount and it springs back elastically. Bend it a lot and it remains permanently bent because the cross section has become plastic. Plastic collapse of a cracked body can occur without crack growth; the presence of a crack simply reduces the cross section. When the ligament has gone permanently plastic no further increase in load can be supported.

Figure 1.32 shows a bar containing an edge crack, subject to a tensile load. Now, although you can use the K calculator to assess whether the applied stress will cause the crack to grow, leading to brittle failure, let's not forget that the material might yield long before that happens. The effective area of the bar is decreased by the presence of the crack, so raising the stress on the remaining ligament. When yield is reached the bar will undergo plastic collapse.

For this geometry I can calculate the load at which plastic collapse occurs:

$$F_{crit} = B(W - a)\sigma_{yield}$$

And, using this idea, I can analyse our plant design to understand its potential for failure by plastic collapse.

The nominal hoop stress at which plastic collapse occurs in our pressure vessel is simply the yield stress of the material factored by the reduction in cross section, a/W. You can think of this in terms of the forces being carried in the wall of the vessel and the areas they act over. The overall force carried will not change, so a reduction in area just increases the stress proportionately.

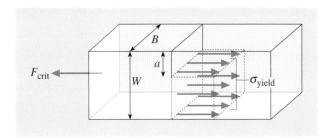

Figure 1.32   Edge-cracked bar under a tensile load

EXERCISE 1.11

If a section with a 3 mm crack yields because of the hoop stress, what is the average stress in an uncracked section? Remember that the yield strength of our material is 500 MPa.

If a cracked section were to yield at a nominal stress of 400 MPa, this gives a reserve factor of 400/300 ≈ 1.3. (The design stress is 300 MPa, remember.)

Based on what you have been doing so far, as an extension to our case study we should consider plastic collapse under the combined loading of the design stresses and the thermal shock stresses, which are in bending.

Our two simple theories, i.e. of brittle fracture and plastic collapse, operate completely independently of each other. The two material properties of K_{IC} and σ_{yield} are independent for any size of section. They are extremes of failure behaviour that do not, in themselves, define their sphere of applicability.

In industry it is routine for engineering analyses to be performed numerically on a computer, using FE analyses. The analyses of important engineering shapes and materials are captured in handbooks and data sheets, so every problem does not require a special solution. The engineering practice of solving for plastic collapse loads for cracked geometries is also supported by solutions in handbooks of common geometries. As with LEFM, if you cannot find a solution in a handbook then you have to buy a specific solution from an FE jockey.

4 SUMMARY

You know now that fracture mechanics is a useful and necessary tool for establishing the safety of structures that may undergo brittle failure if a relatively small flaw combines with high in-service loadings and residual stresses.

I have already mentioned that cracks can extend in service because of fatigue, where cyclic stresses lead to cycling of the stress intensity K. Fortuitously, it turns out that the growth of fatigue cracks can be expressed in terms of the range of K experienced by a crack as it cycles from the minimum to the maximum stress. Part 2 of this block covers the topic of fatigue in more detail, and so that is where we will continue this aspect of the application of LEFM.

LEFM breaks down if there is a lot of plasticity associated with the crack, which is hardly surprising for a theory based on linear-elasticity! Elastic–plastic fracture mechanics (EPFM) lies between the regimes of plastic collapse and LEFM. This is the subject of Part 5 of this block. EPFM is a useful and necessary tool for situations where there is too much plasticity for LEFM to be valid and not enough to cause plastic collapse. It is a complex melange of possible physical events that depends critically on the material, its state, and the geometry of the component. An elastic–plastic numerical analysis is required to solve practical problems in the EPFM regime. In Part 5 you will see enough theoretical discussion to understand the limitations of the approaches and be shown practical EPFM at a level used in current industrial practice.

Fortunately, fracture mechanics in industry combines numerical analyses of EPFM with the more straightforward plastic collapse and LEFM principles to produce a master curve that creates a failure assessment diagram (FAD) that bridges across from LEFM through EPFM to plastic collapse. In Part 5 you will study the theory and practice of EPFM using a state-of-the-art FAD, and emerge equipped to live with cracks.

LEARNING OUTCOMES

After you have studied Block 2 Part 1 you should be able to do the following.

1.1 Explain the meaning of 'plane strain' in the context of fracture toughness, and calculate whether a test sample's dimensions allow for a valid measurement to be made.

1.2 Define the key parameters in the fracture toughness equation.

1.3 Explain that Y varies as a crack grows through a component.

1.4 Calculate values of Y from calibration curves or equations.

1.5 Calculate values of K in components, given appropriate data.

1.6 Assess whether the value of K in a component, from the applied load or stress, is likely to cause brittle failure in the presence of a particular crack.

1.7 Include the likely effects of residual stress in fracture mechanics calculations.

1.8 Assess the overall contributions of K values from different sources of stress.

1.9 Use fracture mechanics concepts in the analysis of components where cracks may be present.

1.10 Describe the importance of NDE/NDT in providing data for fracture mechanics assessments.

1.11 Describe the difference between a brittle and a ductile fracture.

ANSWERS TO EXERCISES

EXERCISE 1.1

Recall from Block 1 that the maximum principal stresses lie at 45° to a state of pure shear (see Figure 1.33) – sketch a Mohr's circle if you need convincing!

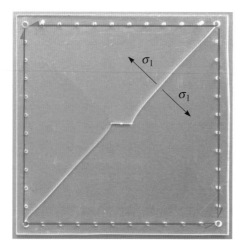

Figure 1.33   Principal stress direction

EXERCISE 1.2

(a) (i)   The 1973 study produces about 39–123 MPa √m.

    (ii)   The SINTAP recommendation produces 32–100 MPa √m.

(b) From the rough-and-ready values in Table 1.1, K_{IC} for steels ranges from 40 to 200 MPa √m, so these recommendations cover about half of the range.

(c) The value would be $(30/12)^2 = 6.25$ J.

EXERCISE 1.3

(a) Referring back to Figure 1.8, $Y = 1$ and, by convention, the length of a surface-breaking flaw is $2a$.

(b) Referring back to Figure 1.9, $Y = 1.12$ and, by convention, the length of a surface-breaking flaw is a.

EXERCISE 1.4

(a) At an a/W of 0.25, Y is about 1.5.

(b) (i)   At an a/W of 0.5, Y is about 2.8, an 87% increase.

    (ii)   At an a/W of 0.75, Y is about 7.3, a 387% increase.

EXERCISE 1.5

The bending stresses go from tension to an equal magnitude of compression (Figure 1.34). The tension stresses are uniform over the depth of the section. So, the combined stress distribution varies from $\sigma_{\text{tension}} + \sigma_{\text{bending}}$ at one surface to $\sigma_{\text{tension}} - \sigma_{\text{bending}}$ at the other surface, where:

$$\sigma_{\text{tension}} = \frac{F}{A} = \frac{F}{BW}$$

and

$$\sigma_{\text{bending}} = \frac{My}{I} = \frac{\pm M\left(W/2\right)}{\left(BW^3/12\right)}$$

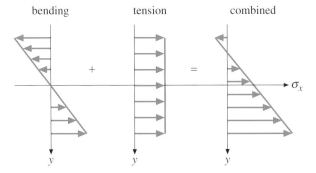

Figure 1.34   Combined stresses under bending and tension

EXERCISE 1.6

I don't need to know the cross section of the specimen in order to evaluate Y, as the Y calibrations are given in terms of a/W. I have already read off Y for $a/W = 0.25$ as about 1.5 in tension and about 1.1 in bending.

The crack length is 7.5 mm (a quarter of 30 mm).

$$K_{I_{\text{tension}}} + K_{I_{\text{bending}}} = Y\sigma_{\text{tension}}\sqrt{\pi a} + Y\sigma_{\text{bending}}\sqrt{\pi a}$$

$$K_{I_{\text{combined}}} = 1.5 \times 100 \text{ MPa} \times \sqrt{\pi\left(0.0075 \text{ m}\right)} + 1.1 \times 100 \text{ MPa} \times \sqrt{\pi\left(0.0075 \text{ m}\right)}$$

$$K_{I_{\text{combined}}} = 40 \text{ MPa } \sqrt{\text{m}}$$

EXERCISE 1.7

In a material of lower toughness, brittle failure would be expected to take place in the presence of a shorter crack.

Putting these numbers in gives a critical crack length of approximately 3.8 mm (Figure 1.35).

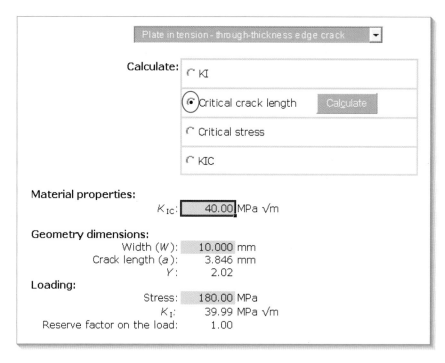

Figure 1.35   Plate in tension with a through-thickness edge crack – the critical crack length is ~3.8 mm

EXERCISE 1.8

The K calculator gives a K_I value of about 50 MPa $\sqrt{m}$, which gives a comfortable reserve factor on load of about 2.8 (Figure 1.36).

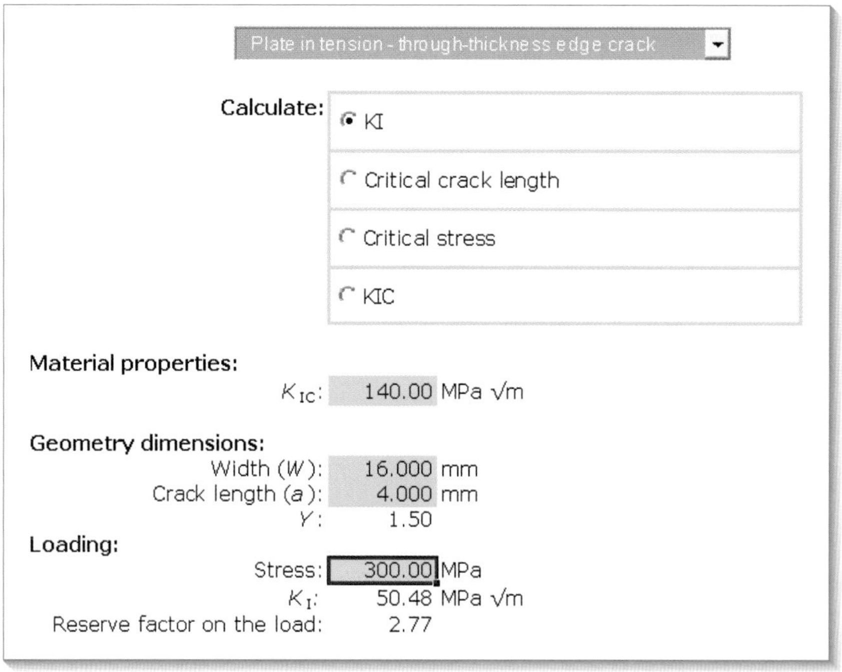

Figure 1.36   Plate in tension with a through-thickness edge crack – the reserve factor is about 2.8

EXERCISE 1.9

The K calculator gives a K_I value of about 76 MPa √m, which reduces the reserve factor on load to about 1.9, so failure is not predicted (Figure 1.37).

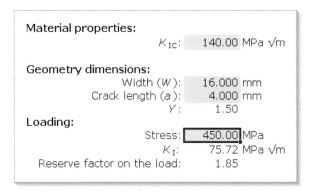

Material properties:
K_{IC}:   140.00 MPa √m

Geometry dimensions:
Width (W):   16.000 mm
Crack length (a):   4.000 mm
Y: 1.50

Loading:
Stress: 450.00 MPa
K_I: 75.72 MPa √m
Reserve factor on the load: 1.85

Figure 1.37   Plate in tension with a through-thickness edge crack – at $K_I \approx 76$ MPa √m the reserve factor is about 1.9

EXERCISE 1.10

A brittle failure analysis indicates a failure stress of over 1000 MPa, i.e. more than twice the yield stress of the material (Figure 1.38).

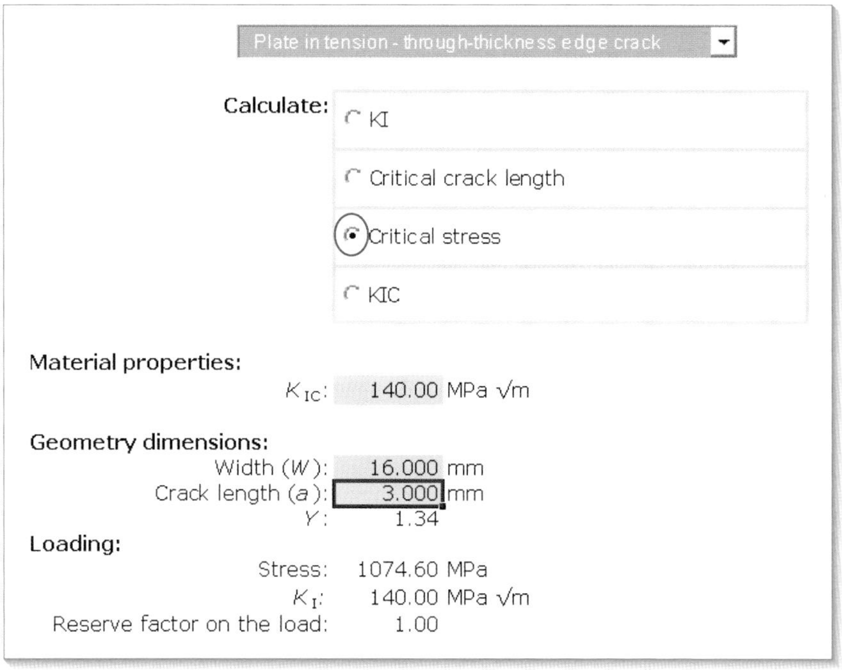

Plate in tension - through-thickness edge crack

Calculate:
○ KI
○ Critical crack length
⦿ Critical stress
○ KIC

Material properties:
K_{IC}:   140.00 MPa √m

Geometry dimensions:
Width (W):   16.000 mm
Crack length (a):   3.000 mm
Y: 1.34

Loading:
Stress: 1074.60 MPa
K_I: 140.00 MPa √m
Reserve factor on the load: 1.00

Figure 1.38   Plate in tension with a through-thickness edge crack – the critical stress is ~1075 MPa

EXERCISE 1.11

a/W is 3 mm/16 mm = 0.19. So the cross section of the cracked region is 81% of the normal wall area.

$$\sigma W = \sigma_{\text{yield}} \left(W - a \right)$$
$$\sigma \times 16 \text{ mm} = 500 \text{ MPa} \times \left(16 \text{ mm} - 3 \text{ mm} \right)$$
$$= \frac{13 \text{ mm}}{16 \text{ mm}} \left(500 \text{ MPa} \right)$$
$$\approx 400 \text{ MPa}$$

ANSWERS TO SELF-ASSESSMENT QUESTIONS

SAQ 1.1

(a) For this material:

$$2.5\left(\frac{K_Q}{\sigma_{yield}}\right)^2 = 2.5\left(\frac{32}{380}\right)^2 m = 0.018 \text{ m}$$

So a sample with a and B greater than 18 mm is needed.

(b)

Table 1.2 **Specimen sizes predicted using the standard (Equation 1.3) for the steel shown in Figure 1.13**

	K_{IC}	σ_{yield}	$2.5\left(\dfrac{K_{IC}}{\sigma_{yield}}\right)^2$
High temperature	153	483	0.25 m
Low temperature	41	765	0.007 m

SAQ 1.2

At an a/W of 0.25, Y is about 1.1.

At an a/W of 0.5, Y is about 1.5, a 36% increase.

At an a/W of 0.75, Y is about 3.3, a 200% increase.

SAQ 1.3

(a) The membrane stress is calculated using Equation (1.4):

$$\sigma = p\frac{r}{t} = 15 \text{ MPa} \frac{0.12 \text{ m}}{0.01 \text{ m}} = 180 \text{ MPa}$$

I estimated Y for a quarter-through-thickness crack under tension in Exercise 1.6 as 1.5.

So:

$$K_1 = Y\sigma\sqrt{\pi a}$$
$$= 1.5 \times 180 \text{ MPa} \times \sqrt{\pi(0.0025 \text{ m})}$$
$$= 24 \text{ MPa } \sqrt{m}$$

(b) A K_1 of 24 MPa √m is well below the range of fracture toughnesses for steels, even old steels, given earlier. So, probably, no.

SAQ 1.4

Although both design stresses and residual stresses are tensile, and so can be added, I shall still add the K values, because it is good practice and the answers come out the same anyway. You may want to prove this to yourself.

From SAQ 1.3:

$$K_{I_{design}} = Y\sigma\sqrt{\pi a}$$
$$= 1.5 \times 180 \text{ MPa} \times \sqrt{\pi(0.0025 \text{ m})}$$
$$= 24 \text{ MPa } \sqrt{m}$$

The residual stress is 400 MPa × 20%, which is 80 MPa.

So:

$$K_{I_{residual}} = Y\sigma\sqrt{\pi a}$$
$$= 1.5 \times 80 \text{ MPa} \times \sqrt{\pi(0.0025 \text{ m})}$$
$$= 11 \text{ MPa } \sqrt{m}$$

The total crack-driving K is therefore 35 MPa √m, which is starting to approach a value of fracture toughness for older steels.

SAQ 1.5

I can reuse the 300 MPa analysis in Exercise 1.8, which gave a K of about 50 MPa √m. However, I also need to calculate a K for a 150 MPa bending stress distribution and add this K to the tension value. Using the pure bending calibration produces a K of about 18 MPa √m (Figure 1.39), so the combined K will be 18 MPa + 50 MPa = 68 MPa √m. Comparing this with the lower-shelf toughness of 80 MPa √m gives a reserve factor on load of 80/68 ≈ 1.18. Some improvement, but not much!

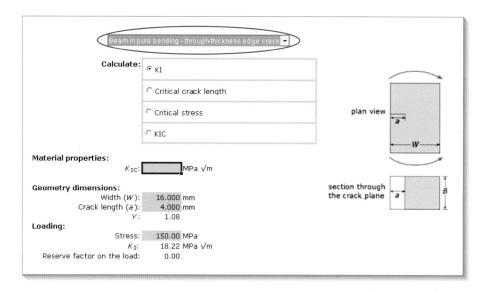

Figure 1.39   Edge-cracked beam in pure bending – $K_I \approx 18$ MPa √m due to 150 MPa

SAQ 1.6

The additional K due to 20% of yield (100 MPa) is about 17 MPa $\sqrt{m}$ (Figure 1.40) and due to 100% of yield (500 MPa) is about 84 MPa $\sqrt{m}$ (Figure 1.41).

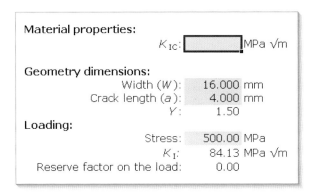

Figure 1.40   Edge-cracked plate in tension – $K_I \approx 17$ MPa $\sqrt{m}$ due to 100 MPa

Material properties:

K_{IC}: ☐ MPa $\sqrt{m}$

Geometry dimensions:
Width (W):	16.000 mm
Crack length (a):	4.000 mm
Y:	1.50

Loading:
Stress:	500.00 MPa
K_I:	84.13 MPa $\sqrt{m}$
Reserve factor on the load:	0.00

Figure 1.41   Edge-cracked plate in tension – $K_I \approx 84$ MPa $\sqrt{m}$ due to 500 MPa

The crack-driving K values are resisted by material K_{IC} values of either 80 MPa $\sqrt{m}$ or 140 MPa $\sqrt{m}$, depending on whether the material is on the lower or the upper shelf.

(a) The combined K values in normal operation are:

   (50 + 17) MPa $\sqrt{m}$ = 67 MPa $\sqrt{m}$ with 20% of yield as a residual stress.

   (50 + 84) MPa $\sqrt{m}$ = 134 MPa $\sqrt{m}$ with 100% of yield as a residual stress.

   If we can assume that the material is on the upper toughness shelf during normal operation, then the reserve factors on load are:

   140/67 ≈ 2.1 with 20% of yield as a residual stress.

   140/134 ≈ 1.0 with 100% of yield as a residual stress.

(b) Adding the thermal shock load:

$(18 + 50 + 17)$ MPa $\sqrt{m} = 85$ MPa $\sqrt{m}$ with 20% of yield as a residual stress.

$(18 + 50 + 84)$ MPa $\sqrt{m} = 152$ MPa $\sqrt{m}$ with 100% of yield as a residual stress.

We can see from this that if the material is on the lower shelf, then failure is predicted on emergency shut-down whatever the assumption about residual stress: the total K always exceeds the lower-shelf value of 80 MPa $\sqrt{m}$.

Under emergency shut-down conditions failure will always occur if there is no heat treatment. Using 100% of yield as a residual stress gives a total K of 152 MPa $\sqrt{m}$, in excess of the upper-shelf toughness.

SAQ 1.7

The options are:

- Use a steel that always has a high value of toughness above 0 °C, combined with pre- and post-weld heat treatment to limit the residual stresses present.

- Use a thicker steel section for the vessel wall. The flaw will then give a smaller value of a/W and all the K values will be smaller.

- Use better NDT to find smaller flaw sizes.

Note that increasing the strength of the steel does not help. Remember that toughness tends to go down as strength goes up; and in any case, a higher strength may just mean higher residual stresses.

SAQ 1.8

(a) The worst case is a design stress of 300 MPa in tension, a thermal shock of 150 MPa in bending and a residual stress of 500 MPa in tension.

With a 3 mm crack these produce K values of 39 MPa $\sqrt{m}$, 15 MPa $\sqrt{m}$ and 65 MPa $\sqrt{m}$ respectively: a total of 119 MPa $\sqrt{m}$. This squeezes under the upper-shelf toughness, but still exceeds the lower-shelf toughness.

(b) With weld heat treatment the loading is a design stress of 300 MPa in tension, a thermal shock of 150 MPa in bending and a residual stress of 100 MPa in tension (20% of the yield stress).

With a 3 mm crack these produce K values of 39 MPa $\sqrt{m}$, 15 MPa $\sqrt{m}$ and 13 MPa $\sqrt{m}$ respectively: a total of 67 MPa $\sqrt{m}$. This clears both the upper-shelf toughness and the lower-shelf toughness, giving reserve factors on load of $140/67 = 2.1$ and $80/67 = 1.2$ respectively.

ACKNOWLEDGEMENTS

Grateful acknowledgement is made to the following sources:

FIGURES

Figure 1.1: Courtesy of US National Transport Safety Bureau.

Figure 1.12: Photograph taken from Accident Investigation Report 9/78, Boeing 707 321C G-BEBP. Department of Trade Accidents Investigation Branch © Crown copyright. Reproduced with the permission of the Controller of HMSO and Queen's Printer for Scotland.

Figure 1.25: Provided by British Energy.

COURSE TEAM ACKNOWLEDGEMENTS

This part was prepared for the course team by Adrian Demaid.

CONTENTS

1 INTRODUCTION

1.1 Fatigue and its effects

Up to now in this course I have talked primarily about structures subjected to static loading. Designing against failure has meant that we want to avoid excessive loads that would exceed the strength of the material, or the rapid extension of a crack when the applied stress intensity reaches a critical level.

But in reality few, if any, load-bearing structures carry truly constant loads. In practice, structures may experience *cyclic loading* conditions, where the loads change with time. Under such conditions it is possible for cracks to initiate and grow, even if the stresses never exceed those caused by the design loads.

This is the phenomenon known as *fatigue*. Fatigue cracks can eventually grow long enough to cause the structure to fail. This occurs when the peak cyclic load is of sufficient magnitude to generate a stress intensity at the crack tip that exceeds the material's fracture toughness.

Failure of components and structures under cyclic loading is very common. A frequently quoted figure is that fatigue accounts for at least 90% of all service failures due to mechanical causes, although that's impossible to quantify with any real accuracy, of course. Certainly fatigue failures can be extremely costly, as can the inspection and component replacement schedules needed to ensure that they do not occur.

Cyclic or oscillating loads will not always lead to failure by fatigue. If the load variation is very small, then fatigue is less likely. When the consequences of failure would be severe, either in financial cost or human suffering, engineers take care to design components or structures to resist fatigue. This is achieved either by ensuring the loads and the load variations are low enough never to initiate fatigue cracks, or by removing the cracked part from service before the crack is long enough to cause failure. We shall study methods for designing against fatigue later in this part.

When failures do occur, the lessons learned are usually incorporated into future design processes. However, fatigue failure is not disastrous for many components and devices, and so fatigue in such components is relatively commonplace. Within our daily lives there is a host of examples of components that are subjected to cyclic loading and that fail unexpectedly, despite having been operating without showing any visible sign of anything untoward: kettle switches, door locks and handles, food mixers, laptop hinges, corkscrews, squash rackets and the hub of a bicycle wheel – and these are just from my own recent experience. You may also have had experience of something 'just falling apart in your hand'!

☑ *Failure and cracking due to fatigue* ☑ illustrates failures that have occurred as a consequence of fatigue that are all in my direct experience. The examples shown in this input are fairly mundane, and caused only mild irritation when the failure occurred. But, as noted earlier, when the component is part of a more crucial piece of a structure or machine, then the consequences can be rather more severe.

▽ Failure and cracking due to fatigue

The following three examples of failure and cracking can be attributed to fatigue; you may be able to relate to these.

The first, shown in Figure 2.1, is the fracture of a plastic WC cistern handle, which parted company from the main body without warning. There was no evidence that a crack had been propagating during use. Notice the very smooth fatigue and fracture surfaces. Such a smooth surface is one of the characteristics of a fatigue failure. The fatigue crack itself grows with no bulk plasticity (although there is local plasticity associated with its growth, as you

will see later). The final failure can then be brittle, as you saw in Part 1 of this block.

The second example is that of a titanium hub of a bicycle wheel, shown in Figure 2.2. The problem was discovered when the tyre began rubbing on the chain stay. Subsequent investigation revealed that a crack had propagated from one of the spoke eyelets, where a combination of tensile loading from the tension in the spoke, the cyclic stress from the rotation of the wheel and the stress concentration of the eyelet had contributed to the initiation and growth of the crack.

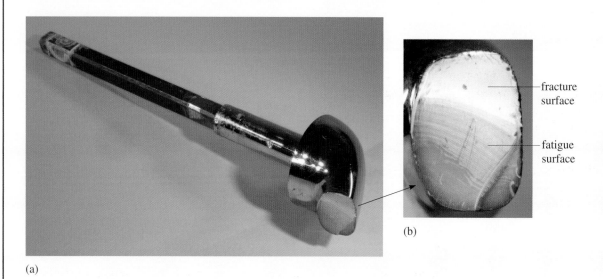

(a)

(b)

fracture surface

fatigue surface

Figure 2.1   (a) Fracture surface of a WC handle; (b) close-up of the failure surface

Figure 2.2   The hub of a bicycle wheel showing a fatigue crack growing from a spoke hole eyelet

The final example is that of the aluminium squash racket shown in Figure 2.3. Here, as you can see, cracks had grown from one of the stringing holes, where a combination of the bending stresses due to impact with the ball plus the string tension had contributed to the overall stress experienced by the racket. The hole has also acted as a stress concentrator, which has amplified the effect of the applied stress.

Figure 2.3   Cracks growing from a stringing hole in a squash racket

Many common examples of fatigue occur in moving machinery: for instance, shafts, axles, connecting rods, valves and springs. However, some very large structures also provide important examples: for instance, the fuselage of an aircraft and the hull of a submarine both experience cyclic loading conditions, as there is a difference in pressure between the inside and outside of the vehicle, which changes with its height (or depth). Even largely static structures such as bridges and buildings undergo cyclic loading in service according to the pattern of traffic flow and the force of the wind.

Despite the best efforts of fatigue design engineers, failure by fatigue leading to loss of life does occur occasionally: see ☑ **Some tragic consequences of fatigue** ☑.

☑ Some tragic consequences of fatigue

The De Havilland Comet disasters

The start of passenger services in jet aircraft in the late 1940s was marked by a series of inexplicable disasters. The Comet, developed by De Havilland after the Second World War, was the first commercial jetliner to initiate the service. It comprised an all-aluminium fuselage made from thin sheet riveted together, and powered by four jet engines. The fuselage was pressurized and streamlined so that it could fly at great height (over 30 000 feet), reducing air resistance and giving improved fuel economy (Figure 2.4).

Problems began as soon as it was introduced into commercial operation: two non-fatal crashes occurred due to poor aerodynamics, but this was

corrected. More serious was the total loss of G-ALYV (code-named Yoke Victor), with its 43 passengers and crew, near Calcutta in a severe thunderstorm on 2 May 1953. The inquiry found that the aircraft had broken up in the storm due to a faulty tailplane, and debris was found scattered over a very wide area. However, later accidents were to suggest that the entire structure was deeply flawed.

Early the following year, on 10 January 1954, Comet G-ALYP (Yoke Peter) took off from Rome and disappeared whil e climbing to 25 000 feet near Etna. There were 35 victims. Three explosions were reported by witnesses on the ground. All the debris was assumed lost in the sea. The inquiry concluded that a bomb or engine failure had caused the disaster. Flights were resumed in March

Figure 2.4 One of the first Comets

after several modifications. But then disaster struck again, less than a month later (8 April 1954) under remarkably similar circumstances. G-ALYY (Yoke Yoke) took off safely from Rome, but radio contact was lost shortly after, when the plane should have been near Stromboli. There were 21 victims. Some debris was found in the sea, but heavier debris was lost in deep water.

The state of the bodies recovered supported explosive decompression as the cause of death in both Yoke Peter and Yoke Yoke.

Meanwhile detailed tests were under way. The fuselage of another Comet (G-ALYU, Yoke Uncle) was pressurized hydraulically in a water tank to simulate the effects of pressure on the structure. The fuselage failed catastrophically and unexpectedly after a low number of pressurization cycles, after cracks grew from the corners of the windows (Figure 2.5).

Furthermore, debris from G-ALYP (Yoke Peter) had by now been lifted from the sea and could be pieced together (Figure 2.6). Detailed analysis suggested that a critical crack had initiated from a corner in a radio-aerial window on the top of the fuselage and grown longitudinally during the explosive decompression.

There were several stress concentrators acting to increase the local stress when the fuselage was under pressure. At the window corner there would be an inevitable increase in stress due to the sharp corner itself. Then there were rivet holes, and there were also small cracks produced during manufacture of the 0.6 mm thick sheet aluminium alloy. The cracks had been found and small holes drilled at their ends to stop further growth. However, small fatigue zones were found on the critical crack that pointed to an origin on a countersunk rivet hole some distance from the corner itself (Figure 2.7).

The tests on Yoke Uncle, which had already been in service, showed that the cabin had failed at a total of 3060 pressurization cycles. This was reckoned at the time to be an overestimate, equivalent to about 2500 for a cabin in service. Yoke Peter had blown apart at 1290 cycles and Yoke Yoke at only 900 cycles.

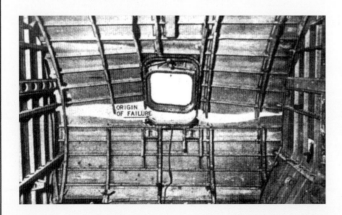

Figure 2.5 Cracks from window corners in test

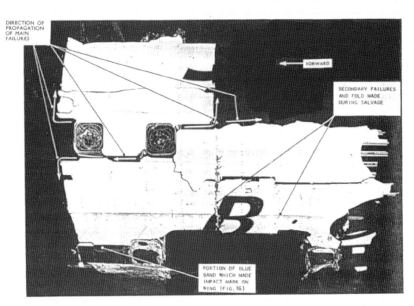

Figure 2.6
Reconstruction of debris
in critical zone of
G-ALYP

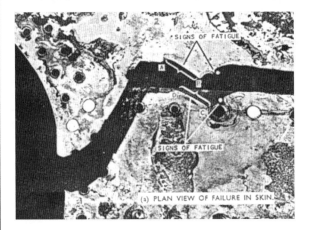

Figure 2.7   Critical crack at edge of aerial window

Tests done before the accidents had indicated failure at a wildly optimistic 18 000 cycles, and it is interesting that these tests also resulted in fatigue failure at a window corner. Reasons for the discrepancies included that the tests had been conducted at a constant temperature, whereas real in-service cycles involved large temperature changes during ascent, and that there were variations in manufacturing quality between different aircraft.

Also, the initial tests were performed on a fuselage that had been given an overpressure proof test, i.e. at higher pressures than met in service, at up to twice the normal cabin pressure of about 60 kPa. This would affect the stress distribution around the stress-concentrating effect of the window corners, by local plastic deformation, and so subsequent fatigue tests would be invalid.

Testing should be as close as possible to real circumstances, and should make allowance for any unknowns. In other words, a larger safety factor should have been used to allow for uncertainties.

The fatigue theory was the most probable cause of failure, although one other, rejected, hypothesis suggested that a phenolic resin glue (Redux®) used for bonding some of the structural elements may have failed prematurely.

The entire Comet fleet was grounded until structural and design changes were made to the fuselage to reduce the severity of the stress raisers, to improve its integrity. The wings and engines had also suffered fatigue cracking and the designs were modified accordingly. The new aircraft re-entered service in 1958, by which time the Boeing 707 and Douglas DC-8 had already been introduced. Both could carry double the number of passengers of the Comet. The British aircraft industry never recovered the ground lost to Boeing and Douglas owing to the design flaws, but the Comet survives today as the Nimrod military surveillance aircraft.

The *Alexander L. Kielland*

The *Alexander L. Kielland* (Figure 2.8a) was a Norwegian oil platform in the Ekofisk field. The platform, located 320 km east from Dundee, was owned by the US company Phillips Petroleum. It was built between 1973 and 1976 in France to an established design. The platform was in fact never used for drilling, but served as living quarters for the crew of the *Edda* platform, located nearby. On 27 March 1980, while most of the crew were in the platform's cinema, a support bracing failed in bad weather (Figure 2.8b). There was then a series of failures of other support braces, and one of the support columns that provided buoyancy to the platform broke off. The platform capsized twenty minutes later. Of the 212 people aboard, 123 were killed. At the time of writing this is the worst disaster in Norwegian offshore history.

(a)

Figure 2.8   (a) *Alexander L. Kielland* oil platform; (b) the failed bracing with detail; (c) fatigue markings on the failed brace

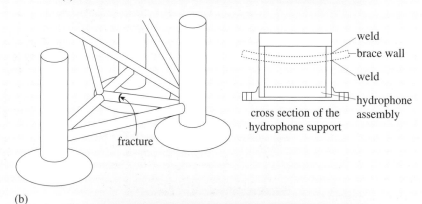

(b)

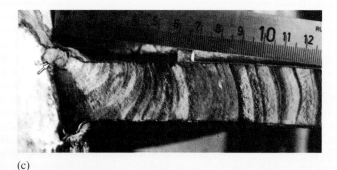

(c)

The investigative report concluded that the platform collapsed owing to a fatigue crack in one of six bracing struts that connected a support column to the rest of the platform. The fatal fatigue crack had initiated from a weld that attached a hydrophone (an underwater microphone) to the structure. The weld was of poor quality and acted as an initiation site for a fatigue crack that grew around the wall of the bracing until final failure occurred by brittle fracture. The report also identified shortcomings in the overall design with respect to its stability and buoyancy, and there was criticism of the emergency-management procedures that were in place.

The process of fatigue can leave characteristic 'beach marks' on a fracture surface, as a result of the gradual propagation of the crack over many cycles of load and the oxidation of the crack faces during this period. The beach marks in this case can be seen on the surface of the failed part in Figure 2.8(c). Marks like this on a failure surface are one of the hallmarks of a fatigue failure. They show the area of the crack that was caused by fatigue, as distinct from the final brittle fracture.

The Eschede train disaster

The Eschede train accident has been described as the world's worst high-speed train disaster. It happened on 3 June 1998, near the village of Eschede in Lower Saxony: 101 people were killed and about 100 were severely injured. An InterCityExpress (ICE) train is shown in Figure 2.9(a).

The ICE trains were originally fitted with one-piece cast 'monoblock' wheels, but this design suffered from severe vibration at high speed. The problem was solved by fitting a steel tyre to the central wheel disc and incorporating a rubber damping ring between the wheel and the tyre (Figure 2.9b). This new design successfully reduced vibration and noise, but it was not tested comprehensively at operating speeds and loads before being put into service. Other users of this design had, in fact, identified as early as 1992 that it seemed to lead to a reduced fatigue life of the wheel.

The fatigue crack in this case initiated at the *inside* rim of the steel tyre. The inspection of wheels

(a)

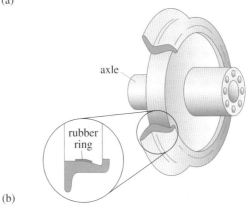

(b)

(c)

Figure 2.9   The German InterCityExpress (or ICE) high-speed train; (b) the wheel design that failed; (c) the failed wheel

traditionally looks at the outer rim, but the revised design, with the rubber spacer, allowed tensile bending stresses to develop on the inner surface of the tyre. This became worse as the tyres were reprofiled during maintenance, which progressively reduces the thickness. With a wheel experiencing typically 500 000 revolutions per day, the possibility for the cyclic loading to cause fatigue cracking is obvious (Figure 2.9c). The tyre that failed had initially been 64 mm thick, but wear and reprofiling had reduced it to 35 mm.

SAQ 2.1 (Learning outcome 2.1)

What were the critical flaws that led to the failures by fatigue in the examples of:

(a) the Comet airliner

(b) the *Alexander L. Kielland* platform

(c) the Eschede train crash?

1.2 The history of fatigue

The first work on fatigue of metals is usually attributed to Wilhelm Albert (1787–1846), who worked in the German mining industry. He noticed the failure of mine chains when they were subjected to repeated loads that were relatively small, and devised a machine to test chains under these conditions (Figure 2.10).

Over the next two decades the concept of metals becoming 'tired' or 'fatigued' was proposed by engineers such as Jean-Victor Poncelet (1788–1867). The first systematic experimental study of fatigue is often attributed to Sir William Fairbairn, 1789–1874 (Figure 2.11), a Scottish engineer who correctly identified that a beam would fail if a load well below its failure load was applied and removed many times. He also discovered the important factor that increasing the magnitude of the load being applied and removed reduced the number of load cycles to failure:

> It is evident that wrought-iron girders, when loaded to the extent of a tensile strain of seven tons per square inch, are not safe, if the strain is subjected to alternate changes of taking off the load and laying it on again …; and what is important to notice is, that from 300,000 to 400,000 changes of this description are sufficient to ensure fracture. It must, however, be borne in mind that the beam from which these conclusions are derived had sustained upwards of 3,000,000 changes with nearly five tons tensile strain on the square inch, and it must be admitted from the experiments thus recorded that five tons per square inch of tensile strain on the bottom of girders, as fixed by the Board of Trade, appears to be an ample standard of strength.

Fairbairn (1864)

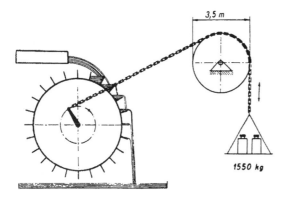

Figure 2.10   Albert's testing machine

Figure 2.11   Sir William Fairbairn (1789–1874)

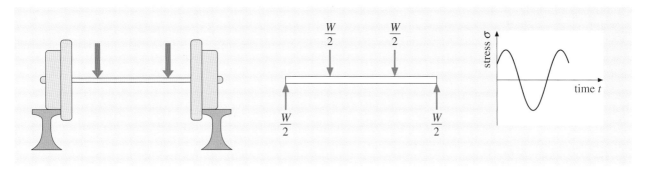

Figure 2.12   Schematic of an axle showing the applied loading

Closely following Fairbairn's research was the work of August Wöhler (1819–1914), an engineer in the German railway system. Wöhler was concerned by the failure of axles after various times in service, where the failures were occurring at much lower loads than expected.

An axle is essentially a cylindrical beam loaded in four-point bending (Figure 2.12). The top surface is in compression and the bottom surface is in tension. Rotation of the axle by a half turn leads to the top becoming the bottom and vice versa. Hence, the stresses on a particular surface region of axle vary sinusoidally between tension and compression. This is known as 'fully reversed' fatigue loading.

1.3 Mechanisms of fatigue

The use of the term 'fatigue' is a shade unfortunate, because it conjures up an image of the material actually becoming 'tired' in service; this simple analogy is a misconception. Another historical misconception was that 'fatigue is a brittle failure', because fatigue failures generally exhibit the sort of flat fracture surface typical of a brittle fracture. You can see this for yourself on the failed keyed shaft shown in Figure 2.13. A fatigue crack has grown from one edge of the key slot and penetrated about two-thirds of the way through before final ductile failure. The area of the shaft where the fatigue crack grew slowly is very flat, like a brittle fracture. The crack was in fact growing in very small plastic steps, but the deformation does not show up on the macroscopic scale.

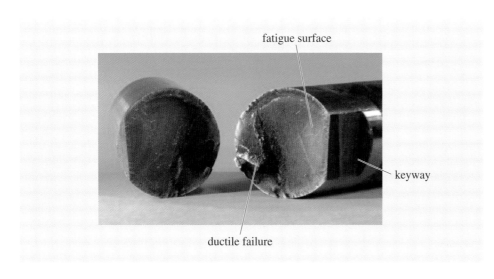

Figure 2.13   Fracture surface of a keyed shaft; the smooth area is the fatigue surface originating from the keyway; the final ductile failure is characterized by the heavily distorted region

For convenience,
I will focus this section
on the fatigue of
polycrystalline metals.
Similar effects are seen
in other materials, but
the mechanisms may be
different; I will touch on
this later in the block.

We will examine the actual microstructural mechanisms that lead to fatigue failure in a range of materials in Part 3 of this block. For now, it is useful if we briefly define the differences between crack *initiation* and crack *growth*.

Crack initiation (also sometimes referred to as nucleation) is the formation of an initial crack. Fatigue failure does not require there to be a macroscopic defect or crack in the material in the first place. In some cases, a sharp crack may already exist in the material when it is first loaded, and then, of course, there is no crack initiation period. More often a fatigue crack will initiate at some flaw or point of stress concentration. If there are no preferential initiation sites, then cracks may form on crystallographic slip bands within the grains of the metal; as they are driven by shear stresses, these are typically at 45° to the principal stress axes. Metallurgists like to call this *Stage I* fatigue cracking, although, as it is rarely seen in engineering practice, this is not a particularly useful definition. Following initiation, the crack will grow (or *propagate*) across the body, usually perpendicular to the maximum principal stress. This stage is referred to as *Stage II* growth. Figure 2.14 illustrates this view of crack initiation and growth, the two stages involved in crack growth.

Cracks growing perpendicular to the maximum principal stress are being opened in mode I loading by that stress (recall this from Part 1: this is the same loading that is used to test K_{IC}).

The *crack initiation life* is the number of cycles it takes to produce a sharp crack. In practice, defining how long that takes depends on how carefully you look for the crack. In an electron microscope we can detect cracks only a few micrometres long, whereas on an undersea oil platform we will do well to detect a crack that is 5 mm long. (One inspection diver found a crack large enough to insert his hand into, and could feel the crack gripping and releasing his hand as the load on the structure cycled, opening and closing the crack mouth.) So, understandably, engineers use a definition of crack initiation that is dependent on the context of the fatigue problem. We shall see later, however, that the concept of crack initiation and growth is essential to fatigue design methods. One of the common descriptions of the assessment of the fatigue life of a component is that it can be assessed by summing the two contributions: the lifetime required to initiate a crack and the lifetime required to grow that crack to failure; thus:

$$N_{total} = N_{initiation} + N_{propagation}$$

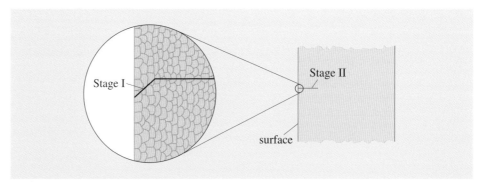

Figure 2.14   An illustration of the two stages involved in crack growth

I have already mentioned, in Part 1, that fatigue is exploited to produce a sharp crack 'to order' in specimens used for measuring the fracture toughness K_{IC}. In these specimens, controlled crack growth occurs under a cyclic stress, where the stress intensity K is kept well below the K_{IC}. Fatigue occurs at values of K that are significantly less than K_{IC} and so fatigue is often referred to as *sub-critical crack growth*.

EXERCISE 2.1

Is this concept of crack growth that occurs slowly cycle by cycle over time, at stress intensity values below K_{IC}, consistent with the ideas on the stability of cracks presented in Part 1 of this block?

So, fatigue is a 'cumulative' form of failure brought about as a result of repeated cyclic loading. Quite often a single crack is the source of a failure, but, depending on the loading, many cracks may form in a component. Figure 2.15 shows a splined shaft where each spline is a stress concentrator and cracks have grown from multiple sites. This occurred because the in-service torque was increased on the component without changing its design, either by making the shaft bigger or using a more fatigue-resistant material.

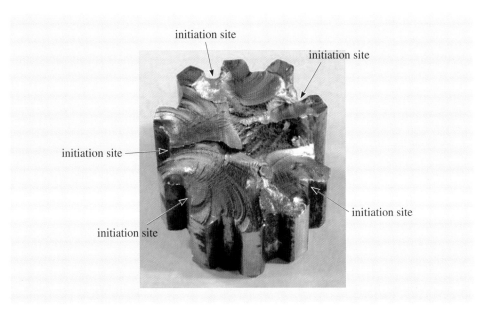

Figure 2.15   Cracks grown from multiple initiation sites led to fracture of this splined shaft

2 FATIGUE BEHAVIOUR OF MATERIALS

One of the aims of this part is to introduce you to the basic characteristics of fatigue and to equip you with an understanding of the design methods needed to avoid failure by fatigue in practice.

Designing against fatigue needs not only a theoretical understanding of the fatigue process, but also data on the fatigue strength of the material under actual operating conditions. This raises a fundamental question. In many cases of fatigue it can be several years before sufficient stress cycles are accumulated to cause fatigue failure. So, do laboratory tests also need to span such a long time scale? For metals the answer is usually 'no'. The fatigue properties of metals can be determined by applying cyclic loads at much higher frequencies than would be experienced in service, without affecting the validity of the results obtained. Although the testing *time* clearly depends on the frequency of loading that is used to test the specimen, it is the number of load *cycles* that is important. Therefore, it is common to test at as high a frequency as is possible, which presents no difficulties for metals (provided time-dependent processes like corrosion or creep do not occur). However, for polymeric materials this may cause accelerated failure due to internal heating – you may have noticed how car tyres become warm in use under the cyclic loading caused by contact with the road. In carrying out accelerated laboratory tests, we must try to match the testing stresses to the service stresses.

Thus, to predict with reasonable accuracy the response and life span of a component subject to cyclic loading before putting it into service, two approaches are used:

1　Simulation of actual operating service conditions on a real or model structure.

2　Tests on standard material specimens that can then be related to service conditions.

During the last 40 years, simulation of in-service behaviour has come into prominence and in many cases now, particularly when human life is at stake, such tests are mandatory before the component or structure is allowed to go into service. Simulation tests are particularly important for civil aircraft and involve the testing to failure of components (e.g. wing panels), sub-assemblies (e.g. a wing or the fuselage, as illustrated in Figure 2.16) or even the complete aircraft.

Testing in this way provides a clear indication of the fatigue life that can be expected of the structure. It can also highlight areas where fatigue cracking is likely to occur, so that inspection regimes can be devised. It can also reveal unforeseen problems where the load paths in a structure lead to fatigue failure earlier than had been anticipated.

However, in many structures and pieces of machinery the actual cyclic loading experienced is complex and, therefore, difficult to simulate. In addition, the in-service load cycling may not be exactly what the designer had anticipated. For example, it may be that additional unexpected stresses are incorporated during assembly. In spite of these difficulties, however, simulation testing can be very informative, albeit very expensive. When simulation testing cannot be carried out, or information has to be obtained for the design of a prototype, we have to depend on fatigue data derived from laboratory tests on standard specimens.

Figure 2.16 Fatigue testing on an aircraft fuselage

2.1 The '*S–N*' curve: stress–life testing

The cyclic stresses that lead to fatigue can arise either from a cyclic applied *load* or from a cyclic *strain* (or deflection). Although it might seem that a deflection has to be associated with a load, recall that thermal effects can cause strains as well.

Historically, fatigue studies have tended to be concerned with conditions of service in which failure occurred at more than 10^4 cycles of stress, so-called *high-cycle fatigue*. However, there is a wide range of engineering applications where components are subjected to large changes in stress and can experience low numbers of cycles to failure, i.e. *low-cycle fatigue*. The Comet disasters are an example of a low-cycle fatigue failure.

Figure 2.17 shows some of the possible forms of applied stress that can be produced by cyclic loading. I will use Figure 2.17 to introduce some of the essential terminology of fatigue.

Let's start with Figure 2.17(a). The stress pattern illustrated here is called an alternating stress, because the stress continuously cycles between tension and compression; this is the sort of stress experienced in a vehicle axle, as I mentioned earlier. The stress range $\Delta\sigma$ is the difference between the maximum stress σ_{max} and the minimum stress σ_{min} in a load cycle, that is:

$$\Delta\sigma = \sigma_{max} - \sigma_{min} \qquad (2.1)$$

We also need to define the mean stress σ_m. This is given by:

$$\sigma_m = \frac{\sigma_{max} + \sigma_{min}}{2} \qquad (2.2)$$

The mean stress is important: changing the mean stress will give a different fatigue life for a particular stress range. For the alternating stress pattern in Figure 2.17(a), the mean stress σ_m during a loading cycle is clearly zero. In Figure 2.17(b), the stress is always tensile and, hence, σ_m will be a net tensile stress; for this reason the stress pattern is called *fluctuating tension*.

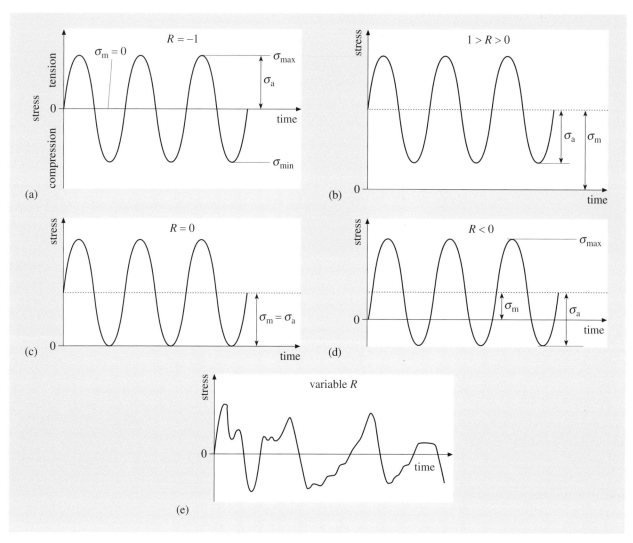

Figure 2.17   Possible forms of fatigue stress arising from cyclic loading: (a) alternating stress; (b) fluctuating tension; (c) pulsating tension; (d) fluctuating mixed; (e) random

It is customary to regard a cyclic stress as having a stress amplitude σ_a. The stress amplitude is simply half the stress range:

$$\sigma_a = \frac{\Delta\sigma}{2} \tag{2.3}$$

A uniform cyclic stress can therefore be described in terms of the stress amplitude, and the mean stress. We can also define a stress ratio R where:

$$R = \frac{\sigma_{min}}{\sigma_{max}} \tag{2.4}$$

Figure 2.17(c) shows the case where $\sigma_m = \sigma_a$, in which the minimum stress is zero.

In Figure 2.17(d), σ_{min} is compressive and σ_{max} is tensile, with σ_m also being tensile.

The purely sinusoidal stress cycles shown in Figures 2.17(a)–(d) are usually seen only in laboratory tests; the stress cycles experienced by components in service are almost invariably far more complex. Figure 2.17(e) is typical of the stress pattern found in most real situations, where the stress is random in both amplitude and frequency. An example of such a pattern might be the loading on a car's suspension as it travels over different road surfaces at different speeds.

EXERCISE 2.2

Determine the stress ratio R for the case when:

(a) the maximum stress is $+\sigma_a$ and the minimum stress is $-\sigma_a$

(b) the maximum stress is 200 MPa and the minimum stress is 40 MPa

(c) the maximum stress is 300 MPa and the minimum stress is 0 MPa

(d) the maximum stress is 200 MPa and the minimum stress is −20 MPa.

The simplest laboratory fatigue tests are those used to obtain a so-called 'S–N fatigue curve' for a specific material, or a part, such as an aircraft skin-stringer assembly (Figure 2.18). These tests determine the number of loading cycles (the N of the section heading) that the sample survives before fracture occurs. By changing the load amplitude, the fatigue life over a range of stress amplitudes (the S of the section heading) can be determined. Typical applied-stress cycles during such a test might be as shown in Figures 2.17(a)–(c).

To generate an S–N curve, a series of samples is tested to failure at a range of stress amplitudes. Typically, the aim of the test is to generate fatigue lives between about 10^3 and 10^7 cycles, and the applied stress ranges will be chosen accordingly. It is rare for engineering components to experience more than 10^7 stress cycles during an operating lifetime, although there are exceptions. A sample that has not failed after 10^7 cycles would be called a 'run-out' and the test halted. Given that 20 Hz (i.e. 20 loading cycles per second) is a typical test frequency, a test that lasts 10^7 cycles

Figure 2.18   Fatigue testing an aircraft skin-stringer panel mock-up

will take nearly 6 days to run. Going to 10^8 cycles would, therefore, take 2 months, which will become very costly.

EXERCISE 2.3

A typical crankshaft in a car engine should survive at least 2×10^9 revolutions before failing (equivalent to about 500 000 miles, or about 805 000 km). On this basis, how long will it take a fatigue machine to break a specimen of the crankshaft material:

(a) at 1 Hz

(b) at 100 Hz?

A typical set of results from a series of S–N fatigue tests is shown in Figure 2.19. There is a very wide range of cycles to failure, so if the number of cycles to failure were plotted on a linear scale, then the data would be too closely packed to analyse effectively; therefore, a logarithmic scale is used, as shown. In this case, several samples were tested at various stress amplitudes at a stress ratio R of 0.1, i.e. the maximum stress was 10 times the minimum stress and the applied stress was always tensile. Note that testing more than once at a particular stress amplitude does not always give the same result: there is scatter in the data obtained, which simply reflects variability in the material and, probably, the surface finish of the samples. There is always an element of statistical variability in fatigue life, as no two cracks will initiate in exactly the same way or at the same rate.

Figure 2.19 shows two material conditions: peened and unpeened. As expected, the material given a shot-peening treatment to improve its fatigue life (see Block 1 Part 7) shows a greater number of cycles to failure at a given stress amplitude.

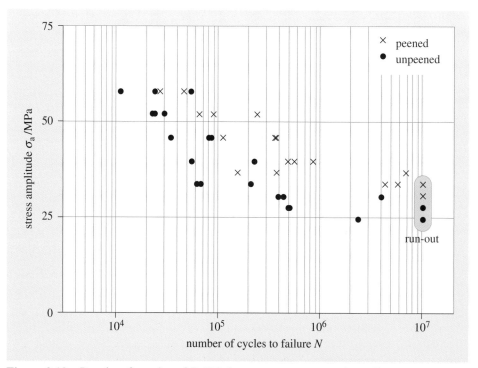

Figure 2.19   Results of a series of S–N fatigue tests on a magnesium alloy

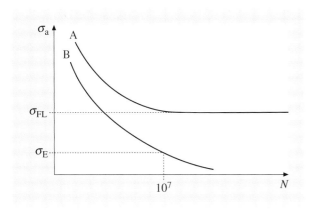

Figure 2.20 Idealized forms of the $S–N$ curve

$S–N$ curves tend to have two basic forms, as shown in Figure 2.20. If the $S–N$ curve runs parallel to the N-axis at high values of N, as does curve A in Figure 2.20, then we can identify a limiting stress amplitude below which failure by fatigue does not occur, irrespective of how many stress cycles the material undergoes. This limit is called the *fatigue limit*, labelled σ_{FL}. This sort of behaviour is typical of ferritic steels (and also a few titanium alloys). As a very rough practical guide, for smooth specimens (i.e. unnotched, with no pre-existing stress concentrators), *the fatigue limit is about 40–50% of the tensile strength of such a material.*

In contrast, most non-ferrous alloys and polymeric materials exhibit an $S–N$ curve that continues to fall gradually as the stress amplitude is lowered; curve B in Figure 2.20 is a typical example. Since the $S–N$ curve is at no point parallel to the N-axis, these materials do not have a fatigue limit and a crack will eventually propagate to failure whatever the stress amplitude. However, in those cases, for convenience we can define an *endurance limit* σ_E as the stress amplitude at which fatigue failure will not occur after a specified number of stress cycles (e.g. $N = 10^7$ cycles) as shown in Figure 2.20.

As I mentioned previously, it is common practice to define two regimes of $S–N$ behaviour arbitrarily:

- The first regime is known as low-cycle fatigue; in this regime failure occurs in less than about 10^4 cycles, where the stress amplitudes are large.

- The second regime is referred to as high-cycle fatigue; here, the number of cycles N exceeds 10^4 cycles and the stress amplitudes are relatively small.

Failures from high-cycle fatigue tend to be more common in practice: 10^5 cycles can be applied in just over a day with a stress cycle of 1 s, or in only a couple of minutes for the crankshaft of a car engine! On the other hand, the stresses arising from the start/stop cycle of a nuclear reactor might occur once every six months, so a lifetime of 1000 cycles might well be acceptable; this is certainly a low-cycle fatigue problem.

I must emphasize that an $S–N$ curve is specific to a particular value of the mean stress level σ_m or the stress ratio R, and one of these should be stated on the curve. Some common tests use an alternating stress where the mean stress $\sigma_m = 0$. In general, the fatigue life will be reduced (and the curve, therefore, will be shifted downwards) by an increase in the value of σ_m, as the value of σ_{max} will increase; thus, failure will occur sooner, as K_{IC} is reached at a shorter final crack length. The fatigue limit can also disappear if the stress cycles are not of constant amplitude, e.g. if an occasional overload occurs that can initiate damage that leads to the development of a crack.

Tests at a constant, non-zero R value will have changing mean stress for different stress amplitudes, but this is realistic for many loading situations. So for $R = 0.1$, for example, a stress range of 100 MPa will be from 11 to 111 MPa with a mean stress of 61 MPa, whereas a stress range of 200 MPa will be from 22 to 222 MPa with a mean stress of 122 MPa.

EXERCISE 2.4

(a) What is the fatigue limit for the steel shown in Figure 2.21?

(b) What is the endurance limit for $N = 10^8$ cycles for the aluminium shown in Figure 2.21?

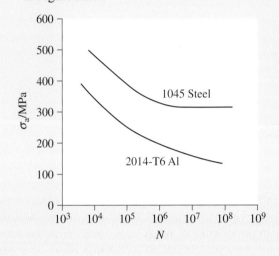

Figure 2.21   S-N curves for steel and aluminium

2.1.1 Test-pieces and test methods

Standard stress-cycle fatigue tests carried out in the laboratory use a range of techniques for applying the cyclic loading, such as:

axial ('push–pull')

rotating bend

cantilever bend

torsion.

Controlling the *stress* in the specimen by varying the applied load is more common than controlling the *strain*. This is partly because the measurement of strain is more difficult – requiring a transducer, such as a strain gauge, to be attached to the sample – and also because knowledge of the stress dependence of the fatigue life is needed in many (but not all) applications.

Unnotched test specimens, such as those in Figure 2.22, are often used; these have generous radii of curvature at changes of section, as well as polished surfaces, to ensure that the crack nucleation stage is not influenced by defects and stress concentrations.

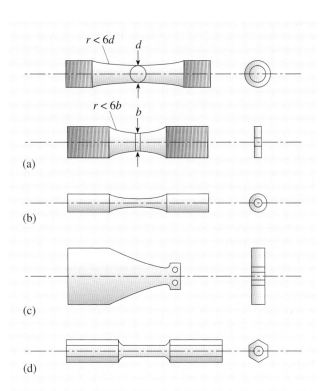

Figure 2.22 Typical fatigue test-pieces: (a) axial loading; (b) rotating bend; (c) cantilever bend; (d) torsion

The rotating cantilever beam (Figure 2.22b) was the basis of one of the first laboratory tests and it is still used to this day. It was devised in 1860 by Wöhler (whom you met earlier) to test samples of railway axles. As shown in Figure 2.23(a), the specimen is rotated by a motor. Weights hung from the bearings apply a constant bending moment to a given section of the specimen. As the specimen rotates at constant speed, the point P (see Figure 2.23b) experiences a bending stress that varies sinusoidally with the angle of rotation θ (and hence with time). In this way Wöhler was able to investigate the effect of the shoulder radius on the fatigue life. His machine closely simulates the regular sinusoidal loading pattern on rotating railway axles (as shown in Figure 2.12). Modern versions of this machine are still used to generate S–N data and are particularly convenient because the specimens are easily manufactured and gripped, while the high rotational speeds used enable 10^6 or 10^7 cycles to be achieved in a relatively short time.

A more sophisticated and versatile type of test machine is the servo-hydraulic testing machine, used in mechanical testing laboratories worldwide. These machines can be used for a range of materials testing, and they are able to apply cyclic loads at high frequencies. Figure 2.24 shows a picture of a fatigue sample on such a machine. In this case the machine is used to apply a tensile load, but the machine can apply compressive loads as well. The lower actuator moves up or down; so, changing the loading jig allows different sample configurations to be tested.

The stress cycles imposed by a fatigue testing machine are usually of constant amplitude and sinusoidal, but it is possible to apply load spectra that vary in both amplitude and frequency during the test. However, bear in mind that laboratory fatigue tests are only idealized representations of what can happen in practice.

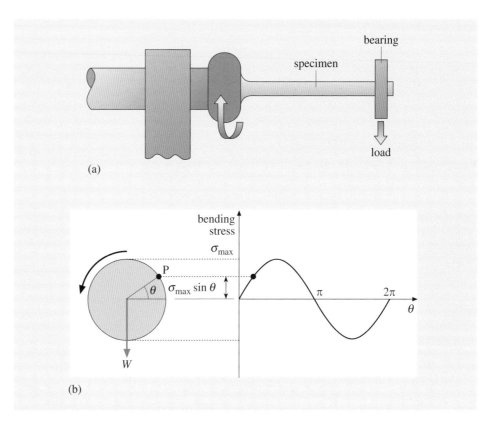

(a)

(b)

Figure 2.23   (a) A rotating cantilever beam test; (b) the change in bending stress at a point on the specimen during rotation

Figure 2.24   A fatigue test specimen in a servo-hydraulic fatigue testing machine

2.1.2 Specimen-size effects

Specimen-size effects are very important in fatigue. Experimental data generated from laboratory tests on small specimens can differ from those observed in the actual components or from the simulated testing of complete structures. It is now well established that larger specimens show lower fatigue or endurance limits; thus, small laboratory specimens can give artificially high values of 'safe' working stress levels that would in practice cause a 'life-size' component to break.

Figure 2.25 illustrates the magnitude of this size effect for unnotched specimens of alloy steel. Clearly, when using fatigue test data from a handbook, a designer must be very aware of all conditions under which the tests were carried out, and particularly of the specimen size.

The size effect has its origin in any or all of the following three factors:

1   A statistical size effect: the larger the specimen is, the greater the probability of a flaw existing in a highly stressed region of the specimen.

2   A microstructural size effect: the microstructure often varies with the size of the component and the position within it. The distribution of features that affect crack nucleation, such as inclusions, may vary with the size of the component.

3   A notch-size effect: the dimensions of any notch in relation to the dimensions of the component section are important. This will affect the volume of material exposed to high stress.

An example of the influence of size effects is that there is often a lack of agreement between the S–N curves determined by the rotating bend test and that determined by a geometrically different test such as the axial 'push–pull' (see Figure 2.26).

EXERCISE 2.5

(a)   What will be the different stress states inside specimens subjected to reversed bending or push–pull?

(b)   Why might this influence how the samples fail?

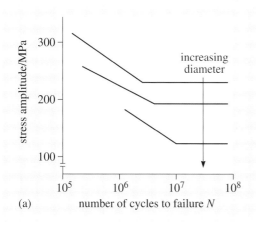

(a)

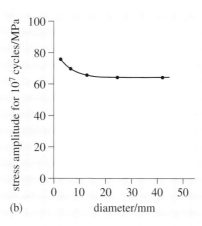

(b)

Figure 2.25   The effect of specimen size: (a) changes in the S–N curve for different sample diameters; (b) changes in the fatigue strength at 10^7 cycles of an alloy steel as the sample diameter is increased

Figure 2.26 *S–N* curve for an alloy steel tested under axial loading compared with that tested in rotating bend

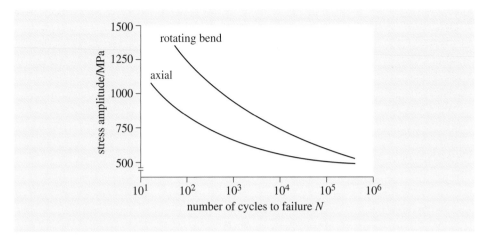

Figure 2.27 Schematic *S–N* diagram showing distribution of lives at various stress levels

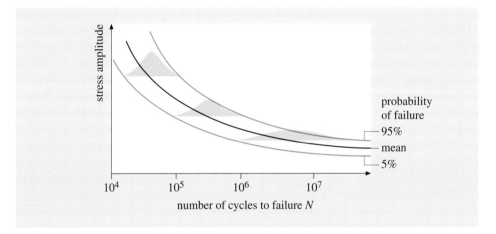

Finally, because the early stages of the fatigue process are random in nature, considerable scatter exists in experimental results. Figure 2.27 illustrates the type of distribution of lives that might be expected if many specimens were tested at each stress level: you saw the type of scatter seen in real data for the magnesium alloy samples I mentioned earlier (Figure 2.19). Some designs might acceptably use the *S–N* curve associated with, say, a 5% probability of failure; but this approach would be clearly unacceptable for a highly safety-critical component. In many cases the *S–N* data alone are not sufficient; what is needed is an understanding of how fast a crack actually grows through the material. More on this later.

2.1.3 *Effect of surface condition*

In most components fatigue cracks propagate from a surface, so the surface condition will have a profound effect on fatigue strength and life. Roughness, porosity and inclusions, such as slag or oxide particles, can all reduce the fatigue life, because they introduce sites from which a fatigue crack can initiate. Figure 2.28 shows schematically the effect of the surface condition on the fatigue limit. Polishing a sample provides the best fatigue life; a machined finish or a sharp notch reduces it. The sensitivity to surface condition increases as the static tensile strength of the material increases; this is due to an effect called ☑ **notch sensitivity** ☑.

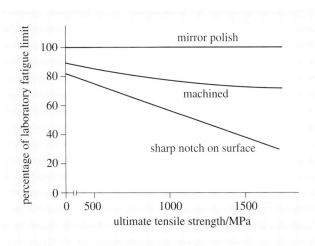

The fatigue performance of components can be enhanced by ensuring that they have smooth, preferably polished, surfaces. But for most products such a good surface finish is either not feasible or not practicable, and even if it can be achieved it is difficult to maintain. However, in some crucial applications, such as in high-performance machinery, surface polishing is used, e.g. the connecting rods in racing-car engines. And you have already seen how residual stress can be introduced into a surface to act against the stresses that would cause fatigue.

☑ Notch sensitivity

You will recall from Block 1 that a notch is a stress concentrator; so are defects such as scratches and inclusions. You may also have noticed that, when talking about fatigue testing, I have been careful to refer to the specimens as being 'unnotched'.

Figure 2.29 shows an example of how the S–N curve of a smooth component is lowered significantly by the presence of a moderate notch (where the stress concentration factor $\alpha_k = 1.76$). (Note that here I am using the α symbol for a stress concentration, not K as in Block 1; this is to avoid confusion with the use of K for stress-intensity factor.)

You might expect the stress concentration to have a relatively simple effect on the fatigue life, where the new maximum stress value could be found from the unnotched S–N curve. But the stress concentration is high at the notch and then decreases away from it; so, a crack, as it initiates and grows away from the notch, experiences a decreasing stress field. The nucleation of a fatigue crack is accelerated in the region of high stress,

and in the region away from the notch the stresses drop to the nominal applied values. The change in stress due to the presence of a stress concentration is illustrated in Figure 2.30.

We can represent the actual fall in fatigue strength by a notch-sensitivity factor q, which clearly depends on both the notch severity and the material:

$$q = \frac{\alpha_f - 1}{\alpha_k - 1} \qquad (2.5)$$

where α_f is the fatigue notch factor:

$$\alpha_f = \frac{\text{fatigue strength of unnotched specimen}}{\text{fatigue strength of notched specimen}} \qquad (2.6)$$

A high notch sensitivity q means that a notched specimen has a low fatigue strength compared with that of an unnotched sample; a low notch sensitivity means that the notch has not affected the fatigue strength to a great degree.   ▷

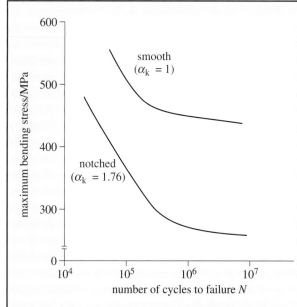

Figure 2.29 *S–N* curves for smooth and notched test-pieces

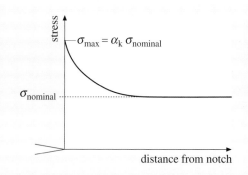

Figure 2.30 Reduction in stress with increased distance from a stress-concentrating notch

At one extreme, a notch may have a greater effect on the fatigue strength than it has on the peak stress from its stress concentrating effect (so $\alpha_f > \alpha_k$ and $q > 1$). At the other extreme, the material would not be sensitive to the presence of notches, i.e. $\alpha_f = 1$ and $q = 0$. The value of q can be anything from zero up to a value in excess of one; however, values are usually between $q = 0$ and $q = 1$.

SAQ 2.2 (Learning outcomes 2.2 and 2.3)

What are the fatigue notch factor α_f and the notch-sensitivity factor q at each value of α_k for the cases given in Table 2.1?

Table 2.1   Reverse axial fatigue limits σ_{FL} for samples of EN 8 steel with various values of α_k

α_k	σ_{FL}/MPa
1	232
1.84	137
2.26	120
3.02	108
4.6	86
7.06	91

Hint: calculate the values of α_f relative to the case of no stress concentration ($\alpha_k = 1$).

The answer to SAQ 2.2 shows how the value of q is not constant, but is dependent on the stress concentration. Interestingly, you can note that there is a bigger reduction in fatigue life for a relatively small stress concentration.

2.1.4 Environmental effects

The environment in which a component operates can have a significant effect on its fatigue properties, particularly in high-cycle (low stress amplitude) fatigue. Even air has a deleterious effect, as moisture and oxygen tend to at least cause some oxidation. Typically, moisture in the air lowers the fatigue strength of most metals and alloys by 5–15%.

Environments that are more corrosive than air attack the surface more vigorously, and this results in a significant decrease in fatigue strength. Increasing the temperature accelerates corrosion and oxidation, so this also lowers the fatigue resistance. The term corrosion fatigue is used to describe failure under the combined effects of cyclic loading and a corrosive environment.

2.1.5 Microstructural effects

The fatigue performance of metals and alloys is greatly affected by their microstructure: in particular by the grain size and by the presence of alloying elements.

However, this is not surprising: these factors affect the strength, ductility and toughness of metals, so there is no reason to assume that their fatigue strength also would not be affected. Any microstructural change that strengthens a metal by increasing its yield stress, thereby making plastic deformation more difficult, will improve the fatigue strength of the metal. However, you cannot assume that the fatigue strength is increased by the same proportion as the yield strength; in general, the proportionate increase in the fatigue strength is smaller.

It is often observed that electroplating a component, i.e. depositing a 'clean' metal layer on its surface, leads to a reduction in fatigue strength. Can we explain this phenomenon? Although electroplating provides a relatively smooth protective layer on the surface, if the new surface is soft, then it will readily undergo plastic flow. So the incidence of plastic flow and the resultant damage and crack initiation outweigh the effect of a smooth surface.

In addition, electrodeposits often contain high residual tensile stresses. In the case of hard chromium plate, the electrodeposits may become riddled with microcracks, each of which is a possible fatigue nucleation site.

EXERCISE 2.6

For a given applied stress cycle, the fatigue endurance of a material normally decreases with increasing temperature. Suggest a reason for this effect.

2.2 Strain–life testing

Laboratory tests can also be carried out where the test-piece is subjected to a constant strain amplitude. For plotting the results of a strain cycling test you can consider the stress amplitude in Figure 2.17 to be replaced by strain amplitude, and by analogy with the S–N curve there is a failure curve for strain cycling consisting of the strain amplitude plotted against cycles to failure N. The strains experienced by the test-piece may be completely elastic or a combination of elastic and plastic; and, in relation to fatigue, it is necessary to distinguish between them.

The total strain range $\Delta\varepsilon$ is made up of elastic and plastic strains $\Delta\varepsilon_e$ and $\Delta\varepsilon_p$ respectively:

$$\Delta\varepsilon = \Delta\varepsilon_e + \Delta\varepsilon_p \qquad (2.7)$$

By definition, the elastic strain range $\Delta\varepsilon_e$ is related to the stress range $\Delta\sigma$ by Hooke's law:

$$\Delta\varepsilon_e = \frac{\Delta\sigma}{E} \qquad (2.8)$$

It follows from Equations (2.7) and (2.8) that the plastic strain range is:

$$\Delta \varepsilon_p = \Delta \varepsilon - \frac{\Delta \sigma}{E}$$

The nucleation and growth of fatigue cracks occurs only when cyclic plastic strains occur, so how is it that cracks initiate at stress levels well below the nominal yield stress? The answer is simply that it is necessary only for plastic strain to occur *locally*; it does not have to occur throughout the section (as it would at the yield stress). In any real component there will always be some stress concentrations due to notches, scratches or microstructural features, and it is here that plastic strain and subsequent fatigue may occur, even though the nominal stress level is below the yield.

When a material is subjected to a constant cyclic strain, it may progressively harden or soften. If it hardens, then the constant strain amplitude is associated with an increasing stress amplitude, referred to as *cyclic hardening*.

Have a look at Figure 2.31, which shows the stress–strain response of a metal deformed cyclically in tension and compression, where there is some plastic deformation. When the metal is deformed from the starting point O to P, it is just like part of a conventional tensile test. Unloading to Q leaves a plastic strain. Loading in compression then causes compressive yielding to S, then unloading to T; the sample does not return to its undeformed state at O when the load is now removed. Loading again in tension will take the sample to R, then the curve will join up again at P, and a *hysteresis loop* is produced.

Figures 2.32(a) and (b) respectively illustrate the behaviour of material that shows cyclic softening and cyclic hardening. Initially, for cyclic softening the peak stress decreases; for cyclic hardening it increases. Eventually, after a sufficient number of cycles, perhaps 1000 or more, the stress amplitude stabilizes at a constant value and a stable or constant hysteresis loop is obtained.

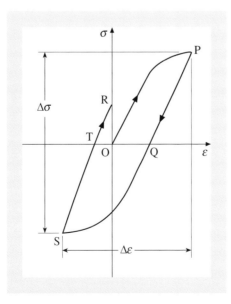

Figure 2.31   Cyclic loading of a metal

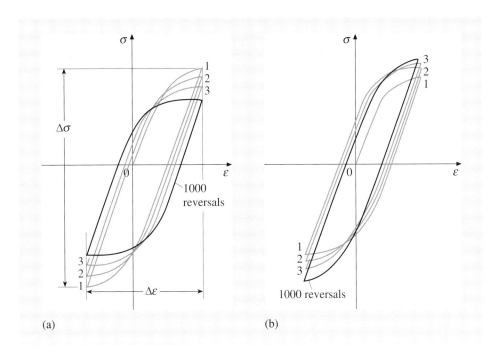

Figure 2.32   (a) Cyclic softening and (b) cyclic hardening

3 USING FATIGUE DATA IN DESIGN

We can conceptually divide the fatigue life of a component into two main stages, i.e. initiation and growth. Although there are a number of specific models that can be used to predict either or both of these phases, and a large number of commercial software packages and finite element programs that claim to make the job easier, there are actually just two fundamental types of predictive fatigue model: safe-life design and damage-tolerant design.

In the *safe-life design* approach, fatigue data are used to calculate how long a component can be used without a critical fatigue crack initiating and growing to the point of component failure. It is assumed implicitly that the majority of the fatigue life is taken up with initiation of the fatigue crack, and that there isn't an identifiable flaw in the component at the start of its life. No analysis is performed on the growth of the crack. However, as mentioned earlier, the definition of precisely when a crack has been initiated is, inevitably, arbitrary. Indeed, in the simplest approaches and tests, a crack is said to have 'initiated' when the specimen fails.

This is the traditional approach to fatigue design. It is particularly well suited to small, highly stressed bodies and it is mathematically simple to use. Thus, the initial 'first pass' design of virtually all components, machines and structures is undertaken using this method. It is also a good way of assessing the inherent fatigue properties of a given material or surface condition.

Conversely, the *damage-tolerant design* approach assumes that a crack always exists at the start of the fatigue life. That is, it assumes that a crack has already initiated and that the fatigue life of the components or structure is dominated and hence controlled by the growth of an initial crack to a size at which failure occurs. When the exact size of the initial crack population is not well known, then an arbitrary, conservative initial crack size is used. The main advantages of this method are that both the kinetics of crack growth and the size when it becomes potentially fatal can be calculated using fracture mechanics. This enables a maintenance schedule to be devised whereby any potentially fatal crack can be identified by inspection well before failure occurs. We will also study this approach later, when you will see that it produces a significant improvement on the structural integrity of safety-critical devices.

Both these fatigue–design philosophies can be incorporated into a so-called *fail-safe design*. If a structure or part of a structure sustains fatigue damage, then there will still be sufficient strength for it to do its job without failing. This can encompass many aspects of a design, including having multiple pathways for load to be transmitted and providing crack stoppers to limit damage to small sections. Fail-safe design, however, did not prevent one of the major fatigue-related accidents in civil aviation, when a transport plane crashed on approach to ☒ *Lusaka* ☒.

3.1 Stress lifing: designing for infinite life

We have seen how the analysis of data from S–N curves is relatively straightforward. If we know the cyclic stress S–N profile in the material, and we can design our component so that the cyclic stress is below the fatigue limit (or a high-cycle endurance limit), then it will not fail by fatigue.

The use of this approach is really designing a component to have an infinite life (at least from a fatigue point of view, and ignoring other mechanisms such as wear and corrosion). It requires the design stresses to be less than the fatigue limit of the material. Of course, if the material has no fatigue limit this approach cannot be used without caution; knowing the endurance limit at 10^7 cycles is no use for a component that may experience 10^8 or 10^9 cycles during its operating life.

Alternatively, if under a particular design loading it is calculated that a component will fail by fatigue after, say, 20 000 cycles, then instigating a replacement scheme where the component is always replaced after 10 000 cycles will ensure safety. Petrol-driven cars that use polymer-based timing belts require that they be changed regularly, typically after 30 000–60 000 miles running. The belts will fail eventually if not replaced. I know: it happened to me and the consequences were expensive.

As a general approximation, fatigue limits and endurance limits (at 10^8 cycles) are about half the ultimate tensile strength (UTS) of the material. The ratios of fatigue strength to UTS for a few of these materials are shown in Table 2.2.

Table 2.2   Ratios of fatigue limit to ultimate tensile strength for various materials

Material	Fatigue or endurance limit at 10^8 cycles Ultimate tensile strength
Cast carbon steels	0.4–0.45
Wrought carbon steels	0.4–0.6
Wrought alloy steels	0.4–0.55
Cast aluminium alloys	0.25–0.35
Wrought aluminium alloys	0.35–0.4
Wrought titanium alloys	0.4–0.55

It is also possible to predict how the fatigue life will vary as the mean stress is altered by using the ☑ *Goodman diagram* ☑.

Of course, many cyclic loadings are not of regular repeating amplitudes and constant mean stress, and the loading is often random. So how is the random nature taken into account during the design process? The answer lies in assessing the damage contribution of each cycle and then linearly summing the damage associated with each cycle by using ☑ *Miner's rule* ☑.

☑ Lusaka

On 14 May 1977 a Boeing 707 transport plane crashed on approach to Lusaka airport, in Zambia, when the right horizontal stabilizer (the small 'wing' part of the tailplane assembly) broke away as the result of the failure of its main spar. The aircraft crashed, killing its six crew.

The aircraft had been designed using a fail-safe approach, which was defined as:

> It shall be shown by analysis and/or tests that catastrophic failure or excessive deformation, which could adversely affect the flight characteristics of the aeroplane, are not probable after fatigue failure or obvious partial failure of a single principal structural element. After such failure, the remaining structure shall be capable of withstanding static loads corresponding with the flight loading condition specified.

Civil Aeronautics Board (1956)

The airframe had been certified as meeting these requirements.

However, the actual behaviour of the structure when there was failure of the critical spar was not as predicted. The design of the spar (Figure 2.33) was effectively an I-beam. The design included a central stiffening bar, at the middle of the web, to act as a crack stopper in the case that the upper flange failed. That was exactly what happened, but the redistribution of load as a result of the failure meant that the crack simply kept going all the way through the entire spar.

The design, therefore, was not fail-safe as its designers had envisaged. Additionally, in this case there had been changes to the stabilizer design that had not been fatigue tested.

A critical conclusion of the accident report was that use of damage-tolerant design, with inspection, could have prevented the accident. This effectively marked the end of the use of fail-safe design in civil aviation, and a move to damage-tolerant design with inspection.

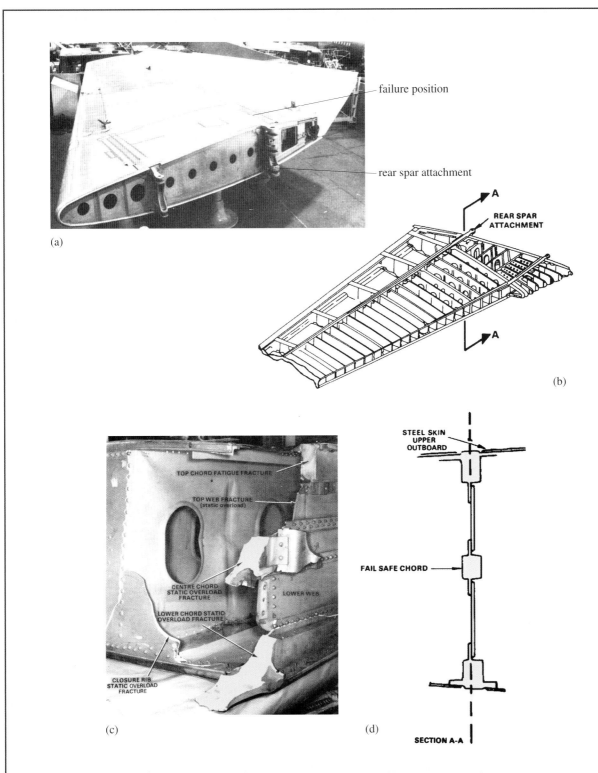

Figure 2.33 The failed component in the Lusaka crash: (a) a picture of the horizontal stabilizer of the type that failed; (b) internal structure of the stabilizer; (c) the fractured component showing the failed, 'fail-safe' chord, plus (d) a schematic of the web cross section at the failure point

☑ Goodman diagram

The *Goodman diagram* is a plot of stress amplitude σ_a against mean stress σ_m, as shown in Figure 2.34(a). The limits of the plot are the maximum possible mean stress on the *x*-axis (i.e. the tensile strength of the material σ_t) and σ_{a0} on the *y*-axis, where σ_{a0} is the fatigue limit when the mean stress is zero (i.e. an alternating stress as in Figure 2.17a). In materials that do not have a fatigue limit this would be the endurance limit. The fatigue and endurance limits under zero mean stress can conveniently be determined from rotating bend tests.

For a material with a fatigue limit to have an infinite life under cyclic loading, the point corresponding to the values of the mean stress and the stress amplitude for the particular case must lie below the

straight line on the Goodman diagram. Since this graph is linear, combinations of stress amplitude σ_a and mean stress σ_m that lie on this line (e.g. the point marked on Figure 2.34a) can be expressed by:

$$\sigma_a = \sigma_{a0}\left(1 - \frac{\sigma_m}{\sigma_t}\right) \qquad (2.9)$$

As the Goodman line effectively describes how the fatigue limit varies with mean stress, it draws a boundary between values of σ_a and σ_m that are 'safe' and the values that will eventually lead to fatigue failure. There are various modifications that can be made to Equation (2.9), and the exact shape of the line, but this is a useful first approximation.

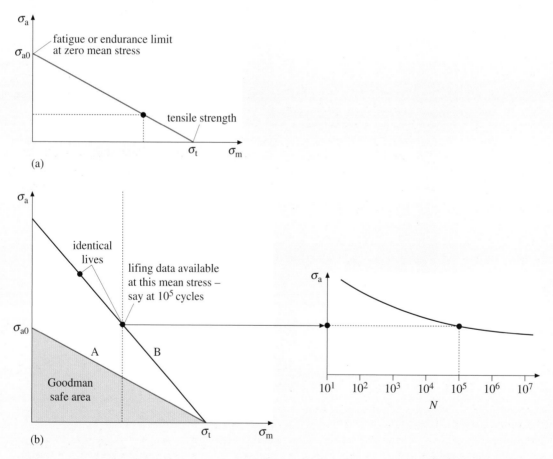

(a)

(b)

Figure 2.34   (a) The effect of mean stress on fatigue strength; (b) using the Goodman construction to calculate fatigue life

Where the Goodman diagram becomes useful is for assessing what happens to a component subjected to fatigue cycles of different mean stresses and stress amplitudes, where fatigue data have been measured at one mean stress only. Have a look at Figure 2.34(b), showing a Goodman plot and an associated S–N curve. The line labelled A is the Goodman line showing the variation of the fatigue limit. The upper line, labelled B, is constructed by taking the point where the S–N curve gives a life of 10^5 cycles and drawing a line down to the tensile strength, which is a known material limit. This line then tells us what values of stress amplitude and mean stress will give the same lifetime.

EXERCISE 2.7

A sample of a titanium alloy is found to have a fatigue limit of 200 MPa when tested with a mean stress of zero. What would be the material's likely fatigue limit when exposed to a mean stress in service of 100 MPa if it has a tensile stress of 500 MPa?

SAQ 2.3 (Learning outcomes 2.2 and 2.4)

An aluminium alloy with a tensile stress of 420 MPa is known to have an endurance limit of 120 MPa when exposed to a mean stress of 200 MPa. What is its likely endurance limit at a mean stress of zero, using the Goodman relation?

◩ Miner's rule

Miner's rule is a numerical method that is used to solve the problem of estimating the life under complex service conditions. Such conditions are quite likely to involve cycles of varying amplitude such as those shown in Figure 2.17(e). Methods exist for counting the cycles within such a complicated spectrum (for example, the so-called 'rainflow' method). To illustrate the problem Figure 2.35(a) shows the load history experienced by a suspension component on a vehicle driven round a test circuit. The resulting load spectrum of this range of data will consist of a number of load cycles of specified amplitude and mean value.

Figure 2.35(b) shows a sample of a complex stress variation, where there are three regions with different stress amplitudes, frequencies, and numbers of cycles. Miner's rule relates each of these to the S–N curve; it is the simplest and oldest empirical law with which to predict (from S–N curves) the fatigue life under varying stresses.

Miner's rule takes each stress amplitude, uses the S–N curve to find the total life at that value (Figure 2.35c) and then assesses how much of the life has been 'used up' by the actual number of stress cycles applied at each amplitude.

Suppose that a specimen undergoes n_1 stress cycles at a stress amplitude σ_{a1} and a mean stress σ_m, and that the expected life under these conditions according to the S–N curve is N_1. The ratio n_1/N_1 is then taken as a measure of the fatigue life that has been 'used up' at that stress amplitude.

Miner's law assumes that failure occurs when the sum of the ratios for all the stress amplitudes involved equals unity. The rule implies that there is a linear accumulation of damage during fatigue and that fracture will occur when:

$$\frac{n_1}{N_1} + \frac{n_2}{N_2} + \frac{n_3}{N_3} + \ldots + \frac{n_i}{N_i} = 1$$

That is:

$$\sum_i \frac{n_i}{N_i} = 1 \qquad (2.10)$$

The major limitation of the law is that it ignores the possible effects of any prior stress history that the component may have experienced.

For example, it is well known that overstressing increases the fatigue life during subsequent cyclic loading. Overloading an existing crack causes plastic blunting of the crack tip, which temporarily slows, or even halts, its growth. One of the crucial factors in the Comet airliner

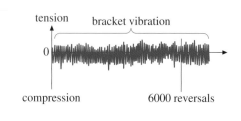

tension   bracket vibration

0

compression   6000 reversals

(a)

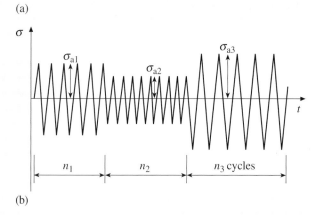

(b)

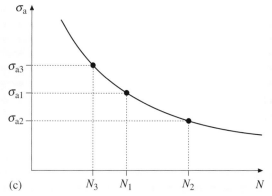

(c)

Figure 2.35   a) The recorded load history of a vehicle suspension component; (b) schematic of different stress cycles within a complex loading pattern; (c) relation of the different stresses to the S–N curve

disasters was exactly that; although the aircraft had undergone simulation fatigue testing, the fuselage used for this testing had also previously been used for an overpressure proof test of the structure. This had caused localized blunting by plasticity at the window corners, i.e. the stress concentrators that initiated the failures; as a result, the fatigue life of the test fuselage was considerably longer than that of the planes released into service.

Miner's rule takes no account of such effects. Therefore, it is not surprising that, in practice, failure after loading at variable stress amplitude does not always occur according to Equation (2.10). In a number of cases when the values of this equation at failure were established, it was found that it did not equate to unity, but can lie both above and below unity, depending upon the sequence of load cycles, the magnitude of the mean stress and the type of material. To take account of this a safety factor has been incorporated, so that the rule states that at failure:

$$\sum_i \frac{n_i}{N_i} = C \qquad (2.11)$$

where 0.3–0.8 would be a typical range for C. Although more effective cumulative damage laws are available, Miner's rule offers a simplified approach for some situations. More modern techniques are based on strain amplitude methods, or using the peak stress experienced in each cycle as a 'damage parameter' to apply a correction to measured data.

3.2 Strain lifing: designing for a finite life

Many components cannot be designed in such a way that the stress within them can be reduced to the point where their fatigue life will be effectively infinite. A challenge for many designers, then, is to assess what the life of a component is likely to be.

You already know that finite element analysis is now ubiquitous in the analysis of structural components. Finite element analysis in itself cannot provide fatigue predictions: elements cannot be assigned fatigue properties in the same way as mechanical properties. Instead, what finite element models can do is to identify regions of a structure where there are high strain amplitudes from which the designer can extrapolate the fatigue life from known data on the material.

Up to this point all our design criteria have been in terms of stress level. So what happens in the low-cycle fatigue regime where plastic strain is predominant, and where the properties are best described using plastic strain amplitude rather than stress amplitude? In this regime the amount of plasticity can be sufficient to cause failure in a very low number of cycles, and in extreme cases one cycle may be sufficient. Some useful empirical relations have been developed, based on the results of extensive testing programmes in which a strain amplitude is imposed on the specimen.

For example, the empirical relation between the cyclic elastic strain range $\Delta\varepsilon_e$ and the number of cycles to failure is found to have the form:

$$\Delta\varepsilon_e = 3.5\left(\frac{\sigma_t}{E}\right)N^{-0.12} \tag{2.12}$$

where σ_t is the tensile strength, E is Young's modulus and N is the number of strain cycles to cause fatigue failure. However, as I have already suggested, it is now well established that, in the low-cycle regime, fatigue lifetime is controlled primarily by the magnitude of the range of *plastic* strain in the material. This plastic component of strain forms the basis of the *Manson–Coffin relation* and is best described by:

$$\Delta\varepsilon_p = N^{-0.6}\varepsilon_f^{0.6} \tag{2.13}$$

where $\Delta\varepsilon_p$ is the cyclic plastic strain range, N is the number of cycles to failure and ε_f is the value of true strain at which fracture occurs in a tensile test.

Equations (2.12) and (2.13) were both determined from an analysis of 29 different materials. However, there was a considerable amount of scatter between the experimental data points and the lines describing the equations. This is why the designer needs to be very conservative in using such equations in predictions!

To model both elastic and plastic components, Equations (2.12) and (2.13) can be added together to give N as a function of the total cyclic strain range:

$$\Delta\varepsilon = \Delta\varepsilon_e + \Delta\varepsilon_p = 3.5\left(\frac{\sigma_t}{E}\right)N^{-0.12} + N^{-0.6}\varepsilon_f^{0.6} \tag{2.14}$$

As Figure 2.36 shows, this combined equation produces a curved graph (plotted on logarithmic scales) of strain amplitude against cycles-to-failure that matches the straight elastic and plastic lines with reasonable fit. In this graph it can be seen that, as might be expected, the total strain curve approaches the plastic strain–life curve at large strain amplitudes and approaches the elastic strain line at low strain amplitudes.

The result of testing this predictive equation against axial fatigue data for a number of low- and high-strength steels is shown in Figure 2.37. You can see that the fit between theory and experiment is good, where the points on the graph are actual data from testing and the solid line has been derived from Equation (2.14).

So, using these empirical equations produces accurate predictions, provided that the material is experiencing similar conditions to those of the tested specimens from which the data were originally derived. Predicting finite life using these techniques

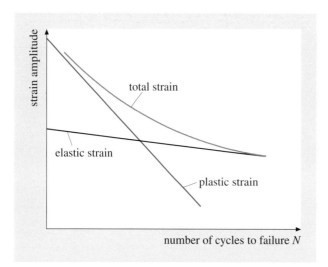

Figure 2.36   A graph of total strain amplitude versus strain cycles to failure, showing the elastic and plastic components of strain

is often referred to as the 'local stress–strain approach'. This procedure relies on accurate modelling of the elastic–plastic stresses and strains at stress concentrators; so, if finite element data are used as the starting point for fatigue analysis of this type, the accuracy of the results is all important.

This has been only the briefest review of empirical methods for estimating the fatigue life. Its purpose has been simply to give you a general impression of what can be done with the results of laboratory tests.

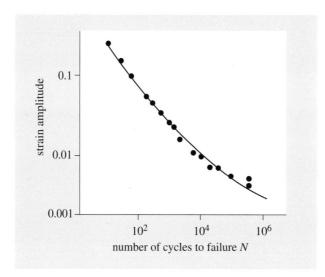

Figure 2.37   Comparison of predicted and experimental fatigue life under strain cycling for various low-alloy and high-strength steels

4 APPLYING FRACTURE MECHANICS TO FATIGUE

At the start of this part, I indicated that the fatigue life of a component can be divided into two stages: the time for a crack to initiate and the time for a crack to grow to a critical length.

When components contain pre-existing flaws, or design features that result in high stress concentrations, the crack-initiation portion of the fatigue life of a component may be significantly reduced to the point where it can effectively be ignored, and it is assumed that a crack will start to grow from the first cycle. As a result, the useful life of these components may be governed by the rate of subcritical crack growth.

In ☑ *the aircraft industry* ☑, for example, designs cannot be overly conservative, simply because the aeroplane would be so heavy that it wouldn't be able to take off! So this leads to highly stressed parts that are susceptible to fatigue. This is well understood in aircraft design, so is not a problem. The fatigue mechanisms are well characterized. Of course, a factor of safety is still used to ensure that the design parameters are relatively conservative, while still allowing the plane to get airborne.

You have seen in the previous sections that in some components the crack-propagation life is neglected during design because strain levels are high, whereas for other components the crack-growth life forms a substantial portion of the total life of the component. For these cases, designing for either an infinite or a finite life can be implemented. Unfortunately, the methods are not totally foolproof, as the Comet case study earlier illustrated, and as does ☑ *the F111 story* ☑.

☑ The aircraft industry

Between the Comet crashes and the Lusaka accident aircraft designers could choose between safe-life approach and fail-safe approaches for their airframe structures. Fail-safe was pretty well universally adopted by commercial aircraft designers. It was very attractive, because the redundant load paths, such as the central stringer chord in the Lusaka 'beam', meant less concern about the details of fatigue crack-growth rates and a more comfortable operating environment. Military folk would not countenance aircraft carrying redundant weight that would affect performance, and were less influenced by cost considerations, so they chose a safe-life approach. Fail-safe, as an airframe design philosophy effectively came to an abrupt halt in 1978, after the Lusaka accident showed that it was severely flawed.

The solution is the methodology known as damage-tolerant design: here, components and structures are made to tolerate limited structural damage in the form of cracking, with inspection carried out on a regular basis to ensure that any damage is within specified limits. Damage tolerance relies on having some element of redundancy in the structure, but it is fundamentally different from the fail-safe approach.

Damage-tolerance prediction relies on the application of linear elastic fracture mechanics (LEFM), which, with some careful manipulation, contributes enormously to the understanding of the behaviour of cracks when subjected to cyclic loading. By knowing the crack-growth rates in any particular material, designers can time inspection and maintenance schedules. This means that, by inspecting at regular intervals, any cracks that do propagate in a component will not have sufficient time to grow to a size sufficiently long to cause catastrophic failure. ▷

In damage-tolerance prediction, crack initiation is not considered significant and the largest proportion of the fatigue life is used up in propagating the crack. So, by applying fracture mechanics to the problem, it is possible to predict accurately the number of cycles it will take to grow the crack to a specific length. Figure 2.38 illustrates schematically how this process works, from the first detectable crack to the predicted length at which the component should be replaced or repaired.

Nowadays the issue is whether damage tolerance is practical or not – effectively, can the part be inspected? If damage tolerance is not practical, then safe-life is the way to go; if it is practical, then our predictive capability for fatigue-crack growth combined with experiment and in-service experience means that damage-tolerance principles are universally used.

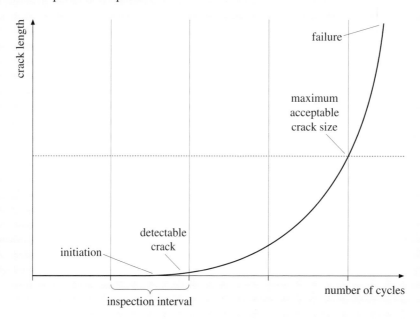

Figure 2.38   Damage-tolerant design, using inspection to detect and monitor growing cracks

✉ The F-111 story

The F-111, shown in Figure 2.39, was one of the first aircraft designed for safe life. However, following several early aircraft losses, it became clear that relatively small flaws not detected during inspection after manufacture could lead to catastrophic failure in the highly stressed, high-strength steel structure, following rapid fatigue-crack growth. One example was the loss of a wing from one aircraft while on a training flight. During a high-stress 'pull-up' manoeuvre, catastrophic failure occurred in the wing-pivot assembly.

The failure was found to have initiated from a forging lap (where the forged material had not flowed evenly into its required form), which was not detected at the manufacturing stage, and from which a crack grew to failure in only 100 flight hours. The safe-life design of the aircraft had predicted a life 100 times longer than this would be achieved, and that included a safety factor of 4. The safe-life approach does not take into account that the high-strength steel used in critical, highly stressed parts of the structure has relatively low toughness and can, therefore, fracture under load in the presence of relatively small defects. Unforeseen, small flaws can, therefore, negate the safe-life design calculations that were used.

Clearly, simply selecting a new safe life of 100 flight hours based on experience was not an option. A new approach was needed.

Since the F-111 was already designed and built, little could be done to change the materials or stresses. The solution to ensuring the integrity of the airframe was a low-temperature proof test, with each airframe individually tested before being passed as safe for service.

The proof test was designed using fracture mechanics principles: the low temperature reduced the toughness of the steel components used, so ensuring a safety factor at operating temperatures; the loads applied would cause an existing defect to propagate to failure if one existed. If the airframe passed the test, then any defects must be below a certain size, and damage-tolerance calculations, based on the rate of growth of such defects if they did exist, could ensure the structure's safety up to the next scheduled test.

Figure 2.39   An F-111 with its wings still attached

4.1 The application of linear-elastic fracture mechanics to fatigue

Fracture mechanics is the mechanics of *cracked* bodies, so it follows that it can be applied only to cases where crack initiation has already occurred. In other words, fracture mechanics can be applied only to crack *growth*. In this approach, we are concerned with propagation of the fatigue crack over distances that are large in comparison with the scale of the atomic structure, i.e. when the crack is in Stage II of its development.

Structural maintenance in the aircraft industry is dictated by the serious economic consequences of major damage or loss of the aircraft, compared with the cost of an inspection programme required to find early damage. Fracture mechanics is vital for the maintenance of aging aircraft, using damage-tolerance principles, by combining inspection with the ability to predict fatigue crack-growth rates based on LEFM principles. The opportunity and ease of inspection is integrated with analysis to ensure that damage is likely to be detected before aeroplane safety is jeopardized. What LEFM brings is the ability to predict the growth rate of long cracks, which is vital to the aircraft industry.

A fatigue crack that grows under cyclic loading is small for most of its life; this is the stage of initiation occurring before we would consider it to be 'detectable'. Once the crack has become 'long' its progress and direction are controlled by the opening stress. Also, the crack's growth rate is also largely independent of the metal's microstructure – metallic microstructures tend to be of the scale of tens of micrometres (a typical grain size), whereas a 'long' crack will be of the order of a few millimetres.

In Part 1 you saw that LEFM can predict whether a crack in a structure will cause brittle fracture. With hindsight, the application of LEFM to fatigue seems to be an obvious extension of the ideas coming from brittle-fracture research. This is because a fatigue crack growing slowly and stably in the body of a metal component has only a small plastic zone surrounded by bulk elastic material. Historically, there has been a lot of resistance to the notion that an elastic parameter could describe an event that is driven by the small plastic events at the crack tip.

The idea is simple: if the cyclic stress range or amplitude is driving a fatigue crack, and stress is related to the stress-intensity factor K and crack length a, then there ought to be a relationship between the stress-intensity factor range ΔK and the change in crack length, i.e. the crack-growth rate.

From Part 1, we know that for static loading the stress-intensity factor K is given by:

$$K = Y\sigma\sqrt{\pi a} \tag{2.15}$$

where Y is a dimensionless factor depending on the geometry, σ is the nominal tensile stress and a is the crack length (for a surface crack) or the half-length (for an internal crack).

In cyclic loading, K varies over the stress-intensity range ΔK, where:

$$\begin{aligned}\Delta K &= K_{\max} - K_{\min} \\ &= Y\left(\sigma_{\max} - \sigma_{\min}\right)\sqrt{\pi a} \\ &= Y\Delta\sigma\sqrt{\pi a}\end{aligned} \tag{2.16}$$

The experimental data supporting this theory are compelling, as shown in Figure 2.40. For a specific metal species it doesn't matter much what the alloy is, or what the heat treatment was; the data for a wide range of values of ΔK fall on a line described by:

$$\frac{\mathrm{d}a}{\mathrm{d}N} = C\left(\Delta K\right)^{m} \tag{2.17}$$

where $\mathrm{d}a/\mathrm{d}N$ is the crack-growth rate, and C and m are material constants. Equation (2.17) is known as the Paris equation. It applies to Region 2 in the centre portion of the graph in Figure 2.40. The Paris equation isn't universally applicable to all fatigue-crack-growth behaviour, though.

- Region 1 is where ΔK is low: the crack is short and its growth is microstructure and load dominated. Only when cracks are larger than the scale of the microstructure by a factor of typically 4–5 does the Paris equation hold true.

- The lower limit of ΔK is called the threshold for crack growth, ΔK_{th}. When the range of stress-intensity factor in a cracked component is less than ΔK_{th}, the crack will not propagate under the existing conditions of, for example, stress and temperature. Clearly, ΔK_{th} has some significance as a possible design criterion for fatigue conditions in components that already contain cracks, such as welded joints. The actual value of ΔK_{th} is very sensitive to mean stress and environment, but a reasonable figure for a typical steel is around 6 MPa $\sqrt{\mathrm{m}}$.

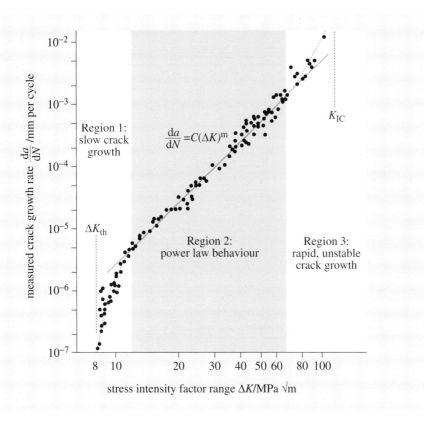

Figure 2.40   Fatigue crack growth

• In Region 3, where K exceeds about $0.7K_{IC}$ and approaches the material's fracture toughness, the growth rate accelerates due to load-controlled 'static' crack-growth mechanisms.

Data such as those in Figure 2.40 have to be obtained by rather more complex testing than generating S–N fatigue data, as described in ☑ *Measuring crack-growth rates* ☑.

☑ Measuring crack-growth rates

Stress–life and strain–life fatigue tests, used to construct an S–N or ε–N curve, are relatively straightforward. Each sample is placed in a test machine, the appropriate cyclic stress or strain amplitude is selected, the operator goes off to do something else and the machine counts the number of cycles until the sample fails.

The measurement of crack-growth rates is more complex, simply because the crack has to be monitored continuously as the applied load is

cycled. This is not only so that the change in crack length over a given number of cycles can be measured, but also because the crack length is needed to calculate the values of K that the crack tip experiences as a result of the applied loading.

One highly tedious method is to apply, say, 1000 load cycles and then measure the crack extension using a microscope with an accurate measuring gauge; but such methods are used only rarely today. Another method is to bond

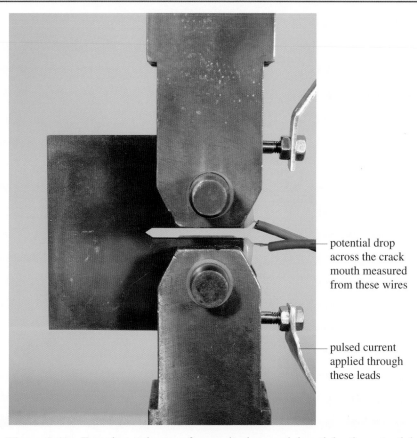

potential drop
across the crack
mouth measured
from these wires

pulsed current
applied through
these leads

Figure 2.41   Experimental set-up for monitoring crack length by the potential-drop method

an array of wires, similar to a strain gauge, to the surface of the test-piece and note the number of cycles as the crack successively cuts each wire.

Most common, though, are so-called 'potential-drop' techniques, where a high electrical current is passed through the sample and the potential drop, i.e. the voltage, is measured across the crack. The potential drop will only be small, given the very low electrical resistance of the metal specimens used, but it is detectable and can be monitored accurately using modern electronics. Figure 2.41 shows a typical experimental set-up.

As the crack grows, there is an increase in the sample's electrical resistance, because the conduction area is smaller. The potential drop across the crack increases.

For a particular sample geometry this effect can be calibrated, allowing continuous monitoring of the crack length. This then allows automation of crack-growth tests, as the data can be logged automatically, and computer control can be used to adjust the loads during the test to maintain a particular value of ΔK, for example.

Throughout the 1960s there was little industrial interest in Paris's work until the major F-111 failure I've already described. The wing was lost when the forging flaw extended only about 10% of its original length due to fatigue. The fleet was grounded for 6 months. Solving the F-111 problem, which was politically and commercially so important, moved fracture mechanics into the vanguard of engineering techniques. And, as I mentioned previously, this accident also introduced the notion of damage tolerance into the military aircraft industry. Certainly, damage tolerance is not possible without the ability to calculate crack-growth rates, and, uniquely, this is what the Paris equation provides.

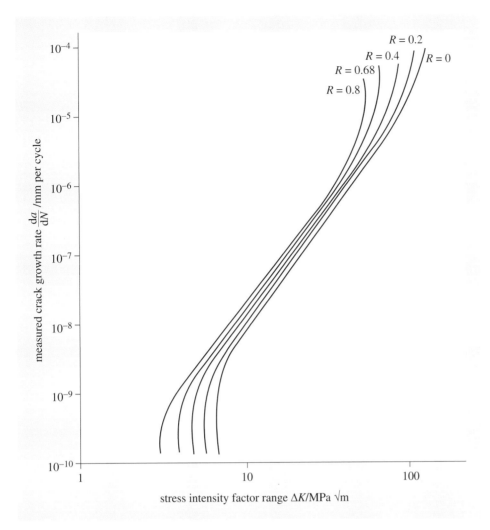

Figure 2.42   Changing the mean stress

Since the 1960s the data confirming the Paris relationship have become overwhelming. The final, compelling piece of experimental evidence in favour of the Paris relationship is shown in Figure 2.42. This shows that varying the mean stress, and therefore R, has only a minimal effect in Region 2 on the Paris results; there is an increase in crack-growth rates as the mean stress increases (we shall see why shortly), but the overall profile is unchanged.

4.2 Using the Paris law

For the Paris relationship (Equation (2.17), the coefficient C and exponent m are, unfortunately, unit dependent: they will be different depending on whether the applied stress is expressed in pascals or pounds per square inch (psi) and on whether the crack is measured in metres or inches. Some branches of engineering, notably those based and supplying to the US markets, still work in imperial units.

For units of metres and megapascals, some common values are shown in Table 2.3.

Table 2.3   Common values of C and m for metals

Material	C	m
Steel	10^{-11}	3
Aluminium	10^{-12}	3
Nickel	4×10^{-12}	3.3
Titanium	10^{-11}	5

Combining the LEFM equation (Equation 2.15) and the Paris equation (Equation 2.17) produces:

$$\frac{da}{dN} = C(\Delta K)^m = C\left(Y\Delta\sigma\sqrt{\pi a}\right)^m$$

This equation, after rearranging for dN, can be integrated directly provided that Y is constant:

$$dN = \frac{da}{C(\Delta K)^m} = \frac{da}{C\left(Y\Delta\sigma\sqrt{\pi a}\right)^m}$$

$$\int_0^{N_f} dN = \int_{a_i}^{a_f} \frac{da}{C\left(Y\Delta\sigma\sqrt{\pi a}\right)^m}$$

where a_i and a_f are the initial and final crack lengths respectively and N_f is the number of cycles to failure.

If Y is not a function of a:

$$N_f = \frac{1}{C\left(Y\Delta\sigma\sqrt{\pi}\right)^m} \int_{a_i}^{a_f} a^{-m/2}\, da$$

So:

$$N_f = \frac{1}{C\left(Y\Delta\sigma\sqrt{\pi}\right)^m} \frac{1}{1-\frac{m}{2}}\left[a_f^{1-(m/2)} - a_i^{1-(m/2)}\right] \tag{2.18}$$

[handwritten annotations in margin:]

$$\frac{1}{1-2}\left[a_f^{-1} - a_i^{-1}\right]$$

$$= \frac{1}{a_i} - \frac{1}{a_f}$$

$$= \frac{a_f - a_i}{a_i a_f} = \frac{1}{a_i}\left(1 - \frac{a_i}{a_f}\right)$$

Substituting a typical value of m into the equation (here I am using $m = 4$, which is common for many steels) and making use of Equation (2.3) gives the result:

$$N_f = \frac{1}{C\left(Y2\sigma_a\right)^4 \pi^2 a_i}\left(1 - \frac{a_i}{a_f}\right) \tag{2.19}$$

Obviously this is a very useful expression, for if we know the initial and final crack lengths, the stress range, and the material's fatigue properties, then we can calculate the number of cycles needed to propagate the crack to any given length.

SAQ 2.4 (Learning outcomes 2.2 and 2.6)

How many cycles would it take to grow a crack from 4 mm to 8 mm in a component that is subjected to a stress range of 80 MPa, in a geometry where Y is a constant 1.2, and the material properties in the Paris equation are $m = 4$ and $C = 10^{-11}$, where $\Delta\sigma$ is in MPa?

Numerical integration is usually required if Y is dependent on a, i.e. Y is not constant.

This approach uses the applied stress range to calculate crack growth, and we will explore this further in the next section. K is then derived from the geometry of the situation via Y. It does assume that there is a direct link between σ_{max} and K_{max}, and between σ_{min} and K_{min}. This is what fracture mechanics tells us is the case, but situations can arise where what happens at K_{min} becomes complicated, as when ☑ *crack closure* ☑ occurs.

☑ Crack closure

The use of the Paris equation to predict successfully the propagation rate of a fatigue crack relies on the assumption that the stress-intensity range ΔK is a true measure of the *crack-driving force* that the crack tip experiences during cyclic loading, which leads to crack advance. So the crack-growth rate does not depend on the absolute values of K_{max} and K_{min}, but only on the difference between them. An obvious exception is when K_{max} approaches or exceeds the fracture toughness K_{IC} of the material. In this case, static, not fatigue, failure is expected. Also, stress-intensity factors cannot take negative values, since the compressive loads are carried by the crack faces, which prevent the crack tip from experiencing any 'opening' loads. Therefore, K_{min} is taken as zero for cyclic loading at negative stress ratios ($R < 0$) on the assumption that the crack will 'close up' at zero load.

However, laboratory tests show that the crack propagation rate does also depend on stress ratio R; this is exemplified by Figure 2.42: increasing the mean stress (which means increasing R) does cause acceleration of the crack-growth rate.

This effect is a result of the permanent plastic deformation that occurs as the crack tip is loaded during each cycle. This leaves a plastic 'wake' behind the growing crack (Figure 2.43), within which contact between the crack faces can occur

even during the tensile portion of the fatigue cycle. The crack faces near the crack tip will require a somewhat larger applied tensile stress to 'open up'. Effectively this means that the crack can be 'closed' during part of the stress cycling, when the nominal K is above K_{min}; hence the term 'crack closure'.

The consequence of crack closure is to decrease the actual stress-intensity range that the crack tip experiences from its nominal (applied) value of ΔK to an effective (lesser) value of ΔK_{eff}, defined as $\Delta K_{eff} = K_{max} - K_{cl}$, where K_{cl} is the stress-intensity factor at which the two fracture surfaces first come into contact during the unloading portion of the stress cycle (Figure 2.44).

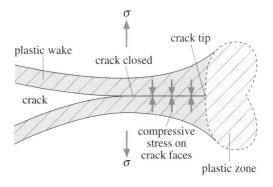

Figure 2.43   Premature closure of crack tip due to plastic deformation in the wake of the crack

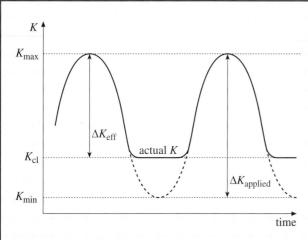

Figure 2.44   Schematic illustration of crack closure

The use of ΔK_{eff} instead of ΔK in the Paris equation enables the crack-growth rates shown in Figure 2.45(a), obtained at different stress ratios, to collapse into a single line as seen in Figure 2.45(b).

K_{cl} is difficult, if not impossible, to determine by analytical modelling methods. Therefore, various experimental methods have been developed for its measurement. The simplest and most reliable ones rely on the measurement of the specimen's compliance by strategically positioned strain gauges around the crack tip. The level at which the crack closes (or opens, depending on whether loading up or down) can be determined by the deviation of the strain gauge reading from linearity (Figure 2.46).

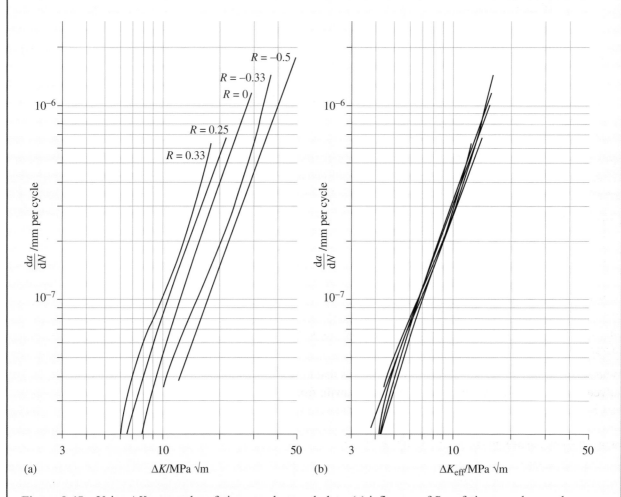

Figure 2.45   Using ΔK_{eff} to analyse fatigue crack-growth data: (a) influence of R on fatigue crack growth; (b) crack-growth rate data correlated by ΔK_{eff}

Besides *plasticity-induced* crack closure, there are other mechanisms that can contribute. Two of the most important of these are shown schematically in Figure 2.47, where it is illustrated that oxide deposits formed on the freshly created crack surfaces (Figure 2.47a), and asperities on uneven crack surfaces (Figure 2.47b), can cause premature crack closure.

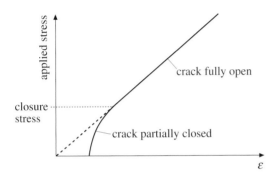

Figure 2.46   Measurement of crack closure from strain data

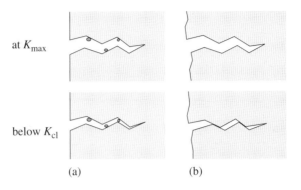

Figure 2.47   Schematic description of other crack-closure mechanisms: (a) corrosion debris; (b) roughness induced (adapted from Suresh, S. and Ritchie, R. O., 1982)

4.3 Practical fatigue analysis

No one carries out manual integration any more – that is what computers are for. Here, I shall use the 'Fatigue calculator' spreadsheet to show the use of the Paris equation.

Open the Fatigue calculator. As for the K calculator, there are purple boxes for entering properties and a drop-down menu for choosing the geometry of interest. If they are not there already, put 10^{-11} and 3, the values for C and m for steel, into the 'Material properties' boxes.

Now put 3 mm and 4 mm for initial crack length and final crack length, for an edge-cracked plate in tension, and 16 mm for width W into the geometry boxes. Put a stress range of 100 MPa into the loading box and an increment of 0.5 mm into the increment box.

When you hit the calculate box, what will happen is that the Paris equation will be solved numerically for two increments of crack growth: from 3 mm to 3.5 mm and 3.5 mm to 4 mm. You should find that the calculator produces an answer of 27 693 cycles (Figure 2.48). So for this geometry, in this material, with this stress range, the spreadsheet tells us a crack will grow from 3 mm to 4 mm length in 27 693 load cycles.

EXERCISE 2.8

Is this increment of 0.5 mm acceptable, or a bit coarse? Use smaller increments to see the effect of changing this parameter. Note down the number of cycles to grow the crack for 0.05, 0.005 and 0.0005 and 0.00005 mm.

Figure 2.48 Screen
dump of the 'Fatigue'
interface for an edge-
cracked plate in tension,
showing 27 693 cycles
to failure

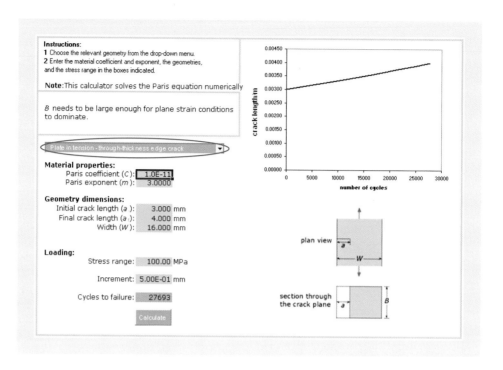

The exercise shows that the increment size is important. This is because the crack accelerates as it grows, i.e. as Y increases. So taking an average over 0.5 mm is not sensible, because in reality the value of Y would have risen sufficiently over that distance to increase the values of K and so ΔK. The calculator shows this: the curving graph of crack length against cycles with the growth rate (the slope of the graph) increases as the crack gets longer (Figure 2.49). Exercise 2.9 also illustrates this.

Figure 2.49 Plate in
tension with a through-
thickness edge crack:
the slope of the graph
increases as the crack
grows from 3 mm to 8 mm

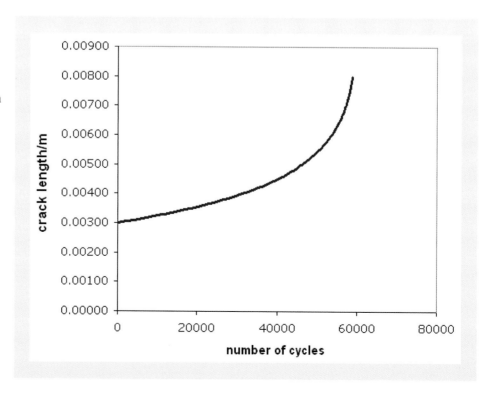

EXERCISE 2.9

Set up your calculator for 1000 (0.0005 mm) increments. How many cycles does it take for the crack to grow from 3 mm to 3.2 mm and how many to grow from 3.8 mm to 4 mm?

The answer to the exercise shows that growing the crack the first 0.2 mm takes something like twice as long as the last 0.2 mm. This is in the nature of fatigue cracks: they spend most of their life being young and accelerate to failure during the latter stages of their life – I know the feeling.

I am now going to return to the pressure-vessel design problem from Section 3.1 of Part 1. I'll make life a bit easier by assuming that we now have a steel supplier who can guarantee that our grade of steel stays on the upper shelf at 0 °C and we have increased the wall thickness of the design to 18 mm. We have also specified pre- and post-weld heat treatment and agreed a fabrication specification that includes 100% inspection for surface flaws – this is an expensive piece of kit we're designing – which guarantees finding any cracks over 3 mm. So the current design parameters are as follows:

- The fracture toughness of the material is a fixed 140 MPa √m.

- Also fixed are the residual stresses, at 100 MPa, the design stresses, at 300 MPa, and the thermal shock stresses, at 150 MPa; the first two are in tension and the third is in bending.

- The wall thickness has increased to 18 mm.

- The length of an unfound crack is 3 mm.

SAQ 2.5 (Block 2 Part 1 revision)

We need to recalculate the K values for the pressure-vessel example in order to produce the new reserve factor on load. Use the K calculator spreadsheet now to do this.

Hint: remember that you have to work out the individual K values from each source, and sum them.

You now have to recommend an inspection cycle for the operation of the plant, to account for the growth, by fatigue, of any pre-existing flaws. The non-destructive evaluation firm will 'guarantee' to find cracks over 3 mm. On start-up there is a surge, and so the plant suffers a one-off cyclic stress excursion of ±50 MPa and start-up happens, on average, 10 times a day. This surge increases the design loading of the plant.

SAQ 2.6 (Block 2 Part 1 revision)

How much stress intensity K does the 50 MPa surge value contribute?

How would you reassess your design's reserve factor in the light of this new information on loading?

The extra 6 MPa √m of crack driver produced by the surge is part of the normal operating cycle so needs to be added to the K values due to operating pressure and residual stresses, giving:

$$K_{operating} = K_{primary} + K_{residual} + K_{surge}$$
$$\approx 38 \text{ MPa } \sqrt{m} + 13 \text{ MPa } \sqrt{m} + 6 \text{ MPa } \sqrt{m}$$
$$\approx 57 \text{ MPa } \sqrt{m}$$

which creates a reserve of:

$$\frac{140 \text{ MPa } \sqrt{m}}{57 \text{ MPa} \sqrt{m}} \approx 2.5$$

My emergency shutdown design gives:

$$K_{emergency} = K_{primary} + K_{residual} + K_{thermal}$$
$$\approx 38 \text{ MPa } \sqrt{m} + 13 \text{ MPa } \sqrt{m} + 15 \text{ MPa } \sqrt{m}$$
$$\approx 66 \text{ MPa } \sqrt{m}$$

which creates a reserve of:

$$\frac{140 \text{ MPa } \sqrt{m}}{66 \text{ MPa } \sqrt{m}} \approx 2.1$$

You now have the plant working at its normal design conditions. There may be a crack 3 mm in length that, because you are a conservative engineer, you assume is oriented in the most dangerous direction under a K crack-driving parameter during normal service of $K_{operating} = 57$ MPa √m.

The question of how fast the crack grows under a cyclic loading of 100 MPa occurring some 10 times a day now presents itself – cue the Paris law. First, though, I have to find the crack length at which brittle failure takes place. Reflect on this problem for a moment; it is not straightforward.

The difficulty is that the primary and residual stresses are tensile and so use the same Y calibration curve (so one can add the stresses); but the thermal shock stresses are in bending and so use a different Y calibration curve. There is no fundamental problem in this: just use the calculator, keep increasing the crack length in increments and calculating the value of $K_{emergency}$ until it equals the material toughness of 140 MPa √m.

This is a little tedious, but I can use conservatism to make life simpler. The thermal shock stresses in bending generate less K than if they were in tension (if you remember this from Part 1, fine; if you don't, then have a play with the K calculator to prove it to yourself). So, if I do this the easy way, using tension for all the components of K, and the result is that design analysis is satisfactory, then I needn't go any further; this saves me time and money.

SAQ 2.7 (Learning outcomes 2.6 and 2.7)

(a) Use the K calculator to find what the critical crack length is for the emergency shutdown procedure, assuming that the thermal shock stresses create a tensile field.

(b) Using your answer to (a), use the Fatigue calculator to find the number of cycles it takes to grow the crack from 3 mm to failure in order to recommend an inspection procedure. If the plant cycles 10 times per day, what is its total lifetime?

(c) The crack is subjected to 10 load cycles per day. Estimate how much the crack will grow in 2 years. (The calculator won't allow a direct calculation of this, but input values of final crack length until you obtain 2 years' worth of cycles.)

I am beginning to like this design! A recommendation for crack detection after 2 years will do as a starter. If no cracks are detected, then the inspection period can probably be increased progressively.

How critical are the values of the initial and final flaw sizes to our calculations? The answer to this can depend on just how much difference there is between the initial and final lengths. In this example, the final crack length is about twice the starting flaw size, which is quite a small difference. If the crack has further to grow, because more cycles are required to grow it when it is small (because ΔK is smaller), then the final crack length is less important. Figure 2.50 shows this effect, where large changes in a_f result in small changes in N_f.

Knowing the initial flaw size is critically important. Without knowing the likely flaw distribution, or being able to measure for flaws accurately, damage-tolerance analysis is either speculative or is forced to be overconservative. It is also difficult to apply damage tolerance to parts (for example, in the F-111) where a relatively small crack extension from a flaw can lead to failure; indeed, there are additional complicating factors associated with the behaviour of ☑ *small cracks* ☑ that are a particular concern within fatigue analysis. ☑ *Trouble on the runway* ☑ gives a recent example of where experience in service has led to a change in inspection and maintenance for a safety-critical component.

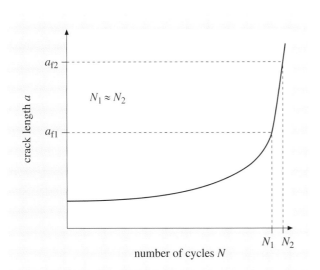

Figure 2.50   Effect of crack size on the fatigue life

☑ Small cracks

The crack propagation data, like the da/dN versus ΔK plots in Figures 2.40 and 2.42, are conventionally obtained using laboratory tests on standard test-pieces, e.g. compact-tension specimens. The procedure in these tests involves growing a fatigue crack away from a starter notch, typically by 1–5 mm, before recording the propagation rate under a constant stress range and ratio. The data obtained for shorter crack lengths are not suitable owing to the stress concentration effect of the notch where the crack begins, and where there may also be some plastic strain. Remember from Part 1 that in calculating the stress intensity the *far-field* stress is used, with no assumption of a stress concentration at the crack tip. So, until they grow out of the stress field of the notch, reaching to the bulk stress field of the specimen, small cracks, especially shorter than a millimetre, grow much faster than expected on the basis of nominal ΔK values, as seen in Figure 2.51. They may even grow at speeds below the threshold value predicted by LEFM. This is primarily due to the failure of LEFM to characterize the crack-driving force in a region with relatively high plasticity. A significant contribution to the difference is believed to be due to crack closure, or more accurately the lack of it, because of the undeveloped crack wake (see the input 'Crack closure') with the small cracks. Reduced crack closure produces a larger ΔK_{eff} and, hence, results in a higher crack-growth rate.

It is also possible for non-propagating fatigue cracks to form at notches, where a crack initiates, grows and then stops, even if the magnitude of the applied load cycle does not change. As the stress concentration effect of the notch decreases with

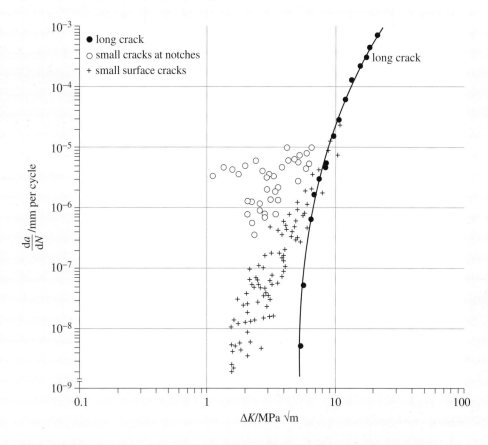

Figure 2.51   Small cracks grow faster than predicted by 'long' crack data

distance from the root of the notch, the magnitude of the stress field at the crack tip may decrease as the crack propagates; and if the remote stress is sufficiently low, the crack may stop altogether within the notch-affected zone.

The small-crack effect is an example of where similitude clearly fails. That is, the stress pattern ahead of a short crack within a notch field is different from that for longer cracks outside the notch stress field. Such small cracks are referred to as 'mechanically short cracks'.

The anomalous behaviour of fatigue cracks at short lengths is not just restricted to notches or stress concentrations. Any newly initiated small crack will at some point be comparable in size to the microstructural dimensions (such as the sizes of grains or strengthening particles) in engineering alloys. Microstructural features such as grain boundaries and second-phase particles can act as effective barriers to crack propagation. As such, they may alter the stress field around the crack tip in various ways, and hence affect the crack propagation rates.

For example, the crack path may deviate from the direction perpendicular to the direction of maximum principal stress and follow structurally weaker paths. Take a look at the path of the small crack in the unnotched specimen, made of an aluminium alloy, shown in Figure 2.52. The crack, which had propagated through a grain (grain A), changes its path when it reaches the grain boundary. Rather than crossing the boundary and propagating in the same direction in the neighbouring grain, propagates along the grain boundary. It seems that the crystallographic orientation of the next grain (grain B) is less favourable to crack propagation than grain A. Since the crack is now propagating at an inclined angle to the direction of maximum principal stress, the crack tip experiences a somewhat lessened stress field and would slow down. At the next junction along the grain boundary, the crack has to choose another favourable path. It seems that the crystallographic convenience of grain C was less than that of the grain boundary, which the crack eventually chose. Even more deviation from the usual direction meant that this crack-growth rate most probably had to fall considerably – growth may even have stopped altogether.

Another example is shown in Figure 2.53, where a crack was stopped several times at microstructural barriers (at particles indicated by the points A–E), before 're-initiating' and continuing to grow. This sort of behaviour does, in fact, provide a clue as to why some alloys exhibit a fatigue limit and some don't.

If the microstructure of the material contains 'natural' crack stoppers, like the iron–iron carbide laths of pearlite in steels (Figure 2.54), then small cracks can be arrested long before they can grow to

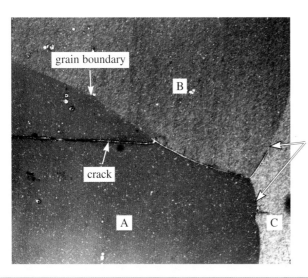

grain boundary

B

crack

grain boundaries

A

C

Figure 2.52 The path of a small crack in an aluminium alloy specimen

a critical length for propagation. This is the origin of the fatigue limit in many steels, which I introduced earlier. But note that the fatigue limit effect can be negated is a single overload causes the crack to break through a barrier and begin to grow anew.

There are very serious practical implications for the small-crack problem. Since most fatigue-life prediction methods rely on long-crack data, and as overall life is most influenced by low propagation rate behaviour, the accelerated and 'sub-threshold'

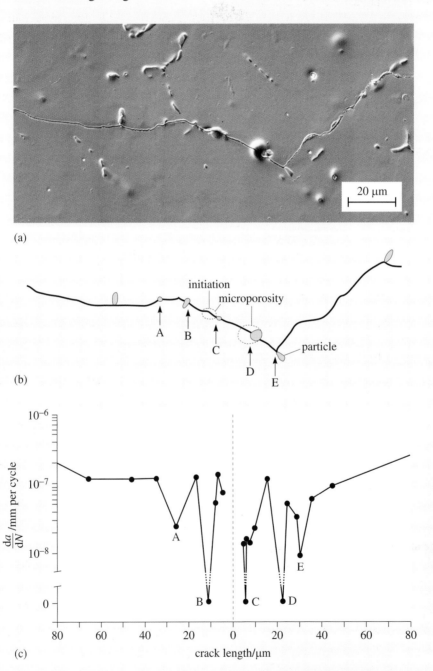

Figure 2.53   Arresting of a crack at microstructural barriers in an aluminium alloy: (a) micrograph of the crack taken using a scanning electron microscope; (b) sketch of the crack; (c) the corresponding crack-growth rate in the microstructure

extension of small cracks can lead to potentially dangerous overpredictions of fatigue life.

Fortunately, new techniques are implementing some aspects of small-crack behaviour into fatigue-life prediction models that have been emerging recently. For example, it is viable to predict the behaviour of mechanically short cracks at stress raisers on the basis of crack closure measurements, and/or correlate the crack propagation rate using parameters that allow some plasticity. Modelling 'microstructurally small cracks' is proving to be more difficult, though. The complex interaction of cracks with microstructure has been only partially successful using complex statistical models.

Better understanding of the behaviour of small cracks will lead to less conservative designs, which will mean lighter and more efficient (using less fuel, so more environmentally friendly) aircraft.

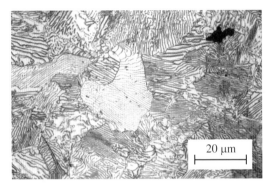

Figure 2.54   Pearlite in steel

▽ Trouble on the runway

On 2 June 2006, a ground test was being performed on an American Airlines Boeing 767 fitted with General Electric engines. The flight crew had reported a power lag in the left engine on its previous flight. The ground crew had powered the engines to maximum twice when there was an explosion in the left engine. The high-pressure turbine stage 1 disc had ruptured, with large pieces of debris being thrown out of the engine housing. One piece bounced off the runway, through the aircraft fuselage and lodged in the engine cowling on the other side of the plane (Figure 2.55). Another fragment was found over 700 m away against an airport perimeter fence; it had crossed two active runways and taxiways to get there! The engine was a total loss, and the plane was damaged substantially. Fortunately, there were no injuries.

Post-incident metallurgical examination revealed that the disk rupture was the result of a radial fracture that originated at a small dent found at the bottom of a blade slot. You will recall from Block 1 that the blade roots in turbine discs are sources of stress concentration. Defects introduced during fabrication or maintenance can make things worse in such highly stressed areas of a component. The examination also revealed two other similar cracks on the disk. The disk had accumulated 9186 flight cycles in service (48 429 h), and had 5814 cycles remaining before compulsory retirement at its design limit of 15 000 cycles.

Clearly, if this failure had happened in flight the aircraft could have crashed, though other such failures in the past have not always had disastrous consequences.

The consequences of the incident were that enhanced inspection regimes were instigated for the engine type concerned, particularly for discs that had previously had repair work in the blade root. All discs that had accumulated more than 3000 cycles required immediate inspection and reworking of the blade root if it had not already been performed. The entire design of the disc was also reviewed to ensure future safety.

Figure 2.55   Part of No. 1 engine lodged in No. 2 after bouncing off the runway

4.4 Linking initiation and propagation

For a fracture mechanics analysis, we must always assume a realistic initial flaw size. If we let the initial crack length shrink to zero, we are faced with a problem: the propagation life tends to infinity, irrespective of stress range, because the initial $\Delta K = 0$! How can we overcome this difficulty?

The mathematical reason for our dilemma is, of course, that if $a = 0$, then $\Delta K = 0$ and the growth rate is zero. The Paris equation is *only valid for Stage II growth,* but initiation and early growth is a Stage I shear-controlled process. Thus, the techniques of fracture mechanics *cannot be applied directly to the initiation phase.* If we want to calculate the total fatigue life, then we will have to split our calculation into two parts. The first stage lumps together initiation and early growth to a crack length a_0; the second calculates the crack growth from a_0 to failure.

Unfortunately, no quantitative theories of initiation exist, so again it is necessary to fall back on an empirical or experimental approach. Test data can be collected under strain-cycling conditions. The number of cycles to initiate and grow a small crack, typically and arbitrarily 0.5 mm long, can be plotted against the applied strain range, as shown in Figure 2.56. The amount of growth depends on the sensitivity of the measurement technique used. Note that this is a strain-cycles curve for *initiation*, not failure.

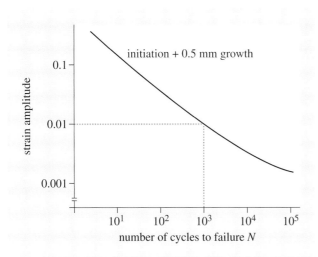

Figure 2.56 A measured relation between strain amplitude and initiation life for smooth, strain-cycled specimens

These data can now be used to calculate the initiation life of a component, if we know the strain range at the site of crack initiation. As an example, if we determine that the strain amplitude at the notch root is 0.01, then we can consult Figure 2.56 to find that this corresponds to an initiation life of 10^3 cycles. We can then use the Paris law to calculate the propagation life in the elastic region away from the notch root.

SAQ 2.8 (Learning outcomes 2.2 and 2.6)

If $a_f = 100$ mm, $\sigma_a = 80$ MPa, $Y = 1.2$ and $C = 10^{-11}$, what is the propagation life if the initial crack length is 0.5 mm?

Hint: use Equation (2.19).

Thus, the total life by this two-stage process is given by:

$$N_f = \text{initiation cycles and propagation cycles}$$
$$\approx 1000 \text{ cycles} + 15\,000 \text{ cycles}$$
$$\approx 16\,000 \text{ cycles}$$

This simplified example, therefore, illustrates how we might link the initiation and propagation stages to calculate the total fatigue life.

SAQ 2.9 (Learning outcomes 2.2 and 2.8)

For a typical steel alloy subjected to an alternating stress of amplitude 100 MPa, what is the maximum length of a centre crack in a large plate that would just fail to grow by fatigue? The fatigue threshold has been measured as 6 MPa √m.

One approach that attempts to look at fatigue safety in terms of stress and crack length is ☑ *the Kitagawa–Takahashi method* ☑.

☑ The Kitagawa–Takahashi method

This approach is best illustrated diagrammatically: see Figure 2.57.

The y-axis is the threshold stress for crack propagation; the x-axis is the length of any existing crack in the material.

At small crack lengths, typically 1 µm or less, the threshold stress is simply the fatigue limit of the material. At longer crack lengths, typically greater than 1 mm, the threshold stress is derived from the Paris equation, using the threshold stress-intensity range ΔK_{th}, below which cracks do not propagate.

Where these two extremes of behaviour intersect is the value of the crack length l_0, which is a critical crack size below which any cracks present do not affect the fatigue limit. This is in line with the concept of small cracks that can be arrested by local microstructural features.

The curved line in between the two extremes is found to fit experimental data reasonably well.

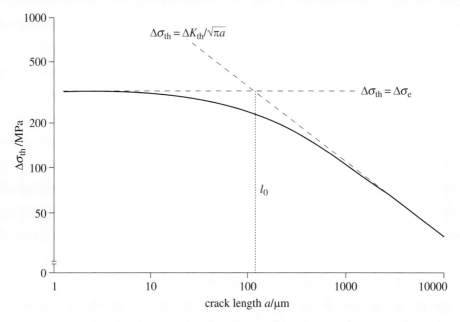

Figure 2.57   Kitagawa–Takahashi diagram for a nodular cast iron; $\Delta\sigma_e = 320$ MPa, $\Delta K_{th} = 6.2$ measured at $R = 0.1$

5 A PRACTICAL EXAMPLE: THE MARKHAM DISASTER

The plan view of the fracture surface of a broken brake rod from a mineshaft lift is shown in Figure 2.58. Its failure cased the death of 14 miners at the Markham colliery in July 1973. The rod had been installed 21 years earlier. Following the accident, an extensive investigation took place to identify the cause of failure.

The rod is simply a long threaded bar, 51.3 mm in diameter with a 3.34 mm deep thread.

Detailed stress analysis found that the axial stress in the threaded portion of the brake rod was 97 MPa. Tests on the steel showed that its yield and tensile strengths were 346 MPa and 600 MPa respectively.

EXERCISE 2.10

What factor of safety does the axial stress represent in respect of the yield strength and the tensile strength? Does this suggest that the load was sufficient to cause failure by static loading?

So the axial stress on its own was too low to cause failure of the brake rod. But further examination of the assembly revealed that a bearing designed to keep the brake rod axially aligned had, through lack of maintenance, seized and was creating a bending moment on the rod. Further stress analysis (using strain gauges on an operating assembly) revealed that the bending stress on the rod was 157 MPa. This, combined with the axial stress, gives a total stress of 254 MPa. This is much higher, but still well within the material's yield strength.

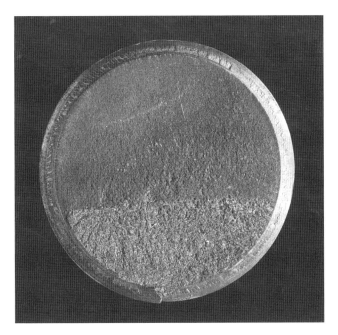

Figure 2.58   The plan view of the fracture surface of a broken brake rod

The investigators then turned to fatigue as the possible cause. Owing to the on/off cyclic nature of the brake rod and because of the way the brake operated, there was always an applied stress on the rod even when the brake was off. It was established that the total cyclic load was 211 MPa (a combination of the axial and bending stresses) and the mean stress was 129 MPa.

SAQ 2.10 (Learning outcomes 2.2 and 2.4)

The closest data that were found for this type of steel gave a tensile strength of 540 MPa and a reverse bending fatigue limit of ±120 MPa.
Using the Goodman relation (either by drawing a diagram or using the equation), establish whether these cyclic stresses would be high enough to cause failure by fatigue.

So, using the Goodman diagram we find that fatigue will occur as a result of the combined bending and tensile stresses. We could stop here and say: 'Well, what do you expect?' The stresses say that it would fail by fatigue, and the fracture surface is consistent with this.

However, to be sure, it would be sensible to confirm that the expected crack-growth rates in the material, and the anticipated load cycling, would lead to the lifetime that was observed in reality.

The brake would have been cycled each time the mine lift was used. An estimation of the number of cycles experienced, given the average daily use of the lift, was 3×10^5 cycles.

SAQ 2.11 (Learning outcomes 2.2 and 2.6)

Using the cyclic stress established earlier, calculate the number of cycles to failure; assume that the initial crack length was 0.1 mm and the final crack length was 29 mm. For this particular steel, take $C = 10^{-11}$ and $m = 3$.

Hint: the geometry does not fit exactly with those in the fatigue calculator, but you should use 'beam in pure bending' geometry.

Although the figure calculated in SAQ 2.11 is very much an estimate (because of the geometry chosen it is more likely to be on the conservative side), it is still in fairly good agreement with the actual number of cycles prior to failure. So everything stacks up: the bending load on the shaft led to fatigue failure pretty much exactly when it would have been predicted had all the factors been known in advance. This is often the case with fatigue failures.

If the applied stress was due only to the axial loading, as the design was intended, then the fatigue life expectancy would have approached an infinite life! The final outcome of the investigation found that the ultimate cause of failure was the ineffective bearing that led to bending of the brake rod, and recommendations were that, in addition to improved design of the bearing, the system should operate in a fail-safe manner.

6 SUMMARY: FATIGUE DESIGN

Hopefully, you are now in a better position to comprehend the difficulties facing the designer who has to tackle situations that involve cyclic loading. It should be evident from studying this part that design against failure by fatigue is far more complex than design against failure by static loading.

Although fatigue can be well characterized by a material's S–N behaviour or the growth rate of a fatigue crack as a result of cyclic loading, it can be challenging to account for safely. Fatigue lives are affected by chemical environments, including air and water vapour, and are sensitive to the surface condition.

It is surprising how frequently fatigue failures are caused simply by poor detailing, e.g. by the use of inadequate radii of curvature at changes of section. Anything that might cause a stress concentration can act as a fatigue initiation point. Fatigue design, in just the same way as designing for strength, is a compromise between the cost and weight of a component and its performance in service. Aircraft that were designed to be entirely fatigue-free would be too heavy to leave the ground.

The successful design of a component or structure reflects a judicious and, where possible, rigorous stress analysis, coupled with due care and attention to the choice of material and control of its microstructure and the selection of an appropriate surface condition for the component. Due regard must also be given to the environment in which the component will operate. Further, the designer must be careful to allow for the statistical scatter associated with fatigue test data and must remember that there is a specimen-size effect in fatigue. Also, the designer must appreciate the need for regular inspection of a critical component when it is in service.

Along with the other failure modes considered in this course, fatigue provides a further example of the need for inputs from both the design engineer and the metallurgist or materials engineer.

LEARNING OUTCOMES

After studying Block 2 Part 2 you should be able to do the following.

2.1 Describe the origin of a fatigue failure, given appropriate information, in terms of a design flaw or other operational problem.

2.2 Perform simple fatigue calculations, given appropriate data.

2.3 Describe the effect of a notch or stress concentrator in fatigue initiation, and describe the effect of notch sensitivity.

2.4 Use the Goodman relation to predict the effect of changes in mean stress on the fatigue limit or fatigue life of a material.

2.5 Describe the applications of 'cycle-counting' methods, such as Miner's rule, in assessing the lifetimes of components subjected to complex loading.

2.6 Use the Paris law to calculate the growth rate of a fatigue crack.

2.7 Use the Fatigue calculator spreadsheet to assess lifetimes of growing cracks.

2.8 Describe and apply the concept of a fatigue threshold, below which cracks do not propagate.

ANSWERS TO EXERCISES

EXERCISE 2.1

In Part 1 you learnt that cracks should not cause failure unless the stress intensity at the crack tip exceeds the material's fracture toughness. Clearly, this isn't what happens in fatigue; somehow the crack is growing because of the cyclic nature of the loading, even though the maximum stress intensity is below K_{IC}. This is what makes fatigue so dangerous.

EXERCISE 2.2

(a) The maximum stress is $+\sigma_a$ and the minimum stress is $-\sigma_a$.
     Therefore, $R = -\sigma_a/\sigma_a = -1$.

(b) The maximum stress is 200 MPa and the minimum stress is 40 MPa.
     Therefore, $R = 40/200 = 0.2$.

(c) The maximum stress is 300 MPa and the minimum stress is 0 MPa.
     Therefore, $R = 0/300 = 0$.

(d) The maximum stress is 200 MPa and the minimum stress is −20 MPa.
     Therefore, $R = -20/200 = -0.1$.

EXERCISE 2.3

(a) At 1 Hz the machine will take 2×10^9 s, i.e. over 63 years!

(b) At 100 Hz the test would take just over 231 days.

So, establishing the fatigue properties precisely at long lives can be very time consuming.

EXERCISE 2.4

Using Figure 2.21:

(a) From the line that is parallel to the x-axis the fatigue limit is about 340 MPa.

(b) Reading from the graph it is about 120 MPa.

EXERCISE 2.5

(a) In push–pull testing, the whole specimen section is subjected to the maximum stress cycle. In the bend test, only the surface layers farthest from the neutral axis experience the peak stress.

(b) The larger volume of highly stressed material in the push–pull test is statistically more likely to contain a flaw, so failure tends to occur earlier in the axial test.

EXERCISE 2.6

The strength of a material tends to decrease with temperature (and conversely the toughness increases). Because the fatigue limit changes with the strength of the material, lowering the strength will increase the susceptibility to fatigue.

EXERCISE 2.7

Using Goodman:

$$\sigma_a = \sigma_{a0}\left(1 - \frac{\sigma_m}{\sigma_t}\right)$$

$$\sigma_{a,100} = 200\ \text{MPa} \times \left(1 - \frac{100\ \text{MPa}}{500\ \text{MPa}}\right)$$

$$= 160\ \text{MPa}$$

Therefore, $\sigma_{a,100} = 160$ MPa.

EXERCISE 2.8

0.05 mm increments produced 30 248 cycles, 100 increments (0.005 mm) produced 31 368 cycles, 1000 increments (0.0005 mm) produced 31 358 cycles. Therefore, choosing too coarse an increment of growth will produce a non-conservative result: one that is too low.

EXERCISE 2.9

It takes 8334 cycles to grow the crack from 3 mm to 3.2 mm (Figure 2.59) and 4523 cycles to grow it from 3.8 mm to 4 mm (Figure 2.60) at a increment of 0.005 mm.

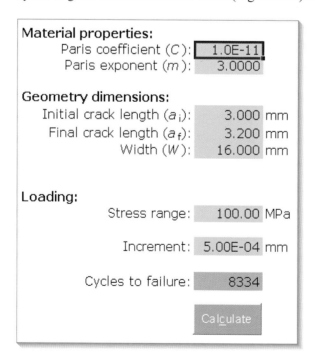

Figure 2.59   Plate in tension with a through-thickness edge crack: 8334 cycles to grow the crack from 3.0 mm to 3.2 mm at an increment of 0.005 mm

EXERCISE 2.10

Against the yield stress, the factor of safety is $346/97 = 3.6$.

Against the tensile strength it is $600/97 = 6.2$.

So failure by the static load seems unlikely.

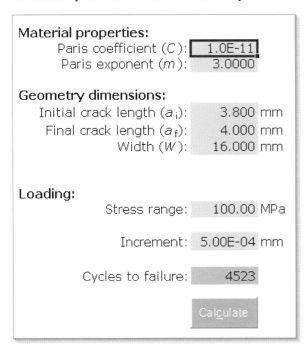

Figure 2.60   Plate in tension with a through-thickness edge crack: 4523 cycles to grow the crack from 3.8 mm to 4.0 mm at an increment of 0.005 mm

ANSWERS TO SELF-ASSESSMENT QUESTIONS

SAQ 2.1

(a) The Comet failed because of various stress concentrators in the structure that could initiate fatigue cracking under cyclic loading. Initial fatigue testing of the structure had not revealed the problem because it had not been undertaken under the same conditions that a real fuselage structure would experience.

(b) The *Alexander L. Kielland* platform collapsed after a fatigue crack grew from a hydrophone mounting. The weld securing the hydrophone was of poor quality, and a crack grew from the weld, eventually fracturing the brace to which it was attached. Poor design then led, through a series of failures of other connecting structures, to the capsizing of the platform.

(c) The cause of Eschede train crash can be traced to the design of wheel used. The original monoblock design was changed to a design using a separate tyre on the central wheel, with a rubber insert to reduce noise. Unfortunately, the external tyre could then flex in bending, particularly as its thickness reduced by wear. A fatigue crack grew from the inner tyre surface and caused the failure of the wheel.

SAQ 2.2

From the data in Table 2.1, the fatigue limit of unnotched samples is 232 MPa ($\alpha_k = 1$); the value for notched samples varies with the sharpness of the notch, i.e. with α_k.

For $\alpha_k = 3.02$, the fatigue limit is 108 MPa, thus:

$$\alpha_f = 232/108 = 2.15$$

and

$$q = \frac{(232/108) - 1}{3.02 - 1} = 0.57$$

Values of α_f and q can be determined in the same way for each α_k given; the results appear in Table 2.4. The values of q vary depending on the stress concentration values, but they all indicate that the material is notch-sensitive.

Table 2.4   Values of fatigue notch factor α_f and the notch sensitivity factor q for the values of a_k given in Table 2.1

α_k	σ_{FL}	α_f	q
1	232	–	–
1.84	137	232/137 = 1.69	0.82
2.26	120	232/120 = 1.93	0.74
3.02	108	232/108 = 2.15	0.57
4.6	86	232/86 = 2.70	0.47
7.06	91	232/91 = 2.55	0.26

SAQ 2.3

Using Goodman:

$$\sigma_{a,200} = \sigma_{a0}\left(1 - \frac{\sigma_m}{\sigma_t}\right)$$

$$120 \text{ MPa} = \sigma_{a0}\left(1 - \frac{200}{420}\right) \text{ MPa}$$

$$\sigma_{a0} = \frac{120 \text{ MPa}}{0.52} = 231 \text{ MPa}$$

SAQ 2.4

Substituting these values into Equation (2.19) gives:

$$N_f = \frac{1}{C\left(Y2\sigma_a\right)^4 \pi^2 a_i}\left\{1 - \frac{a_i}{a_f}\right\}$$

$$= \frac{1}{10^{-11}\times\left(1.2\times80\right)^4\times\pi^2\times0.004}\times\left(1 - 0.5\right)$$

$$\approx 15\,000 \text{ cycles}$$

Therefore, the number of cycles to failure will be approximately 15 000.

SAQ 2.5

Using the calculator gives $K_{primary} \approx 38$ MPa $\sqrt{m}$ (Figure 2.61), $K_{residual} \approx 13$ MPa $\sqrt{m}$ (Figure 2.62) and $K_{thermal} \approx 15$ MPa $\sqrt{m}$ (Figure 2.63), giving a total crack-driving parameter of:

$$K_{emergency} \approx \left(38 + 13 + 15\right) \text{ MPa } \sqrt{m} \approx 66 \text{ MPa } \sqrt{m}$$

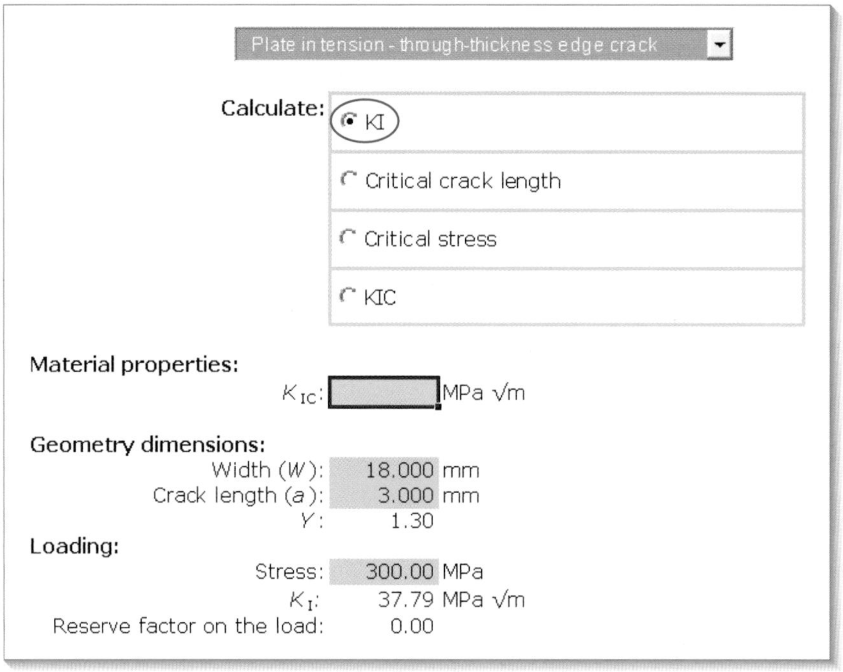

Figure 2.61 Plate in tension with a through-thickness edge crack – $K_{\text{primary}} \approx 38$ MPa $\sqrt{m}$

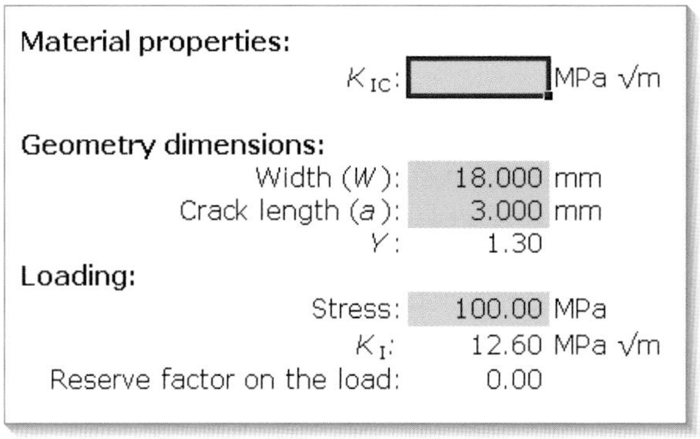

Plate in tension - through-thickness edge crack

Calculate: ● KI

○ Critical crack length

○ Critical stress

○ KIC

Material properties:

K_{IC}: [   ] MPa $\sqrt{m}$

Geometry dimensions:
Width (W):   18.000 mm
Crack length (a):   3.000 mm
Y: 1.30

Loading:
Stress: 300.00 MPa
K_{I}:   37.79 MPa $\sqrt{m}$
Reserve factor on the load: 0.00

Figure 2.62 Plate in tension with a through-thickness edge crack – $K_{\text{residual}} \approx 13$ MPa $\sqrt{m}$

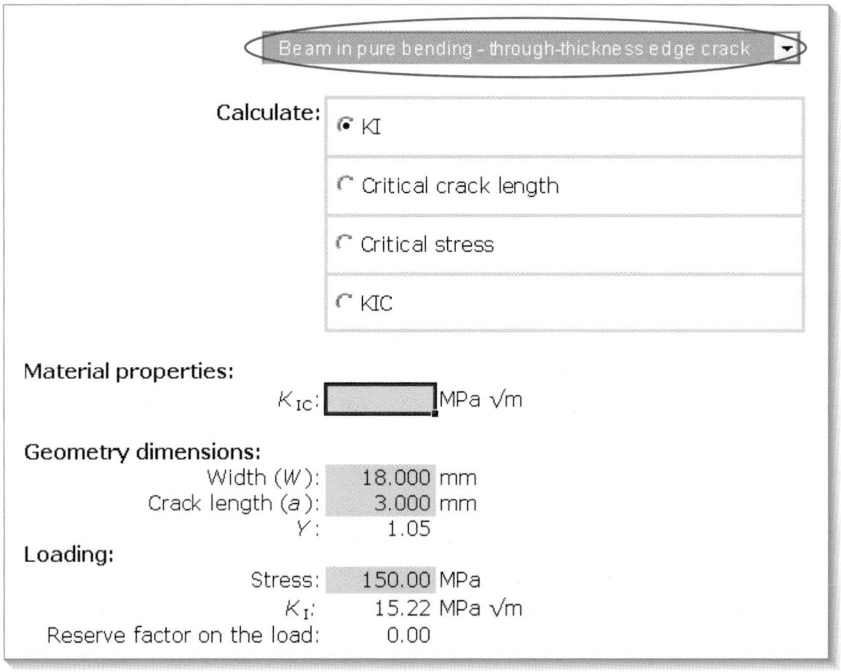

Material properties:

K_{IC}: [   ] MPa $\sqrt{m}$

Geometry dimensions:
Width (W):   18.000 mm
Crack length (a):   3.000 mm
Y: 1.30

Loading:
Stress: 100.00 MPa
K_{I}:   12.60 MPa $\sqrt{m}$
Reserve factor on the load: 0.00

Figure 2.63 Plate in pure bending with a through-thickness edge crack – $K_{\text{thermal}} \approx 15$ MPa $\sqrt{m}$

Beam in pure bending - through-thickness edge crack

Calculate: ● KI

○ Critical crack length

○ Critical stress

○ KIC

Material properties:

K_{IC}: [   ] MPa $\sqrt{m}$

Geometry dimensions:
Width (W):   18.000 mm
Crack length (a):   3.000 mm
Y: 1.05

Loading:
Stress: 150.00 MPa
K_{I}:   15.22 MPa $\sqrt{m}$
Reserve factor on the load: 0.00

The toughness of the steel is 140 MPa √m, so the reserve factor on load is
140 MPa √m/66 MPa √m ≈ 2.1.

SAQ 2.6

Another 50 MPa worth of K in terms of crack driving would contribute 6 MPa √m to
the K-driving parameter (Figure 2.64).

Do I add this on to the existing K values, giving a total of $66 + 6 \approx 72$ MPa √m and
so reducing the reserve to 140 MPa √m/72 MPa √m ≈ 1.9 on emergency shutdown?
I think not: this is a surge on start-up, which is part of the normal cycle of use;
if I were to sum the start-up surge K and the emergency shutdown K, I would be
assuming that start-up and shutdown could hit peak conditions simultaneously. I
think this is incredible, so I choose not to do it.

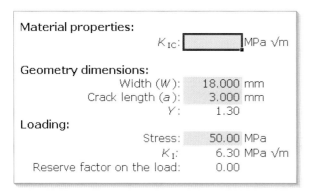

Material properties:
K_{IC}: ☐ MPa √m

Geometry dimensions:
Width (W): 18.000 mm
Crack length (a): 3.000 mm
Y: 1.30

Loading:
Stress: 50.00 MPa
K_{I}: 6.30 MPa √m
Reserve factor on the load: 0.00

Figure 2.64   Plate in tension with a through-thickness edge
crack – $K_{\text{I}} \approx 6$ MPa √m

But note that in the nuclear industry there is a 'condition of incredibility' that
demands you use anything possible, no matter how incredible.

So, if you have factored for the surge on the grounds of conservatism that is fine by
me – there are no correct answers in this game. You just have to be able to justify
your approach to your boss, regulator, conscience or God!

SAQ 2.7

(a) I have a design primary stress of 300 MPa, a thermal shock stress of 150 MPa
    and a secondary residual stress of 100 MPa, giving a total of 550 MPa, all in
    tension. The K calculator produces a critical crack length of about 6.2 mm
    (Figure 2.65).
(b) The Fatigue calculator produces about 64 000 cycles, (Figure 2.66), which if
    cycling at 10 times a day means that it will be about 17 years before the crack
    grows long enough to fail under emergency shutdown conditions. There is no
    point in refining this analysis, as we clearly have plenty of time to play with and
    no immediate cause for concern.
(c) Two years is some 7300 cycles. The Fatigue calculator does not allow a direct
    calculation, but it is easy enough to try a few values of final crack length until
    about 7300 cycles are returned. I get a crack length of about 3.2 mm, which is
    just long enough to move into the detectable zone for non-destructive testing.

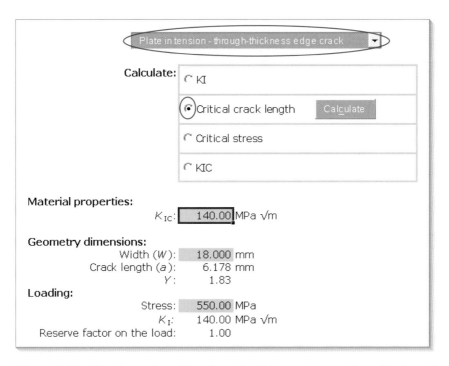

Figure 2.65   Plate in tension with a through-thickness edge crack – critical crack length ≈ 6.2 mm

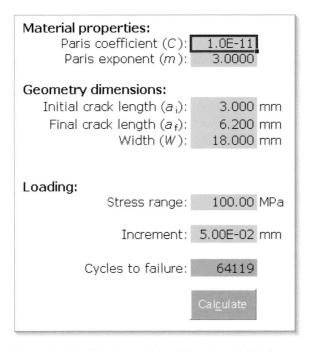

Figure 2.66   Plate in tension with a through-thickness edge crack – number of cycles = 64 119

SAQ 2.8

There is a little trick here to make the calculation easier. As $a_f \gg a_i$, $(1 - a_i/a_f)$ is 0.995, i.e. close to unity, so we can reduce Equation (2.19) to:

$$N_f = \frac{1}{C(Y2\sigma_a)^4 \pi^2 a_i}$$

Substituting the values given and taking $a_i = 0.5$ mm we get $N_f \approx 15\ 000$ cycles.

SAQ 2.9

The crack will not grow if the applied stress-intensity range ΔK is less than the threshold value ΔK_{th}. For a centre crack in a large plate, $Y = 1$, and in this case $\Delta\sigma = 100$ MPa and $\Delta K_{th} = 6$ MPa $\sqrt{m}$. So, using $\Delta K = Y\Delta\sigma\sqrt{\pi a}$:

$$\sqrt{\pi a_0} = \frac{\Delta K_{th}}{\Delta\sigma} = 0.06\ \sqrt{m}$$

Therefore:

$$a_0 = 1.15\ \text{mm}$$

where a_0 is the length of the largest crack that would just fail to grow.

SAQ 2.10

I have plotted a Goodman diagram using this data in Figure 2.67. The straight line joins a point on the y-axis corresponding to the fatigue limit and a point on the x-axis corresponding to the tensile strength. I have also plotted the point with the value of $\Delta\sigma/2$ and σ_m corresponding to the conditions within the threaded region of the rod. The point lies above the Goodman line, and so I conclude that fatigue at the root of the threads is likely.

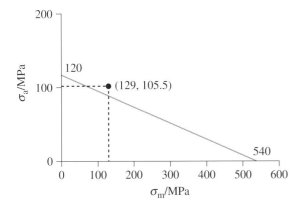

Figure 2.67   Goodman diagram for the answer to SAQ 2.9

SAQ 2.11

Using 211 MPa as the load range and the values given, the number of cycles should calculate as 2.50×10^5 when using a growth increment of 0.05 mm and 2.64×10^5 when using an increment of 0.01 mm.

REFERENCES

Civil Aeronautics Board (March 1956) Airplane Airworthiness Transport Categories, Part 4b-3, para 270.

Fairbairn, W. (1864) 'Experiments to determine the effect of impact, vibratory action, and long-continued changes of load on wrought-iron girders', *Philosophical Transactions of the Royal Society of London*, vol. 154, pp. 311–25.

Suresh, S. and Ritchie, R. O. (1982) 'A geometric model for fatigue crack closure induced by fracture surface roughness', *Metallurgical and Materials Transactions A*, vol. 13A, pp. 1627–1631.

ACKNOWLEDGEMENTS

Grateful acknowledgement is made to the following sources:

FIGURES

Figure 2.4: © The Flight Collection/Alamy.

Figure 2.8(a): © STR/AP/EMPICS.

Figure 2.8(c): Maier G. (ed) (1985) Case Histories in Offshore Engineering, CISM.

Figure 2.9: © Alex Grimm/Reuters/Corbis.

Figure 2.11: © Getty Images.

Figure 2.16: © Peter Menzel/Science Photo Library.

Figure 2.18: Courtesy of Cranfield University.

Figure 2.19: Courtesy of Dr Sarah Hainsworth, University of Leicester.

Figure 2.26: Electro General Corporation for D.F. Socie, Fatigue Life Estimation Techniques, Technical Report, No. 145.

Figure 2.28: McGraw Hill (1967) for A.T. Benedetto, 'The Structure & Properties of Materials'.

Figure 2.33(a): Photograph taken from Accident Investigation Report 9/78, Boeing 707 321C G-BEBP. Department of Trade Accidents Investigation Branch © Crown copyright. Reproduced with the permission of the Controller of HMSO and Queen's Printer for Scotland.

Figure 2.33(c): Photograph taken from Accident Investigation Report 9/78, Boeing 707 321C G-BEBP. Department of Trade Accidents Investigation Branch © Crown copyright. Reproduced with the permission of the Controller of HMSO and Queen's Printer for Scotland.

Figure 2.39: © Purestock/Getty Images.

Figures 2.51–3: Courtesy of Dr Salih Gungor, The Open University.

Figure 2.55: Blakey, M.C., (2006) US National Transportation Safety Board, Safety Recommendation Report, 28 August 2006. Taken from http://www.ntsb.gov

COURSE TEAM ACKNOWLEDGEMENTS

This part was prepared for the course team by Jim Moffatt, Adrian Demaid and Michael Fitzpatrick, with contributions by Salih Gungor.

T357 COURSE TEAM

Dr Michael Fitzpatrick (course team chair)

Andy Harding (course manager)

ACADEMIC STAFF

Dr Alun Armstrong

Professor Adrian Demaid

Professor Chris Earl

Professor Lyndon Edwards

Dr Salih Gungor

Michael Hush

Dr Peter Lewis

Dr Jim Moffatt

Dr Ed Murphy

Dr Martin Rist

EXTERNAL ASSESSOR

Professor Lindsay Greer, University of Cambridge

CONSULTANTS

Martin Goldthorpe

David Sefton (critical reader)

Olivier Zanellato (critical reader)

SUPPORT STAFF

Debbie Derbyshire (course team secretary)

Colin Gagg

Stan Hiller

Pete Ledgard

Rehana Malik

PRODUCTION TEAM

Kirsten Barnett

Annette Booz

Philippa Broadbent

Lisa Carrick

Teresa Cox

Sarah Crompton

Daphne Cross

Vicky Eves

Chris French

Carol Houghton

Jonathan Martyn

Katie Meade

Lara Mynors

Deana Plummer

Lynn Short

Susanne Umerski